THE COMPLETE GUIDE TO
TOEIC®

by

Bruce Rogers

INTERNATIONAL

THOMSON
ASIA ELT

Thomson Singapore Pte Ltd

Singapore • Albany • Belmont • Bonn • Boston • Cincinnati • Detroit • London
Madrid • Melbourne • Mexico City • New York • Paris • Tokyo • Toronto

First published 1997 by:
International Thomson Asia ELT
60 Albert Street
#15-01 Albert Complex
Singapore 189969

TOEIC® is a registered trademark of Educational Testing Service. The publisher of this text is in no way affiliated with ETS, nor has ETS endorsed the contents of this text in any way.

Designed by Raketshop Design Studio, Philippines
Printed by Chong Moh Offset Printing Pte Ltd, Singapore

1 2 3 4 5   01 00 99 98 97

ISBN 0-534-83520-1

Contents

Acknowledgments

I would like to thank the following professionals for their invaluable comments and suggestions during the development of this text:

James Boyd, *ECC Foreign Language Institute, Osaka, Japan*

Gary Hussey, *Temple University, Japan*

Junko Imai, *Tokyo Foreign Language College, Japan*

Joud Jabri-Pickett, *Kanda Institute of Foreign Languages, Japan*

Jae Ho Kim, *Pagoda Academy, Seoul, South Korea*

Park Jong Yeon, *Moonjinmedia, Seoul, South Korea*

David Progosh, *Kanda School of Foreign Languages, Japan*

Jean L Turner, *Monterey Institute for International Studies, California, USA*

I would also like to thank David Lee, Ken Mattsson, and the other members of the Global Innovations Publishing Team at Heinle & Heinle.

Thanks to Kyung-Seop Sim and Kae-Hong Park of International Thomson Publishing Asia, Satoshi Saito of Imprint, and Hideki Kanna of International Thomson Publishing Japan for special assistance.

Photo Credits

The following photos were taken by the author: Exercise 1.2, #3 and #4; Exercise 1.3, #2, #3, #5, #7, #8, and #10; Exercise 1.4, #8; More Practice, #18; Practice Test, #14 and #16. Exercise 1.3, #9 is by Raketshop Design Studio. All other photos are by Jonathan Stark, Heinle & Heinle Publishers.

Getting Started

A Guide to the *Guide* : How to Use This Book

About This Book

TOEIC is an increasingly important test. Nearly a million people around the world take this test annually. In an era of globalization, a knowledge of English, the global language, is a key to success. One measure of English proficiency is a high score on TOEIC. And a high score on TOEIC can be an important factor in being hired, promoted, or selected to travel and work internationally.

However, preparing for this test is not easy. Some of the books written to help you are badly organized, incomplete, or poorly written. Some of the "practice tests" have little resemblance to actual exams.

You need a guide you can depend on. That is why this book was written.

The Complete Guide to TOEIC® is a complete, accurate, and up-to-date preparation book. It is based on extensive research and on years of classroom experience in test preparation. It offers a step-by-step program that provides test-taking strategies and the development of language skills. It is based on the following simple philosophy:

- The same points are tested over and over on every TOEIC.
- Each of these testing points is based on a clearly defined language skill.
- These skills can be mastered by practice.

Organization of the Guide

1. **Getting Started** This is an introduction to the exam.
    - **Questions and Answers About TOEIC** This provides basic background about the format and scoring of the test.
    - **Eight Keys to High Scores** This helps you become a smarter test taker by suggesting ways to arrange your preparation time, use the process of elimination, mark your answer sheet, control test anxiety, and learn other important test-taking techniques.
2. **Guide to Listening Comprehension (Lessons 1 – 4)** This part of the book is designed to prepare you for the Listening Comprehension part of TOEIC (Sections I – IV). In order to complete the exercises for this part of the book, you must have the accompanying audio cassette tapes. (See "Guide to Listening Comprehension," page 12, for more information about using the cassette tapes.)
3. **Guide to Reading (Lessons 5 – 7)** This part is designed to prepare you for the Reading part of TOEIC (Sections V – VII).
    Each of the seven lessons consists of these components:
    - **Preview: Lesson Outline** This provides a brief overview of the lesson.
    - **Format** This describes in detail the form of the problems in this section.
    - **Tactics** This component discusses the best techniques for maximizing your score on each section.
    - **Sample Test** This is a shortened version of the test section that familiarizes you with the directions and the most common types of items for each section of the test. Items for this section are used as examples in the next component.
    - **Testing Points and Skill-Building Exercises** This is the main component of each lesson. It breaks down the testing points into

understandable individual units and offers numerous exercises designed to increase your skills.

- **More Practice** This component offers a full-length test section so that you can practice testing points, not in isolation but in combination. Together, the seven "More Practice" components provide you with the equivalent of another full-length practice test.

4. **A Complete Practice Test** This duplicates actual tests in terms of format, content, and level of difficulty. To get the most of this exam, follow the suggestions in the section titled "How to Take the Practice Test."

5. **Tapescript and Answer Key** This provides a written version of all the taped material in the audio program, answers for all the exercises and tests, and explanations when appropriate.

Suggestions for Using the *Guide*

The Complete Guide to TOEIC® is designed to be used either as a textbook for a TOEIC preparation course or as a tool for individual learners who are preparing for the test on their own. If you are working alone, you will need to obtain the audiotapes that accompany the book.

Whether working in a class or alone, you should begin preparing for TOEIC by reading the introductory lessons ("Getting Started"). Then you can work through the lessons one by one, or begin with the parts in which you feel you need improvement. You can usually make the fastest progress by working in the areas in which you are weakest.

When using the book in the classroom, the exercises work well as small-group or pair activities. Students may either work on the exercises together or complete them individually and then check and discuss them afterward.

Following are the amounts of time required to cover each part of the *Guide*. Keep in mind that these times are very approximate and do not include review sessions.

Getting Started .. 1–3 hours	Lesson 5 .... 8–10 hours
Lesson 1 .... 2–3 hours	Lesson 6 .... 7–9 hours
Lesson 2 .... 5–7 hours	Lesson 7 .... 5–7 hours
Lesson 3 .... 4–6 hours	Practice Test .... 3–4 hours
Lesson 4 .... 5–7 hours	

If you have any questions, comments, or suggestions regarding this book or the TOEIC test itself, I would very much appreciate hearing from you. Please contact me in care of the publisher:

International Thomson Publishing Asia
60 Albert Street, #15–01, Albert Complex
Singapore 189969

Or you can contact me directly:
E-mail address: brogers@colorado.edu
Fax number: 303/443-3006

And good luck on TOEIC!

Bruce Rogers
Boulder, Colorado
October 1995

Questions and Answers About TOEIC®

Q: What is TOEIC?

A: TOEIC (Test of English for International Communication) is a standardized test designed to measure a person's ability to understand English as it is used in international business situations.

TOEIC is designed and written by Educational Testing Service (ETS) of Princeton, New Jersey. ETS produces many other standardized tests, such as TOEFL (Test of English as a Foreign Language), GMAT (Graduate Management Aptitude Test), and GRE (Graduate Records Exam).

TOEIC was first administered in Japan in 1979 and in Korea in 1982. It is now given in over 50 countries all over the globe. In 1995, more than 600,000 candidates took the test. Every year, four new forms of the test are administered.

Q: How is TOEIC administered?

A: Most TOEIC testing is arranged by a sponsoring organization (a multinational corporation, for example) and by a local representative. The dates, times, and locations of the testing are generally set by the sponsoring organization. In some locations, persons who are not affiliated with a sponsoring organization may also take the test on a regular basis. Contact the TOEIC representative's office in your area for more information. (There is a list of representatives at the end of this section.)

Q: What format does TOEIC follow?

A: All the questions on the current TOEIC examinations are multiple choice questions. Items in most parts have four answer choices; in Part II, there are three answer choices. The test is divided into two main sections: Listening Comprehension and Reading. Each section contains 100 items and takes one hour and fifteen minutes to complete. Listening Comprehension is divided into four parts, Reading into three. Each part has its own directions. The entire test takes about two and a half hours to complete.

TOEIC Format			
Section 1: Listening Comprehension			
Part I: Questions About Photographs	20	items	
Part II: Questions/Responses	30	items	
Part III: Dialogs	30	items	
Part IV: Short Talks (6–8 talks)	20	items	
	100	items	
Approximately	1	hour	15 minutes
Section 2: Reading			
Part V: Sentence Completion	40	items	
Part VI: Error Identification	20	items	
Part VII: Short Passages (13–16 passages)	40	items	
	100	items	
	1	hour	15 minutes
Totals:	200	items	
Approximately	2	hours	30 minutes

Q: Who takes TOEIC?

A: Anyone who travels abroad on business or who has contact with international visitors is a likely candidate for TOEIC. All types of employees of international organizations may be asked to take the test: managers, marketing experts, sales representatives, customer service agents, flight attendants, hotel employees, customs officials, and others. Many organizations also require job applicants to take TOEIC. Some individuals take it on their own and include their test scores as part of their résumés.

Q: Who uses TOEIC?

A: TOEIC clients include trading and manufacturing companies, government agencies, international banks, hotel chains, and airlines. Within these organizations, personnel directors, training managers, human resource managers, and English language program administrators use the scores.

Q: How is TOEIC scored?

A: Three scores are reported: a score for Listening Comprehension, a score for Reading, and a total score. To calculate these scores, the number of correct answers in each of the two main sections is first counted. These scores are called raw scores. Then the raw scores are changed to scaled scores by means of a conversion chart similar to the one on page 198. The scaled scores for the two sections are added together to obtain a total score. Scores on each of the two sections range from 5 to 495. Total scores range from 10 to 990.

The chart below provides an approximate guide to interpreting TOEIC scores:

805 – 990	High advanced	305 – 400	High beginner
655 – 800	Advanced	205 – 300	Beginner 2
555 – 650	High intermediate	10 – 200	Beginner 1
405 – 550	Intermediate		

Q: How does TOEIC differ from TOEFL?

A: The names of the two tests sound quite similar. Both are produced by ETS, and both measure a person's ability to understand English. Both are multiple choice tests. However, there are a number of differences between the two exams, as shown in the following chart:

	TOEFL	**TOEIC**
Purpose	To measure the English-language proficiency of applicants for North American universities	To measure the English-language proficiency of employees, trainees, or prospective employees of international organizations
Format	150 questions 3 sections: 　**1.** Listening Comprehension 　**2.** Structure and Written Expression 　**3.** Reading Comprehension	200 questions 2 sections: 　**1.** Listening Comprehension 　**2.** Reading

Time Limits	1 hour, 40 minutes	2 hours, 30 minutes
Range of Scores	200 – 677	10 – 990
Language	Academic English as used in campus settings and university textbooks.	International English as used in business settings.

Q: What contexts are used for TOEIC questions?

A: Common contexts for TOEIC questions are business situations (marketing, sales, contract negotiations, meetings), travel (airlines, taxis, hotels), entertainment (restaurants, movies, plays, museums), and health and fitness (doctors, dentists, exercise programs).

Q: Where can I get more information about TOEIC?

A: You can contact the appropriate department of your organization or the TOEIC representative for your country:

Argentina
    Telephone: 541/322-4557
    Fax: 541/322-2106

Canada
    Telephone: 1/613-542-3368
    Fax: 1/613-542-2907

Colombia
    Telephone: 57/2-6 673 539
    Fax: 57/2-6 684 695

Dominican Republic
    Telephone: 1/809-582-6627
    Fax: 1/809-587-3858

Egypt
    Telephone: 20/2-355-3170
    Fax: 20/2-355-2946

France
    Telephone: 33/1-40 74 05 21
    Fax: 33/1-42 56 65 27

Germany
    Telephone: 49/69-58 096 0
    Fax: 49/69-58 096 50

Greece
    Telephone: 30/1-362 9886
    Fax: 30/1-363 3174

Hong Kong
    Telephone: 852/2603-5771
    Fax: 852/2603-5765

Indonesia
    Telephone: 62/21-520 0364
    Fax: 62/21-520 0365

Italy
    Telephone: 39/55 672 580
    Fax: 39/55 669 446

Japan
    Telephone: 81/3 3581-5663
    Fax: 81/3 3581-5608

Korea
    Telephone: 82/2-274-0509
    Fax: 82/2-277-2610

Kuwait
    Telephone: 965/532-7794
    Fax: 965/532-7796

Madagascar
    Telephone: 261/2-202 38
    Fax: 261/2-345 39

Malaysia
    Telephone: 60/3-238 0133
    Fax: 60/3-232 4585

Mexico
    Telephone: 52/5-273-8190
    Fax: 52/5-203-9524

Paraguay
    Telephone: 595/21-24 831
    Fax: 595/21-214-544

Portugal
    Telephone: 351/1-387 89 11
    Fax: 351/1-388 95 27

Spain
    Telephone: 34/1-345-7026
    Fax: 34/1-345-8608

Switzerland
    Telephone: 41/37 41 26 26
    Fax: 41/37 41 26 27

Taiwan
    Telephone: 886/2-362-6385
    Fax: 886/2-362-2809

Thailand
    Bangkok
    Telephone: 66/2-260-7061 or
                260-7189
    Fax: 66/2-260-7061
    Chiang Mai
    Telephone: 66/053-248-208

United Kingdom
    Telephone: 44/181-740-6282
    Fax: 44/181-740-5207

United States
    Telephone: 1/607-748-9500
    Fax: 1/607-748-9614

Venezuela
    Caracas
    Telephone: 58/2-951-0356
    Fax: 58/2-951-0592
    Maracaibo
    Telephone: 58/61-911 436
    Fax: 58/61-921 098

Yemen
    Telephone: 967/1-216-975
    Fax: 967/1-216-975
                (after office hours)

If no representative is listed for your country, contact the U.S. representative.

More information is available at:
    http://www.toeic-usa.com

Eight Keys to Higher Scores on TOEIC®

Key 1: Increase Your General Knowledge of English

There are two types of knowledge that will help you improve your scores on TOEIC:
- A knowledge of the format of the test and the tactics used by good test takers.
- A general command of English (which must be built up over a long period of time).

A step-by-step TOEIC preparation program such as the one in this book can supply the first type of knowledge. The best way to increase your background knowledge of English is simply to use English whenever you can. If possible, take English language classes. Outside of class, look for opportunities to speak English, especially with native speakers of the language. Read newspapers and magazines in English. Listen to English language news programs and talk shows on the radio. Attend lectures and movies in English.

Key 2: Learn Your Strengths and Weaknesses and Work on Improving Your Weaknesses

You probably already have a fairly clear idea of the areas of English in which you need improvement. You may want to use the Sample Tests that are part of each lesson in this book as diagnostic tools. Take each of these sample sections before you begin your studies. Did you find one or more of the samples particularly difficult? If so, focus more of your time and attention on the corresponding lesson or lessons of this book.

Key 3: Make the Most of Your Preparation Time

Taking an important test such as TOEIC is like facing any other challenge in your life. You need to train for it, and your training should be systematic.

Before you begin studying for the test, prepare a time-management chart. Begin by drawing up an hour-by-hour schedule of your current weekly activities. Then pencil in times for TOEIC preparation. You'll remember more of what you study if you schedule an hour or so daily or three or four times weekly than if you schedule all your study time in large blocks on weekends. After following this schedule for a week, make whatever adjustments are needed. Then keep to your schedule as much as possible until a few days before the test. At that point, studying won't have much effect on your score. It's better for you to relax.

If possible, reserve a special study space where you do nothing but study for TOEIC, separate from the place where you do your regular homework or other paperwork. This space should be as free of distractions as possible.

Use the "30–5–5" method of studying:
- First, study for thirty minutes.
- Take a five-minute break. Leave your desk and do something completely different.
- When you return, take five minutes to review what you studied during the last thirty minutes and preview what you are going to study next.

It's also a good idea to meet regularly with a small group of people who are also preparing for TOEIC. Research has shown that this "study group" approach is highly effective.

Key 4: Be Familiar with the TOEIC Format and the Directions for Each Section

If you have a clear "map" of TOEIC in your mind, you won't have any surprises on test day. You'll always know exactly where you are in the test and what will come next. You can become familiar with the format by studying the chart on page 4 and by taking the practice test in this book.

The directions for each part of the test are always the same; even the same examples are used. If you have familiarized yourself with these directions, you won't need to waste precious testing time by reading them. For copyright reasons, the directions that appear in this book are not the same, word for word, as those used on official versions, but they are similar, and if you understand these directions, you will understand those on ETS tests.

Key 5: Know How to Mark Your Answer Sheet

One of the worst surprises you can get during a test is to suddenly discover that the number of the item you are working on does not correspond to the number of the answer you are marking for that item. You have to go back to find where you first got off track, then change all the answers after that number. You can avoid this problem by using the test book itself as a marker. Cover the unanswered items in each column on the answer sheet with the book and then, as you mark each item, move the test book down one number.

Bring several number 2 black-lead pencils, a good eraser, and a small pencil sharpener. Don't use a pen or a liquid-lead pencil to mark your answers. Mark the answers by filling in the space completely. Don't mark answers in any other way.

Correct

1. Ⓐ   Ⓑ   Ⓒ   ●

Incorrect

1. Ⓐ   Ⓑ   Ⓒ   Ⓧ

1. Ⓐ   Ⓑ   Ⓒ   Ⓓ

1. Ⓐ   Ⓑ   Ⓒ   ⊛

Always be sure that you have filled in the blank completely and have only filled in one blank per item. If you have to erase an answer, be sure to erase completely.

Key 6: No Matter What, Always Guess!

On TOEIC, unlike on certain standardized tests (such as GMAT), there is no penalty for guessing. In other words, no points or fractions of points are subtracted for incorrect answers. What this means to you is that you should *always* guess at the answer and *never* leave any items unanswered at the end of the test. Remember, even if you are guessing blindly, you have a one-in-four chance (25%) of guessing the answer correctly in most sections. (In Part II, your odds go up to one in three, or 33.3%.)

If you have no idea which answer is correct, it's probably better to use a standard guess answer such as (C) than to guess at random.

⚿—π Key 7: Use the Process of Elimination to Make the Most of Your Guess

In Key 6, you learned that you should *always* guess. However, until the last few minutes of the test, it's not a good idea to guess blindly. Instead, you want to make the best guess that you possibly can, and to do so, you need to use the process of elimination. In other words, if you are unable to find the correct answer, you should eliminate unattractive or unlikely choices and then, if more than one cannot be eliminated, guess from the remaining choices. This is not as difficult as it may seem because of the way test writers design many of the items on standardized tests.

Let's look at a diagram of a typical multiple-choice item:

Stem................................

> (A) Answer choice
> (B) Answer choice
> (C) Answer choice
> (D) Answer choice

Only one of the four answer choices, of course, can be the best one. This choice is called the **key**. The three incorrect choices are called **distractors** because their function is to distract (take away) your attention from the key.

Stem..............................

> (A) Distractor
> (B) Distractor
> (C) Key
> (D) Distractor

However, many items are written so that the distractors are not equally attractive. One or two choices are often clearly incorrect and are easy to eliminate. Another one of the distractors is usually less easy to eliminate because it is somehow closer to the key. This is the choice that most people choose if they answer an item incorrectly. It is called the **main distractor**.

Stem..........................

> (A) Main distractor
> (B) Distractor
> (C) Key
> (D) Distractor

Even if you can eliminate only one distractor from a four-choice item, you have improved your chance of guessing the key from one in four (25%) to one in three (33.3%), and if you can eliminate two distractors your chances become pretty good — one in two, or 50%.

What should you do if you can eliminate one or two choices but can't decide which of the remaining choices is correct? If you have a "hunch" (an intuitive feeling) that one answer is better, choose that one. If not, just mark your standard guess answer or, if you've eliminated that choice, choose any remaining letter and go on.

Let's see how this process works in practice by looking at an example from Part V:

I am eager _____ the new member of the product development team.

> (A) meeting
> (B) will meet
> (C) to meet
> (D) met

You'll probably be able to eliminate choices (B) and (D), because these are both main verbs and the sentence already has a main verb (*am*). Also, choice (D) incorrectly refers to the past. It may be more difficult to choose between (A), a gerund (*meeting*) and (B), an infinitive (*to meet*), but even so, you've improved your chances of getting this answer correct by making an educated guess. And one of the remaining answer choices may sound better than the other. If you guessed (C), you're right!

Not all items on TOEIC follow this pattern exactly, and it is not always easy to eliminate two distractors or even one. Still, the process of elimination is a powerful tool for good test takers.

Key 8: Learn to Control Test Anxiety

There is nothing unusual about being nervous before a test. Standardized tests such as TOEIC can have a definite impact on your future plans. If you were participating in a big athletic event or giving an important business presentation, you would feel the same. There is an expression in English that describes this feeling of anxiety very well: "butterflies in your stomach." These "butterflies" will mostly disappear once the test begins. And a little nervousness can actually work to your advantage by making you more alert and focused. However, too much nervousness can slow you down and cause you to make simple mistakes.

One way to avoid stress on the day of the test is to give yourself plenty of time to get to the testing site. If you have to rush or if you're late, you'll be even more nervous during the testing period.

If you find yourself nervous during the second section of the test (Reading), give yourself a short break — take a "fifteen-second vacation." Sit back, close your eyes, take a few deep breaths, relax as completely as possible — then get back to work. (Don't try this technique during the Listening Comprehension part of the test — you will miss items on the tape!)

In general, the best way to overcome test anxiety is through a positive, confident attitude toward the test. You can develop this attitude if you become familiar with all aspects of the exam, polish the skills that are required to do well, and take a realistic practice test. *The Complete Guide to TOEIC®* was developed to help you fulfill these goals.

Guide to Listening Comprehension

The first section of TOEIC consists of four separate parts. Each has its own directions and format:

Part I: Questions About Photographs .... 20 items
Part II: Questions/Responses .... 30 items
Part III: Dialogs .... 30 items
Part IV: Short Talks (6–8 talks) .... 20 items

This section tests your ability to understand informal spoken English, but only Part II is a "pure" test of listening. Part I also tests your ability to quickly interpret photographs, and Parts III and IV test your reading skills, since you must read the questions and answer choices before you can answer.

You can make quite a few errors on this section and still get a good score. Errors count less against your total score than errors in the Reading section do. (See Score Conversion Chart on page 198.)

Concentration is very important to success in this section. You need to focus your attention on the tape, on the test booklet (except in Part II), and on your answer sheet. In Parts I and II, particularly, you need a very close, almost word-for-word understanding of the items on the tapes, and you will have to be able to distinguish between words with similar sounds.

The Listening section of the *Guide* is divided into 4 lessons, each corresponding to one of the parts of the test. Each lesson provides familiarity and practice for that part of the test.

Using the Audio Program

The audio portion of the four lessons in this section are on the audiotapes that accompany this book. The symbol [____] in your book indicates that you should turn on the tape. Almost all the exercises in this section are also on the tape. However, directions for the exercises are *not* recorded. You should read the directions before you begin to work on an exercise. The audio portion of the Practice TOEIC Test is also recorded on the tapes.

The "Tapescript and Answer Key" section at the end of this book provides a written version of the material on the tapes, as well as answers for the exercises and tests. If you have trouble with an exercise, rewind the tape and listen to it again before you look at the tapescript and the answer. Don't stop the tape in the middle of an exercise; always complete each exercise before rewinding or looking at the tapescripts.

Sentences About Photographs

 Preview: Lesson Outline

- Part I Format
- Tactics for Part I
- Sample Test
- Testing Points and Skill-Building Exercises
    - A. Sentences with Meaning Problems
    - B. Sentences with Sound Problems
    - C. Sentences with Sound and Meaning Problems
- More Practice

Part I **Format**

The first part of TOEIC consists of twenty numbered photographs that are in your test book. For each photograph, you hear on the tape four sentences that refer to it. You must decide which of the sentences best describes something you can see in the photograph. The photographs are pictures of ordinary situations. Around two-thirds of the photographs involve a person or people; around one-third involve an object or a scene without people.

The sentences are short and grammatically simple. They generally deal with the most important aspects of the photographs, but some focus on small details or on objects or people in the background.

Each item is introduced by a statement that tells you to look at the next numbered photograph. The pacing for this part is fast: There is only a six-second pause between items, and there is *no* pause between sentences (A), (B), (C), and (D).

Tactics for Part I

1. Always complete each item as quickly as possible so that you can preview the photograph for the next item. Don't wait for the statement that says, "Now look at photograph number ____."

2. If you are previewing a photograph that involves a person or people, look for certain aspects of the photographs that are often mentioned in the sentences:
   - What are the people doing?
   - Where are they?
   - Who are they? (Is there a uniform or piece of equipment or anything else that indicates their profession or role?)
   - What distinguishes them? (Is there a hat, a mustache, a purse, a pair of glasses, a tie, or anything else that differentiates the people?)
   - What do the people's expressions tell you? (Do they look happy? Unhappy? Excited? Bored? Upset?)

3. If you are previewing a photograph of an object, focus on these aspects:
   - What is it?
   - What — if anything — is it doing?
   - What is it made of?
   - Where is it?

4. If you are previewing a photograph of a scene, focus on these aspects:
   - Where is it?
   - What is in the foreground (the "front" of the picture)?
   - What — if anything — is happening?
   - What is in the background (the "distant" part of the picture)?

5. Keep looking at the photograph as the sentence is being read. If you think the right answer is one of the first three sentences — (A), (B), or (C) — put a light pencil mark in that circle, but don't fill in the blank completely. In that way, you will remember which of the three sentences you think is correct. However, if you change your mind, you can erase the mark easily. If you think the answer is (D), simply fill in the blank for (D). When all four sentences have been read, finish filling in the (A), (B), or (C) blank if you didn't change your mind, or erase the mark if you did.

6. Try to eliminate choices with problems in *meaning, sound,* and *sound + meaning.* (There is more information about recognizing these problems in the main part of this lesson.) Mark one of the remaining answers.

7. Never leave any blanks. Always guess before going on to the next item.

8. As soon as you have finished marking the answer, stop looking at and thinking about that photograph and move on to the next item.

Sample Test

 Start the audio program and read along as the directions are read.

Directions: For each item, there is a photograph in the book and four short sentences about it on the tape. The sentences are NOT written out, so you must listen carefully.

You must choose the one sentence — (A), (B), (C), or (D) — that is the best description of what can be seen in the photograph. Then mark the correct answer.

Look at the example

Listen to the four sentences:
Choice (C) — "He's waving to someone" — is the best description of what can be seen in the photograph.

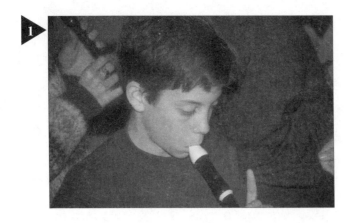

(A)   (B)   (C)   (D)

(A)   (B)   (C)   (D)

(A)   (B)   (C)   (D)

4

    Ⓐ   Ⓑ   Ⓒ   Ⓓ

5

    Ⓐ   Ⓑ   Ⓒ   Ⓓ

6

    Ⓐ   Ⓑ   Ⓒ   Ⓓ

Testing Points and Skill-Building Exercises

The correct answer for a Part I item is one that correctly describes what can be seen in the photograph. The distractors — incorrect answers — are incorrect for one of the following reasons:

A. **Meaning** — The sentence does not correctly describe what is shown in the photograph.

B. **Sound** — The sentence contains a word that sounds like — but is not the same as — something visible in the photograph.

C. **Meaning + Sound** — The sentence is not only an incorrect description of what is shown in the photograph but also contains a sound-alike word.

Let's look at the first item from the Sample Practice Test to see examples of each type of distractor.

Sample Item

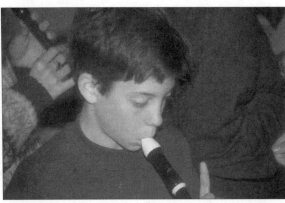

(A) The boy is holding the fruit.

(B) He's playing a game by himself.

(C) The boy is preparing some food.

● He's playing music on the flute.

Choice (A) involves a **sound** problem — the boy is holding a *flute*, not a *fruit*. (*Flute* and *fruit* are sound-alike words.) Choice (B) is a problem of **meaning**. He's not playing a game; he's playing a musical instrument, and he's not by himself. Choice (C) involves a **meaning + sound** problem: The boy is not preparing food; he is playing a flute. (*Flute* and *food* sound somewhat alike.) Choice (D) best describes what is pictured in the photograph.

Exercise 1.1

Focus: Identifying types of distractors for Part I items.

Directions: There are five photographs taken from the Sample Test section. The sentences spoken about them are printed out beneath the photograph. Identify each sentence according to the following system:

M	=	**Meaning** problem
S	=	**Sound** problem
M + S	=	**Meaning + sound** problem
C	=	Correct answer

Now start the audio program.

1

_____ (A) She's painting the wall.
_____ (B) She's pushing the stroller.
_____ (C) She's climbing the ladder.
_____ (D) She's planting flowers by the wall.

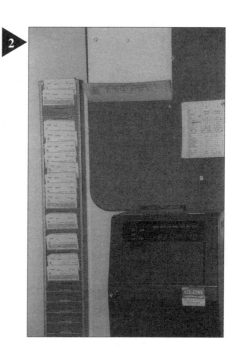

2

_____ (A) The cards are on the rock.
_____ (B) The lock is on the machine.
_____ (C) The time clock is below the bulletin board.
_____ (D) The cars are in a line.

3

_____ (A) The barges appear to be empty.
_____ (B) Trees grow on both sides of the river.
_____ (C) The boat is passing under a bridge.
_____ (D) The river is too narrow for the boat.

4

_____ (A) He's pushing a steel barrel.
_____ (B) He's going the wrong way.
_____ (C) He has just stepped out of the shadow.
_____ (D) He's waiting at a stop sign.

5

_____ (A) The man is holding the book open.
_____ (B) They're standing by themselves.
_____ (C) The books are all of different sizes.
_____ (D) The woman is pointing at the page.

A. Sentences with Meaning Problems

This is the most common type of distractor. Sentences of this type in some way contradict what is seen in the photograph. Some common types of meaning problems are listed below, but many other types are heard during the test.

Meaning Problem	Example
1. The sentence misrepresents the location.	The photograph shows a man eating in a hospital bed. The sentence says, "He's eating out at a restaurant."
2. The sentence misrepresents the photograph's "environment."	The photograph shows people in light clothing sitting in the sun. The sentence says, "It's cold and rainy today."
3. The sentence misrepresents the spatial arrangement.	The photograph shows a car parked behind a fence. The sentence says, "The car is in front of the fence."
4. The sentence misrepresents a person's activity.	The photograph shows a person writing a note. The sentence says, "She's reading from her notebook."
5. The sentence misrepresents a person's facial expression or "body language."	The photograph shows people in an audience with interested and attentive expressions. The sentence says, "They seem to be bored by what they're seeing."

6. The sentence assigns characteristics of one person or thing to another person or thing.	The photograph shows a tall man wearing a hat and a shorter man with glasses. The sentence says, "The tall man is wearing glasses."
7. The sentence misidentifies an object.	The photograph shows a scientist looking through a microscope. The sentence says, "He's using a telescope."
8. The sentence identifies people in a scene with no people.	The photograph shows an empty swimming pool. The sentence says, "The pool is crowded with swimmers today."
9. The sentence misidentifies the material something is made of.	The photograph shows a woman sitting on a stone wall. The sentence says, "The wall is made of wood."
10. The sentence misidentifies a background detail as a central feature of the photograph.	The photograph shows a man walking through an airport. There is a telephone in the background. The sentence says, "The man is talking on the telephone."

Exercise 1.2

Focus: Identifying distractors involving errors in meaning and recognizing sentences with correct meanings.

Directions: Look at each of the photographs below. You will hear a number of sentences describing each one. Decide if the sentence is true (T) or false (F) according to what you see in the picture. There may be more than one true sentence about each photograph, or there may be no true sentence.

▭ Now start the audio program.

1

(a)	T	F
(b)	T	F
(c)	T	F
(d)	T	F
(e)	T	F
(f)	T	F

2

(a)	T	F
(b)	T	F
(c)	T	F
(d)	T	F

3

(a) Ⓣ Ⓕ
(b) Ⓣ Ⓕ
(c) Ⓣ Ⓕ
(d) Ⓣ Ⓕ
(e) Ⓣ Ⓕ
(f) Ⓣ Ⓕ

(a) Ⓣ Ⓕ
(b) Ⓣ Ⓕ
(c) Ⓣ Ⓕ
(d) Ⓣ Ⓕ
(e) Ⓣ Ⓕ
(f) Ⓣ Ⓕ

4

5

(a) Ⓣ Ⓕ
(b) Ⓣ Ⓕ
(c) Ⓣ Ⓕ
(d) Ⓣ Ⓕ
(e) Ⓣ Ⓕ

(a) T F
(b) T F
(c) T F
(d) T F
(e) T F

(a) T F
(b) T F
(c) T F
(d) T F

(a) T F
(b) T F
(c) T F
(d) T F
(e) T F

(a) T F
(b) T F
(c) T F
(d) T F
(e) T F
(f) T F

(a)	Ⓣ	Ⓕ
(b)	Ⓣ	Ⓕ
(c)	Ⓣ	Ⓕ
(d)	Ⓣ	Ⓕ
(e)	Ⓣ	Ⓕ
(f)	Ⓣ	Ⓕ

B. Sentences with Sound Problems

These sentences test your ability to distinguish similar-sounding words. For example, the photograph may show a man taking a letter out of a file. The spoken sentence says, "He's taking the letter from the pile." To avoid choosing the incorrect answer, you must be able to hear the difference between *pile* and *file*.

Remember: If you hear a sentence with a sound-alike word, that sentence is not the right answer.

Also remember that, if you hear a sentence that seems strange or unrelated to what you see in the photograph, it probably involves a sound problem, even if that problem is not clear to you. These unusual sentences will not be correct answers.

Exercise 1.3

Focus: Identifying distractors involving sound problems and recognizing correct answers.

Directions: There are two parts to this exercise. For Part A, look at the photographs and listen to the sentences — (A) and (B) — about them. Mark the letter of the sentence that best describes what can be seen in the photograph.

▭ Now start the audio program.

Ⓐ   Ⓑ

Ⓐ   Ⓑ

Ⓐ   Ⓑ

Ⓐ   Ⓑ

Ⓐ   Ⓑ

6   Ⓐ   Ⓑ

7   Ⓐ   Ⓑ

8   Ⓐ   Ⓑ

9   Ⓐ   Ⓑ

Ⓐ   Ⓑ

Part B Directions: Rewind the tape to the beginning of Exercise 1.3. Write down the "sound-alike" word from the incorrect answer and the "correct" word from the correct answer. You may want to stop the tape between items to give yourself time to write. In a couple of cases, the "correct" word is not actually spoken in the answer, or appears in a different form. You'll have to guess what the correct word is in those cases.

	Sound-Alike Word	**"Correct" Word**
1.	_____	_____
2.	_____	_____
3.	_____	_____
5.	_____	_____
6.	_____	_____
7.	_____	_____
8.	_____	_____
9.	_____	_____
10.	_____	_____

C. Sentences with Sound and Meaning Problems

This type of item is more common than those involving pure sound problems. A sentence of this type contains a sound-alike word, but the sentence is also an inaccurate description of what can be seen in the photograph. For example, a photograph shows a man putting a lock on his bicycle. One sentence says, "He's blocking the path." Another sentence says, "He's swimming in the lake." In the first sentence, *blocking* sounds like *locking*, and in the second sentence, *lake* sounds like *lock*. Neither sentence describes what is happening in the picture.

Sentences of this type can be eliminated either by the sound-alike word or the incorrect meaning.

Exercise 1.4

Focus: Identifying distractors involving sound + meaning problems and recognizing correct answers.

Directions: There are two parts to this exercise. In the first part, look at the photographs and listen to the two sentences — (A) and (B) — about them. Mark the letter of the sentence that best describes what can be seen in the photograph.

▭ Now start the audio program.

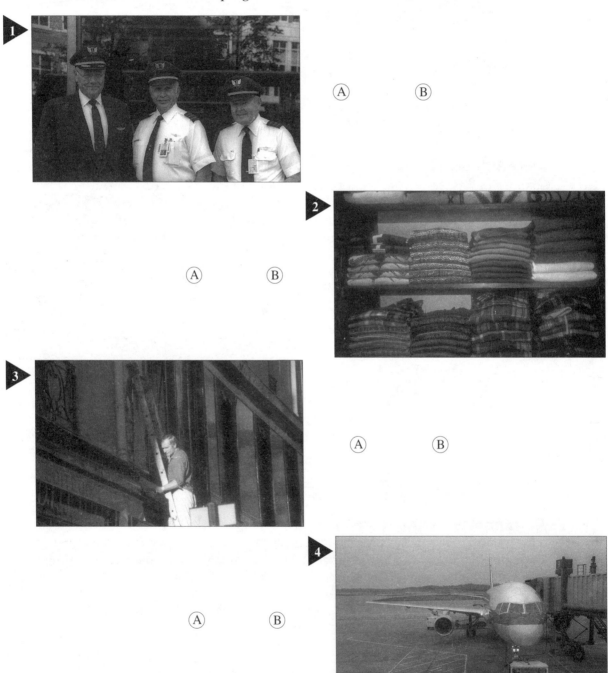

5

Ⓐ   Ⓑ

6

Ⓐ   Ⓑ

7

↓ Hall 4
Aeroflot
Air India
All Nippon Airways
Meridiana
Ukraine International

Ⓐ   Ⓑ

8

Ⓐ   Ⓑ

9

Ⓐ   Ⓑ

10 ▶

Ⓐ   Ⓑ

Part B Directions: Rewind the tape to the beginning of Exercise 1.4. Write down the "sound-alike" word from the incorrect answer and the "correct" word from the correct answer. You may want to stop the tape between items to give yourself time to write. In a couple of cases, the "correct" word is not actually spoken in the answer, or appears in a different form. You'll have to guess what the correct word is in those cases.

Sound-Alike Word	**"Correct" Word**
1. _____	_____
2. _____	_____
3. _____	_____
4. _____	_____
5. _____	_____
6. _____	_____
7. _____	_____
8. _____	_____
9. _____	_____
10. _____	_____

More Practice

Directions: For each item, there is a photograph in the book and four short sentences about it on the tape. Choose the one sentence — (A), (B), (C), or (D) — that is the best description of what can be seen in the photograph. Then mark the correct answer.

🔲 Now start the audio program.

1 ▶

Ⓐ   Ⓑ   Ⓒ   Ⓓ

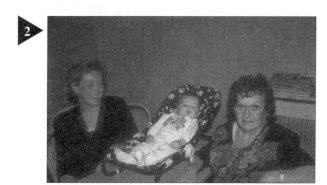

Ⓐ　　Ⓑ　　Ⓒ　　Ⓓ

Ⓐ　　Ⓑ　　Ⓒ　　Ⓓ

Ⓐ　　Ⓑ　　Ⓒ　　Ⓓ

Ⓐ　　Ⓑ　　Ⓒ　　Ⓓ

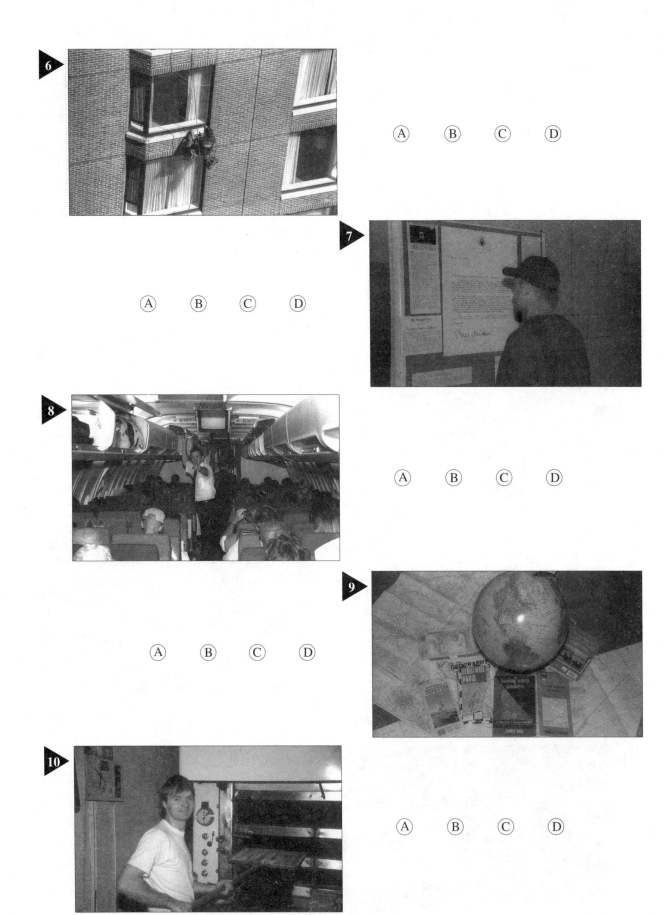

6 ▸

Ⓐ Ⓑ Ⓒ Ⓓ

7 ▸

Ⓐ Ⓑ Ⓒ Ⓓ

8 ▸

Ⓐ Ⓑ Ⓒ Ⓓ

9 ▸

Ⓐ Ⓑ Ⓒ Ⓓ

10 ▸

Ⓐ Ⓑ Ⓒ Ⓓ

    Ⓐ   Ⓑ   Ⓒ   Ⓓ

    Ⓐ   Ⓑ   Ⓒ   Ⓓ

    Ⓐ   Ⓑ   Ⓒ   Ⓓ

    Ⓐ   Ⓑ   Ⓒ   Ⓓ

    Ⓐ   Ⓑ   Ⓒ   Ⓓ

16   Ⓐ   Ⓑ   Ⓒ   Ⓓ

17   Ⓐ   Ⓑ   Ⓒ   Ⓓ

18   Ⓐ   Ⓑ   Ⓒ   Ⓓ

19   Ⓐ   Ⓑ   Ⓒ   Ⓓ

20   Ⓐ   Ⓑ   Ⓒ   Ⓓ

Questions/Responses

 Preview: Lesson Outline

- Part II Format
- Tactics for Part II
- Sample Test
- Testing Points and Skill-Building Exercises
    - A. Information Questions
    - B. Yes/No Questions
    - C. Other Types of Questions
    - D. Recognizing Sound/Meaning Distractors
    - E. Recognizing Other Types of Distractors
- More Practice

 Part II **Format**

This part of TOEIC consists of thirty items. Each item consists of a question spoken on the tape, followed by three possible responses (answers) to the question, also spoken on the tape. Your job is to decide which of these three best answers the question. Between each item is a six-second pause. Part II problems do not involve any reading skills; therefore, this part is considered a "pure" test of listening skills. Your test book simply tells you to mark an answer for each problem.

Tactics for Part II

1. There are no answer choices to consider before or while the item is being read. You should concentrate entirely on the question and the three responses on the tape, and pay no attention at all to the test book.
2. Try to identify the type of question (information question, yes/no question, choice question, and so on). The correct response, of course, often depends on the type of question being asked.
3. Try to eliminate distractors. Parts D and E of the "Testing Points and Skill-Building Exercises" section of this lesson, pages 51–52, will help you recognize distractors.
4. As you listen to the three responses, put a small dot with your pencil in the circle marked (A) or (B) if you believe one of those responses is correct. Don't completely fill in the space until you've heard all three responses.

    Ⓐ   Ⓑ   Ⓒ

    This is to remind you which of the two you thought was correct. If you change your mind and choose (C), be sure to erase the dot that you made.
5. If you hear all three responses and none of the three seems correct, make a guess and get ready for the next problem.
6. There is very little time (only six seconds) between items in Part II. You need to decide on an answer and fill in the blank quickly to be ready for the next item.

Sample Test

Start the audio program and read along as the directions are read.

Directions: In this part of the test, you hear a question asked on the tape. After that, you hear three possible responses to the question. Each question and response is given only once and is not written out in your book, so listen carefully. Mark the answer that corresponds to the best response to the question.

Listen to a sample

You hear: Where have you been, Steve?

You then hear: (A) At the gymnasium.
(B) Very well, thanks.
(C) Yes, I have.

Choice (A), "At the gymnasium," is the best response to the question "Where have you been, Steve?" You should mark (A).

1. Mark your answer.	(A)	(B)	(C)	7. Mark your answer.	(A)	(B)	(C)
2. Mark your answer.	(A)	(B)	(C)	8. Mark your answer.	(A)	(B)	(C)
3. Mark your answer.	(A)	(B)	(C)	9. Mark your answer.	(A)	(B)	(C)
4. Mark your answer.	(A)	(B)	(C)	10. Mark your answer.	(A)	(B)	(C)
5. Mark your answer.	(A)	(B)	(C)	11. Mark your answer.	(A)	(B)	(C)
6. Mark your answer.	(A)	(B)	(C)	12. Mark your answer.	(A)	(B)	(C)

Testing Points and Skill-Building Exercises

The questions you hear on this part of TOEIC can be broken down roughly as follows:

Information questions (*wh-* questions)	50%
Yes/No questions	25%
Other types of questions	25%

Information questions begin with a *wh-* question word:

When can we begin?
Where's the post office?
How are you today?

Yes/No questions begin with an auxiliary verb or a form of the main verb *to be*.

Did Hiroshi attend the lecture?
Would you like to come with us?
Were you in Nairobi last year?

Other types of questions include questions with embedded sentences, choice questions, tag questions, and negative questions.

Do you know who wrote this report? (question with embedded sentence)
Do you want to play chess or checkers? (choice question)
You've been to Seoul before, haven't you? (tag question)
Isn't this interesting? (negative question)

Exercise 2.1

Focus: Distinguishing between information questions, yes/no questions, and other types of questions.

Directions: Decide whether the question you hear is an information question, a yes/no question, or some other type of question (embedded question, choice question, tag question, or negative question) and then mark the appropriate blank. The first one has been done as an example.

Now start the audio program.

	Information Question	Yes/No Question	Other Type of Question
1.	✓		
2.			
3.			
4.			
5.			
6.			
7.			
8.			
9.			
10.			
11.			
12.			

A. Information Questions

Nearly half the questions in Part II are information questions. These questions ask for specific pieces of information. Questions with *what . . . ?* and *how . . . ?* are the most common.

1. What . . . ?	**5.** Why . . . ?
2. How . . . ?	**6.** Who . . . ?
3. When . . . ?	**7.** Whose . . . ?
4. Where . . . ?	**8.** Which . . . ?

Responses to *wh-* questions may be either short answers (a word or phrase) or complete sentences.

What color is your new car?
- Ⓐ I bought a sports car.
- Ⓑ New cars are expensive.
- ● It's bright blue.

This question asks about color. Only (C) provides this information.

How was that party Friday night?
- ● Very enjoyable.
- Ⓑ By car.
- Ⓒ Until around midnight.

This question asks a person for his or her general impression of the party. Choice (A) provides this.

What do you think of the plan to open an office in Yokohama?
- ● I think it's a great idea.
- Ⓑ I'll leave the office open.
- Ⓒ I'm going next month.

The question asks for an opinion of the plan, such as the one expressed in (A).

How many suitcases are you bringing?
- Ⓐ Quite expensive.
- Ⓑ They're very full.
- ● Two or three.

A *how many . . . ?* question asks about quantity (number). The only response containing a quantity is (C).

Questions with *What . . . ?*

The question word *what . . . ?* is used to ask about things, names, actions, ideas, definitions, and many other concepts.

Sample Questions	Possible Responses
What are you thinking about?	I'm thinking about my family.
What did Cathy say to you?	She just said, "Good morning."
What is George going to do tomorrow?	He's going to a job interview.
What's her name?	It's Joyce Wong.
What happened here?	There was an accident.

What type of . . . ? and *What kind of . . . ?* are used to ask about classification.

Sample Questions	Possible Responses
What kind of music does he listen to?	He usually listens to jazz.
What type of people read this magazine?	Well-educated people, generally.

What time . . . ? is used to ask about the time of day.

Sample Questions	Possible Responses
What time does your flight leave?	At 7:30.
What time is the news on television?	It's on at 11.

What do/did you think of . . . ? asks for an opinion.

Sample Questions	Possible Responses
What do you think of Scott Graham's latest novel?	It's a real thriller.
What do you think of your new supervisor?	I don't know her well enough to say.

What . . . like? is used to ask for a general description or impression. It is also used to ask about the weather.

Sample Questions	Possible Responses
What are your co-workers like?	They seem very pleasant.
What does your house look like?	It's a two-story, red-brick bungalow.
What's the weather like here in the winter?	It's cool and often rainy.

What does . . . do for a living? is used to ask about a person's occupation.

Sample Question	Possible Response
What does your brother do for a living?	He's an accountant.

What's the matter with . . . ? and *What's wrong with . . . ?* are used to ask about problems.

Sample Questions	Possible Responses
What's the matter with Joe?	He ate too much, and he doesn't feel well.
What's wrong with this microphone?	I don't know; it just doesn't seem to work.

What . . . ? is also used before many nouns to ask questions.

Sample Questions	Possible Responses
What size sweater do you wear?	Medium, usually.
What sports do you enjoy?	Tennis and volleyball.
What color is your new suit?	It's dark blue.
What flavor ice cream do you want?	Strawberry, please.

Exercise 2.2

Focus: Answering information questions beginning with *what*.

Directions: You will hear a number of questions, each followed by three possible responses to the question. For each item, choose the letter of the response that best answers the question.

▭ Now start the audio program.

1. Mark your answer. (A) (B) (C)   6. Mark your answer. (A) (B) (C)
2. Mark your answer. (A) (B) (C)   7. Mark your answer. (A) (B) (C)
3. Mark your answer. (A) (B) (C)   8. Mark your answer. (A) (B) (C)
4. Mark your answer. (A) (B) (C)   9. Mark your answer. (A) (B) (C)
5. Mark your answer. (A) (B) (C)   10. Mark your answer. (A) (B) (C)

Questions with *How . . . ?*

The question word *how . . . ?* is used to ask about manner and methods.

Sample Questions	Possible Responses
How did she get to Melbourne?	By plane.
How did you get in touch with Mr. Suyoto?	By faxing him.
How does he drive?	Slowly and carefully.
How did you make these holes?	With a drill.
How did they get a loan for their business?	By providing collateral.
How do you know Christina?	She works in my office.

How . . . ? can be used to ask about the general condition of someone or something.

Sample Questions	Possible Responses
How's your father doing?	He's doing well, thanks.
How has Ellen been?	As far as I know, just fine.
How was dinner?	Great — we went to a good Mexican restaurant.

How much . . . ? is used to ask about cost or amount. *How many . . . ?* is used to ask about quantity (number).

Sample Questions	Possible Responses
How much is a motorcycle like that one?	Around $5,000.
How much water should we bring?	A couple of liters each.
How many guests were at the party?	There were twenty or thirty.

How do/did you like . . . ? is used to ask for an opinion of someone or something.

Sample Question	Possible Response
How did you like that new movie?	I enjoyed it, but my husband didn't.

How . . . get to . . . ? is used to ask for directions.

Sample Question	Possible Response
How do I get to the post office from here?	Walk down Liberty Avenue until you come to Third Street.

How about . . . ? is used to offer something to someone or to invite someone to do something.

Sample Questions	Possible Responses
How about some French pastries?	I'd love to have some, but I'm on a diet.
How about coming to a barbecue at our house on Saturday?	Sure, that sounds great.

How . . . ? is used with adverbs and adjectives to ask about age, duration, frequency, size, distance, and other characteristics.

Sample Questions	Possible Responses
How old is Fritz?	He's twenty-seven.
How long will this session last?	For another hour, perhaps.
How often does Michelle go skiing?	Once or twice a month.
How far is it from Boston to Washington, D.C.?	It's around 400 miles.
How late is this store open tonight?	Until nine o'clock, I believe.
How soon can you be here?	In about fifteen minutes.

Exercise 2.3

Focus: Answering information questions beginning with *how*.

Directions: You will hear a number of questions, each followed by three possible responses to the question. For each item, choose the letter of the response that best answers the question.

🔲 Now start the audio program.

1. Mark your answer.   (A)   (B)   (C)
2. Mark your answer.   (A)   (B)   (C)
3. Mark your answer.   (A)   (B)   (C)
4. Mark your answer.   (A)   (B)   (C)
5. Mark your answer.   (A)   (B)   (C)
6. Mark your answer.   (A)   (B)   (C)
7. Mark your answer.   (A)   (B)   (C)

8. Mark your answer.   (A)   (B)   (C)
9. Mark your answer.   (A)   (B)   (C)
10. Mark your answer.   (A)   (B)   (C)
11. Mark your answer.   (A)   (B)   (C)
12. Mark your answer.   (A)   (B)   (C)
13. Mark your answer.   (A)   (B)   (C)
14. Mark your answer.   (A)   (B)   (C)

Questions with *When . . . ?* and *Where . . . ?*

The question word *when . . . ?* is used to ask about time: times of day, days, dates, years, decades.

Sample Questions	Possible Responses
When did Christos arrive?	Last Wednesday.
When will the planning session take place?	Tomorrow at eleven.
When is Maria's birthday?	On March 3.

The question word *where . . . ?* is used to ask about locations: rooms, buildings, streets, cities, countries, and so on.

Sample Questions	Possible Responses
Where is the television studio?	It's downtown on Wells Street.
Where is your passport?	In my briefcase.
Where are you going?	To the drugstore.
Where are my glasses?	Over there, on your desk.

Where . . . from? is used to ask about place of origin.

Sample Question	Possible Response
Where is Jaewoo from?	He's from Pusan, South Korea.

Exercise 2.4

Focus: Answering information questions beginning with *when* and *where*.

Directions: You will hear a number of questions, each followed by three possible responses to the question. For each item, choose the letter of the response that best answers the question.

[cassette icon] Now start the audio program.

1. Mark your answer. (A) (B) (C)   5. Mark your answer. (A) (B) (C)

2. Mark your answer. (A) (B) (C)   6. Mark your answer. (A) (B) (C)

3. Mark your answer. (A) (B) (C)   7. Mark your answer. (A) (B) (C)

4. Mark your answer. (A) (B) (C)   8. Mark your answer. (A) (B) (C)

Questions with *Why . . . ?*, *Who . . . ?*, *Whose . . . ?*, and *Which . . . ?*

The question word *why . . . ?* is used to ask about reasons and purposes.

Sample Questions	Possible Responses
Why did she go to Brussels?	To attend a conference.
Why did you leave your last job?	Because of the low wages.

Why don't you . . . ? is used to make suggestions.

Sample Question	Possible Response
Why don't you order the soup?	Good idea — soup sounds great.

The question word *who . . . ?* is used to ask questions about people.

Sample Questions	Possible Responses
Who were you talking to on the phone?	To my wife.
Who is that woman in the blue raincoat?	That's Patricia Wedgewood.

The question word *whose . . . ?* is used to ask about possession.

Sample Question	Possible Response
Whose scarf is this?	It's Fran's.

The question word *which . . . ?* is used to ask about choices from a limited number of selections.

Sample Questions	Possible Responses
Which salesperson won the award?	Mr. Ishimura did.
Which floor is your office on?	It's on the fourth floor.

Which way . . . ? is used to ask about directions.

Sample Question	Possible Response
Which way is it to Concourse E?	Walk straight ahead and you'll see a sign.

Exercise 2.5

Focus: Answering information questions beginning with *why*, *who*, *whose*, and *which*.

Directions: You will hear a number of questions, each followed by three possible responses to the question. For each item, choose the letter of the response that best answers the question.

▨ Now start the audio program.

1. Mark your answer.	(A)	(B)	(C)	5. Mark your answer.	(A) (B) (C)
2. Mark your answer.	(A)	(B)	(C)	6. Mark your answer.	(A) (B) (C)
3. Mark your answer.	(A)	(B)	(C)	7. Mark your answer.	(A) (B) (C)
4. Mark your answer.	(A)	(B)	(C)	8. Mark your answer.	(A) (B) (C)

Exercise 2.6

Focus: Reviewing and practicing all types of information questions.

Directions: Listen to the question on the tape. You will then hear three responses. Decide which of the responses best answers the question, and mark that response.

▨ Now start the audio program.

1. Mark your answer.	(A)	(B)	(C)	9. Mark your answer.	(A) (B) (C)
2. Mark your answer.	(A)	(B)	(C)	10. Mark your answer.	(A) (B) (C)
3. Mark your answer.	(A)	(B)	(C)	11. Mark your answer.	(A) (B) (C)
4. Mark your answer.	(A)	(B)	(C)	12. Mark your answer.	(A) (B) (C)
5. Mark your answer.	(A)	(B)	(C)	13. Mark your answer.	(A) (B) (C)
6. Mark your answer.	(A)	(B)	(C)	14. Mark your answer.	(A) (B) (C)
7. Mark your answer.	(A)	(B)	(C)	15. Mark your answer.	(A) (B) (C)
8. Mark your answer.	(A)	(B)	(C)	16. Mark your answer.	(A) (B) (C)

B. Yes/No Questions

Basic Yes/No Questions

Yes/no questions begin with auxiliary verbs (*do, are, has, should, can,* for example) or with a form of the main verb *be* (*is, are, was,* and *were*). Responses may be short answers or full sentences.

Sample Questions	Possible Responses
Did you watch television last night?	No, I was out last night.
Is Herbert out of town?	I believe he is.
Will Mr. Cho attend the meeting?	Probably not.

Some yes/no questions contain the words *yet* and *still*. *Yet* is used in questions and negative sentences to mean that an activity is continuing. *Still* has a similar meaning in some questions and in affirmative sentences.

Sample Questions	Possible Responses	
Is the game over yet?	No, it's still going on.	**Or**
	No, it's not over yet.	**Or**
	Yes, it's already over.	
Are you still working at TRC Electronics?	Yes, I still work there.	**Or**
	No, I don't work there anymore.	

Some yes/no questions contain the word *ever*. *Ever* means "at any time in the past."

Sample Question	Possible Response
Have you ever been to Kuala Lumpur?	Yes, several times. **Or** No, never.

Some yes/no questions begin, "Have you had the chance to. . ." This means "Have you had the opportunity to do something yet?"

Sample Question	Possible Response
Have you had a chance to read that letter?	No, not yet.

In Part II, the correct responses for yes/no questions are often not simple short answers such as "Yes, I do" or "No, I'm not." There is a range of affirmative, negative, or neutral responses, as shown:

Question: Has Martin finished writing the report?		
Possible Affirmative Responses	**Possible Negative Responses**	**Possible Neutral Responses**
I think so. Of course he has. Yes, he finished this morning. I believe he has. Sure, he's a fast worker. Probably.	No, I don't think he has. Not yet, but he's hard at work on it. No, but he should finish soon. No, he gave up on it. No, he's doing something else now.	I have no idea. Why don't you ask him? Maybe. Perhaps. I'm not sure.

Exercise 2.7

Focus: Answering yes/no questions.

Directions: You will hear a number of questions, each followed by three possible responses to the question. For each item, choose the letter of the response that best answers the question.

Now start the audio program.

1. Mark your answer. (A) (B) (C)
2. Mark your answer. (A) (B) (C)
3. Mark your answer. (A) (B) (C)
4. Mark your answer. (A) (B) (C)
5. Mark your answer. (A) (B) (C)
6. Mark your answer. (A) (B) (C)
7. Mark your answer. (A) (B) (C)
8. Mark your answer. (A) (B) (C)
9. Mark your answer. (A) (B) (C)
10. Mark your answer. (A) (B) (C)

Requests, Invitations, and Offers

Some yes/no questions have special functions. These functions include making requests, giving invitations, and making offers. A **request** involves asking someone to do something or asking someone to help.

Sample Requests	Possible Responses
Will you come here a minute?	Of course —what do you need?
Would you hand me that pair of scissors?	Sure, here you are.
Can you take a look at this new schedule?	I'll be glad to.
Could you help me move this box?	I can't, I'm afraid — I have a sore back.
Can I have some more ice water?	Yes, here's some.
Could I get a copy of that?	This is the only copy I have, I'm afraid.
May I borrow twenty dollars?	Yes, if you promise to pay me back tomorrow.
Would you mind if we didn't go out tonight?	No, I don't care — I don't want to go out either.*
Do you mind if I turn on the radio?	No, go ahead.*

*A positive response to questions beginning *do you mind if . . . ?* or *would you mind if . . . ?* may begin with the word *No.* For example, the response "No, go ahead" means "Yes, you may turn on the radio."

An **invitation** is a suggestion that someone go somewhere or do something with the person asking the question.

Sample Invitations	Possible Responses
Would you like to join us for a game of tennis?	We'd love to — thanks!
Will you be able to come to the garden show this afternoon?	I'm afraid not, but perhaps tomorrow.
Should we get something to eat now?	Sure — I'm getting hungry.
Do you want to come skiing with us this weekend?	That would be great.
Should we get something to eat now?	All right, let's do.

An **offer** is a proposal to help someone or to allow someone to do something.

Sample Offers	Possible Responses
Could I get you a glass of water?	Thanks, I could use one.
Can I help you?	Yes, I'm looking for some printer paper.
May I show you our new line of fall clothes?	I just want to look around, thank you.
Should I get you a taxi?	No, I believe I'll walk.
Would you like to use my computer?	Yes, if you don't mind.
Is there anything I can do for you?	You could make a phone call for me.
Would you like me to take you to the airport?	Thanks — it's kind of you to offer.

Exercise 2.8

Focus: Answering yes/no questions involving requests, invitations, and offers.

Directions: You will hear a number of questions, each followed by three possible responses to the question. For each item, choose the letter of the response that best answers the question.

⊡ Now start the audio program.

1. Mark your answer. (A) (B) (C)　　7. Mark your answer. (A) (B) (C)

2. Mark your answer. (A) (B) (C)　　8. Mark your answer. (A) (B) (C)

3. Mark your answer. (A) (B) (C)　　9. Mark your answer. (A) (B) (C)

4. Mark your answer. (A) (B) (C)　　10. Mark your answer. (A) (B) (C)

5. Mark your answer. (A) (B) (C)　　11. Mark your answer. (A) (B) (C)

6. Mark your answer. (A) (B) (C)　　12. Mark your answer. (A) (B) (C)

C. Other Types of Questions

Sample Items: Other Types of Questions

Can you tell me when the next planning meeting will be?
    (A) Every month.
    ● This Monday at ten.
    (C) Yes, that's the plan.

This is an embedded question. It really asks, "When will the next planning meeting be?"

Do you prefer tennis or golf?
    (A) All right, let's play.
    (B) I like both.
    ● I'd rather play tennis.

This is a choice question. The correct answer indicates which of the two choices the respondent prefers.

That presentation wasn't very long, was it?
    (A) No, it wasn't difficult.
    ● You're right — it was quite short.
    (C) Thanks, I enjoyed it.

This is a tag question. Choice (B) responds to the question of whether or not the presentation was long or not.

Wasn't that a fascinating article?
    (A) Yes, he was fascinating.
    (B) It will be over quickly.
    ● Yes, it was very interesting.

This is a negative question. The questioner believes the article was fascinating, and in (C), the respondent agrees.

Questions with Embedded Sentences

This type of question usually begins with one of the following phrases:

Do you know . . .   Do you think . . .   Did you decide . . .
Did you hear . . .   Are you sure . . .   Did anyone tell you . . .
Have you heard . . .   Can you tell me . . .   Will you let me know . . .

The embedded question may be an information question:

Sample Questions	Possible Responses
Did you decide where you're going for your honeymoon?	We're going to Tahiti.
Can you tell me how to get to the Continental Express office?	Sorry, I'm not sure where it is.

Responses to this type of questions are not simply yes/no answers; they must answer the embedded information questions.

The embedded question may be a yes/no question. These questions are introduced by the word *if* or *whether*.

Sample Questions	Possible Responses
Do you know if Mr. Kwon is in his office?	I believe he is — let me check.
Have you heard whether interest rates will go up again?	I haven't heard anything, but they probably will.

The embedded sentence may also be a statement. These statements can be introduced by the word *that*, but *that* is often omitted.

Sample Questions	Possible Responses
Did you hear that Bill was laid off?	Oh, no — poor Bill!
Are you sure this is a bargain?	Yes, it's the best price I think you'll get.

Choice Questions

Choice questions ask listeners to choose one of two (sometimes three) possibilities. They contain the word *or*.

Sample Questions	Possible Responses
Will you arrive in the morning or the evening?	In the morning, I think.
Do you want coffee or tea?	Coffee for me.

Responses to these questions usually name one of the choices. Answers may also include the words *either*, *neither*, or *both*. A yes or no response is seldom appropriate for a choice question.

Sample Question	Possible Response
Do you want milk or sugar in your coffee?	Neither one. **Or** Both please.

Exercise 2.9

Focus: Answering questions with embedded sentences and choice questions.

Directions: You will hear a number of questions, each followed by three possible responses to the question. For each item, choose the letter of the response that best answers the question.

Now start the audio program.

1. Mark your answer. (A) (B) (C)
2. Mark your answer. (A) (B) (C)
3. Mark your answer. (A) (B) (C)
4. Mark your answer. (A) (B) (C)
5. Mark your answer. (A) (B) (C)
6. Mark your answer. (A) (B) (C)
7. Mark your answer. (A) (B) (C)
8. Mark your answer. (A) (B) (C)

9. Mark your answer. (A) (B) (C)
10. Mark your answer. (A) (B) (C)
11. Mark your answer. (A) (B) (C)
12. Mark your answer. (A) (B) (C)
13. Mark your answer. (A) (B) (C)
14. Mark your answer. (A) (B) (C)
15. Mark your answer. (A) (B) (C)
16. Mark your answer. (A) (B) (C)

Tag Questions

Tag questions consist of an affirmative statement with a negative tag (. . . *doesn't he?*, . . . *isn't it?*, . . . *haven't you?*) or a negative statement with an affirmative tag (. . . *will you?*, . . . *did she?*, . . . *are there?*).

Sample Questions	Possible Responses
This is a beautiful beach, isn't it?	It's lovely.
You enjoyed the play, didn't you?	As a matter of fact, I found it boring.
This won't take long, will it?	Just a few minutes.
He didn't miss his plane, did he?	I don't think so.

Expressions such as . . . *wouldn't you say?*, . . . *don't you think?*, *okay?*, and . . . *right?* are sometimes used in place of negative tags.

Sample Questions	Possible Responses
You remember Rachel, right?	Oh, sure, I remember her well.
This is a good place to camp, don't you think?	Yes, it's a nice spot.

Negative Questions

Negative questions begin with negative contractions: *Doesn't . . ., Hasn't . . ., Aren't. . . .* The expected answer is affirmative, but the actual answer may be either affirmative or negative.

Sample Questions	Possible Responses
Isn't this beautiful weather?	It certainly is.
Weren't you tired after the race?	No, not too tired.

Some negative questions are used in special functions:

Won't you . . . is used in invitations.

Sample Question	Possible Response
Won't you come to the party with us?	Sure, I'd love to.

Shouldn't you/we . . . is used to make suggestions.

Sample Question	Possible Response
Shouldn't you take your umbrella?	No, I think the weather is going to clear up.

Wouldn't you like . . . ? is used to make offers.

Sample Question	Possible Response
Wouldn't you like some tea?	Thanks, I'd love some.

Exercise 2.10

Focus: Answering tag questions and negative questions.

Directions: You will hear a number of questions, each followed by three possible responses to the question. For each item, choose the letter of the response that best answers the question.

Now start the audio program.

1. Mark your answer. (A) (B) (C)
2. Mark your answer. (A) (B) (C)
3. Mark your answer. (A) (B) (C)
4. Mark your answer. (A) (B) (C)
5. Mark your answer. (A) (B) (C)
6. Mark your answer. (A) (B) (C)
7. Mark your answer. (A) (B) (C)
8. Mark your answer. (A) (B) (C)
9. Mark your answer. (A) (B) (C)
10. Mark your answer. (A) (B) (C)
11. Mark your answer. (A) (B) (C)
12. Mark your answer. (A) (B) (C)

D. Recognizing Sound/Meaning Distractors

Some responses are incorrect because of problems involving sound and meaning.

Sample Items: Sound/Meaning Problems

Did you catch the plane?
- (A) No, I didn't change my plan.
- ● Yes, but I almost missed it.
- (C) No, I didn't catch a cold.

The question contains the word *plane*. Choice (A) contains the sound-alike word *plan* and is incorrect. The question also includes the word *catch*. Choice (C) contains the word *catch* too, but it has another meaning (to contract an illness).

How did you hear about this event?
- ● My brother told me.
- (B) The event is not held here.
- (C) It starts at nine.

Choice (B) contains the word *here*, which sounds exactly like the word *hear* in the question. However, choice (B) does not answer the question. Choice (C) answers the question "When does the event start?"

There are three types of sound/meaning problems:

1. **Sound-alike words:** The question and one of the responses have words with similar sounds but different meanings (such as *plane* and *plan* in the first sample item).
2. **Words with multiple meanings:** The question contains a word that has more than one meaning. The word is used one way in the question and another way in one of the responses (*catch* and *catch* in the first sample item).
3. **Homonyms:** The question and one of the responses contain homonyms — words that have the same pronunciation but different meanings (*hear* and *here* in the second sample item).

Exercise 2.11

Focus: Identifying distractors based on sound/meaning problems, and choosing correct answers.

Directions: You will hear a number of questions, each followed by three possible responses to the question. For each item, choose the letter of the response that best answers the question.

⌷⌷ Now start the audio program.

1. Mark your answer. (A) (B) (C)   6. Mark your answer. (A) (B) (C)

2. Mark your answer. (A) (B) (C)   7. Mark your answer. (A) (B) (C)

3. Mark your answer. (A) (B) (C)   8. Mark your answer. (A) (B) (C)

4. Mark your answer. (A) (B) (C)   9. Mark your answer. (A) (B) (C)

5. Mark your answer. (A) (B) (C)   10. Mark your answer. (A) (B) (C)

E. Recognizing Other Types of Distractors

Some responses are incorrect for the following reasons:

1. **Incorrect verb tense**
   > Where did Jacques go?
   >> (A) He'll go tomorrow.

   The question asks about the past (*did . . . go*), but the response involves the future. (*He'll go tomorrow.*)

2. **Incorrect person**
   > Do you plan to go with her?
   >> (A) Yes, she plans to.

   The question asks about *you*, so the response should use the word *I* or *we*. Instead, it incorrectly involves the word *she*.

3. **Response to the incorrect type of question**
   > When did Maria leave?
   >> (A) I think she went to the bank.

   The question asks about time (*When . . . ?*), but the response provides a destination (at the bank). This response is incorrect because it answers a *where . . . to?* question, not a *when . . . ?* question.

   > Were you here at noon?
   >> (A) At a restaurant.

   The question asks for a yes/no reply, but the response answers an information question ("Where were you at noon?").

   > Do you want one scoop of ice cream or two?
   >> (A) Yes, please.

   The question asks the listener to choose between one scoop or two, but the response is a simple affirmative. This is a proper answer for a yes/no question, not for a choice question.

Exercise 2.12

Focus: Identifying common types of distractors for Part II items.

Directions: You will hear a question followed by a response. In each case, the response is an inappropriate one. Choose the category that most correctly explains why the response is not an appropriate one, and mark the blank accordingly.

	Wrong Tense	Wrong Person	Wrong Type of Question
1.	_____	_____	_____
2.	_____	_____	_____
3.	_____	_____	_____

4.   _____   _____   _____

5.   _____   _____   _____

6.   _____   _____   _____

7.   _____   _____   _____

8.   _____   _____   _____

9.   _____   _____   _____

10.   _____   _____   _____

More Practice

Directions: You will hear a number of questions, each followed by three possible responses to the question. For each item, choose the letter of the response that best answers the question.

Now start the audio program.

1. Mark your answer. Ⓐ Ⓑ Ⓒ		16. Mark your answer. Ⓐ Ⓑ Ⓒ
2. Mark your answer. Ⓐ Ⓑ Ⓒ		17. Mark your answer. Ⓐ Ⓑ Ⓒ
3. Mark your answer. Ⓐ Ⓑ Ⓒ		18. Mark your answer. Ⓐ Ⓑ Ⓒ
4. Mark your answer. Ⓐ Ⓑ Ⓒ		19. Mark your answer. Ⓐ Ⓑ Ⓒ
5. Mark your answer. Ⓐ Ⓑ Ⓒ		20. Mark your answer. Ⓐ Ⓑ Ⓒ
6. Mark your answer. Ⓐ Ⓑ Ⓒ		21. Mark your answer. Ⓐ Ⓑ Ⓒ
7. Mark your answer. Ⓐ Ⓑ Ⓒ		22. Mark your answer. Ⓐ Ⓑ Ⓒ
8. Mark your answer. Ⓐ Ⓑ Ⓒ		23. Mark your answer. Ⓐ Ⓑ Ⓒ
9. Mark your answer. Ⓐ Ⓑ Ⓒ		24. Mark your answer. Ⓐ Ⓑ Ⓒ
10. Mark your answer. Ⓐ Ⓑ Ⓒ		25. Mark your answer. Ⓐ Ⓑ Ⓒ
11. Mark your answer. Ⓐ Ⓑ Ⓒ		26. Mark your answer. Ⓐ Ⓑ Ⓒ
12. Mark your answer. Ⓐ Ⓑ Ⓒ		27. Mark your answer. Ⓐ Ⓑ Ⓒ
13. Mark your answer. Ⓐ Ⓑ Ⓒ		28. Mark your answer. Ⓐ Ⓑ Ⓒ
14. Mark your answer. Ⓐ Ⓑ Ⓒ		29. Mark your answer. Ⓐ Ⓑ Ⓒ
15. Mark your answer. Ⓐ Ⓑ Ⓒ		30. Mark your answer. Ⓐ Ⓑ Ⓒ

LESSON 3

Dialogs

 Preview: Lesson Outline

- Part III Format
- Tactics for Part III
- Sample Test
- Testing Points and Skill-Building Exercises
    - A. Overview Questions
    - B. Detail Questions
    - C. Inference Questions
- More Practice

Part III **Format**

This part of TOEIC consists of thirty short dialogs (conversations), either between a man and a woman or between two men. The dialogs are three-part exchanges: The first speaker says something, the second speaker responds, and the first speaker says something else. Two typical patterns are given below:

Speaker 1:   Asks a question.
Speaker 2:   Responds to the question.
Speaker 1:   Comments on the response.

Speaker 1:   Makes a statement.
Speaker 2:   Questions the statement.
Speaker 1:   Responds to the question.

In your test book, a question is written out, followed by four possible answer choices. Your job is to decide which one of these best answers the question. Then you need to mark the corresponding answer on your answer sheet.

Tactics for Part III

1. Between each dialog there is a twelve-second pause. This may not sound like a long time, but you can actually accomplish quite a bit during this pause. You need to mark the answer for the item that you just heard and then preview the next item. Previewing the item consists of reading the question — this tells you what to listen for — and of quickly looking over the four answer choices.
2. While listening to the dialog, keep your eyes on the answer choices. Don't close your eyes or look away. Try to evaluate the four choices as you are listening.
3. Remember that distractors are sometimes mentioned in the dialogs but do not answer the questions. Don't choose an answer just because you hear a word or two from the answer in the dialog.
4. If the correct answer is not obvious, try to eliminate answers that seem to be incorrect. If more than one answer choice is left, make a guess.
5. Mark your answers as quickly as possible so that you can preview the next item.
6. Never leave any answers blank. Always guess.

Sample Test 🎧

Start the audio program and read along as the directions are read.

Directions: In this part of the test, you hear short dialogs involving two speakers. Each dialog is spoken only once and is not written out in the book, so listen carefully.

In your book, you read a question about each dialog. Following each question are four answer choices. Choose the best answer — (A), (B), (C), or (D) — and mark the answer.

Example

You will hear: Man: My wife and I plan to visit the Grand Canyon when we're in the United States.

Woman: You'll love it — it's a beautiful sight! Are you going on a bus tour?

Man: No, we're going to rent a car at the Los Angeles airport and drive there ourselves.

You will read: How will the man and his wife travel to the Grand Canyon?
- (A) By plane.
- ● In a rental car.
- (C) By bus.
- (D) In a taxi.

Choice (B), "In a rental car," is the best answer to the question, "How will the man and his wife travel to the Grand Canyon?" You should choose (B).

1. What is the problem?
   - (A) The contract cannot be found.
   - (B) The man did not know the way.
   - (C) The contract is confusing.
   - (D) The man arrived too soon.

2. When will Rita leave?
   - (A) Monday
   - (B) Tuesday
   - (C) Wednesday
   - (D) Thursday

3. Where are they?
   - (A) At a theater
   - (B) At a party
   - (C) At an airport
   - (D) At a restaurant

4. What are they discussing?
   - (A) A new outfit that the woman is wearing
   - (B) How people dress at the man's company
   - (C) Where to buy clothes for work
   - (D) A social event that the man attended

5. Why is Mr. Tupton calling?
   - (A) To complain about an order
   - (B) To discuss a legal problem
   - (C) To reassure a customer
   - (D) To place an order

6. What is George planning to do?
   - (A) Watch a video
   - (B) Talk to the manager
   - (C) Change his style
   - (D) Read a book

Dialogs **55**

7. What advice does the woman give?
   - (A) To stay on the job
   - (B) To take a risk
   - (C) To apply for another position
   - (D) To give someone a present

8. Who is the first speaker?
   - (A) A hotel clerk
   - (B) A lawyer
   - (C) A journalist
   - (D) A dry cleaner

9. What do the speakers think of the book?
   - (A) It is very enjoyable.
   - (B) It is too critical.
   - (C) It is difficult to find.
   - (D) It is hard to understand.

10. What is Brian doing now?
    - (A) Designing products
    - (B) Working as a manager
    - (C) Studying management
    - (D) Teaching a class

Testing Points and Skill-Building Exercises

Many kinds of questions may be asked about the dialogs, but they can be divided into these general categories:
   - A. Overview questions
   - B. Detail questions
   - C. Inference questions

A. Overview Questions

These questions require you to have a "global" or overall understanding of the dialogs that you hear. There are four kinds of overview questions:

Types of Overview Questions	Typical Question Words
1. Questions about locations	1. Where . . . ?
2. Questions about occupations	2. Who . . . ?
3. Questions about activities	3. What . . . doing?
4. Questions about topics	4. What . . . talking about?

Questions About Locations

These ask where the conversation occurs. There are a number of ways these questions can be asked:
   - Where are they?
   - Where are the speakers?
   - Where is the man/woman?
   - Where is the conversation taking place?

The answer choices for these questions are the names of four locations of various types — for example, a restaurant, a bank, an advertising agency, a tailor shop. To answer these questions, you can't simply listen for the name of the location, which is seldom provided in the dialog. You need to listen for vocabulary that is tied to a certain location. For example, if you hear the words *reservations, first class,* and *tickets,* the answer will probably be "In a travel agency." However, don't choose an answer on the basis of just one of these words. The word *reservations* could also be heard in a restaurant or hotel; the word *first class* could also be heard at a post office; the word *tickets* could also be heard at a concert, movie, or sporting event.

Sample Item: Location Question

Man: We don't have any reservations. Is it possible for us to get a table?
Woman: You're in luck — a party of two just canceled their reservations. We can
             seat you in a few minutes.
Man: Great.

Where are they?

    Ⓐ At a theater.
    Ⓑ At a party.
    Ⓒ At an airport.
    ● At a restaurant.

The mention of *reservations*, *table*, and *party of two* indicates that they are at a restaurant.

Exercise 3.1

Focus: Linking vocabulary to locations.

Directions: Match the locations in the column on the right with the appropriate group of vocabulary by writing the letter of the location in the blank. The first one is done as an example.

There is no audio program for this exercise.

1. __C__ rolls cake bread	7. _____ terminal hangars gate	**a)** airport **b)** apartment complex **c)** bakery **d)** bank
2. _____ stage exit usher	8. _____ wave towel umbrella	**e)** beach **f)** computer store **g)** construction site **h)** court room
3. _____ bulldozer hard hat crane	9. _____ pens envelopes letterhead	**i)** farm **j)** football stadium **k)** freeway **l)** grocery store
4. _____ chain ring bracelet	10. _____ lanes toll booth exit	**m)** hair salon **n)** hardware store **o)** hotel **p)** jewelry store
5. _____ menu terminal keyboard	11. _____ suite front desk reservations	**q)** laundromat **r)** post office **s)** restaurant **t)** stationery store
6. _____ dryer hangers detergent	12. _____ field barn fertilizer	**u)** theater **v)** travel agency

Occupation Questions

These questions are very similar to the ones asked about locations, but they ask about the job or profession of one or both of the speakers. There are various ways these questions can be asked:

- Who is the man/woman?
- Who are they?
- What is he/she?
- What are they?
- What is the man's/woman's profession?
- What is the man's/woman's occupation?
- What is the man's/woman's job?

The answer choices for these questions are the names of four occupations: banker, bus driver, airline reservationist, secretary, and so on. The occupations are seldom given directly in the dialogs. As with location questions, you must listen for key vocabulary that ties the speaker or speakers to one of the answers. For example, if you hear the terms *fare, transfer,* and *next stop,* the correct answer will be "bus driver." Again, don't choose an answer based on just one term; the word *fare* could also be used by an airline reservationist.

Sample Item: Occupation Question

1st Man:	Front desk.
2nd Man:	Yes, I'd like to have my suit cleaned and pressed.
1st Man:	Certainly. I'll have someone come by your room in a few minutes to pick it up.

Who is the first speaker?

- ● A hotel clerk
- Ⓑ A lawyer
- Ⓒ A journalist
- Ⓓ A dry cleaner

The words *front desk* and *room* indicate that the first speaker is the clerk at the front desk of a hotel.

Exercise 3.2

Focus: Linking vocabulary to occupations.

Directions: Match the locations in the column on the right with the appropriate group of vocabulary by writing the letter of the occupation in the blank.

There is no audio program for this exercise.

1. _____ anesthesia scalpel operation	4. _____ first class frequent flyer reservation	7. _____ alterations tape measure suit	10. _____ arrangement delivery bouquets	**a)** carpenter **b)** dentist **c)** florist **d)** hair stylist **e)** manicurist
2. _____ transmission spark plug tune–up	5. _____ drill polish cavity	8. _____ first class stamps parcel post		**f)** mechanic **g)** musician **h)** painter **i)** postal clerk **j)** secretary
3. _____ nails file drill	6. _____ brushes rollers coat	9. _____ notes arrangement orchestration		**k)** student **l)** surgeon **m)** tailor **n)** taxi driver **o)** travel agent

Exercise 3.3

Focus: Answering overview questions about locations and occupations.

Directions: Listen to the dialog. Read the question about the dialog and then choose the one answer — (A), (B), (C), or (D) — that best answers the question.

Now start the audio program.

1. Who is the second speaker?
   (A) An electrician
   (B) A banker
   (C) An engineer
   (D) A jeweler

2. Where are they?
   (A) In a grocery store
   (B) On a farm
   (C) At an outdoor market
   (D) In a vegetable garden

3. Where is this conversation taking place?
   (A) At a men's clothing store
   (B) In a courtroom
   (C) At an art gallery
   (D) In a paint store

4. Who are they?
   (A) Printers
   (B) Architects
   (C) Fashion designers
   (D) House painters

5. Who is Thomas?
   (A) A sailor
   (B) A mechanic
   (C) A plumber
   (D) A carpenter

6. Where are they?
   (A) At a coffee shop
   (B) On an airliner
   (C) In an automobile
   (D) In a clothing store

7. Who is the man?
   (A) A police officer
   (B) A gardener
   (C) A security guard
   (D) A pilot

8. Where is this conversation taking place?
   (A) On a bus
   (B) In a taxi
   (C) At the library
   (D) On Clifton Avenue

9. Where are the speakers?
   (A) At a cinema
   (B) At a television studio
   (C) At a bookstore
   (D) At a video rental store

10. Who is Lisa?
    (A) An interior designer
    (B) The director
    (C) A painter
    (D) A newspaper reporter

11. Where are they?
    (A) In a hardware store
    (B) In a dentist's office
    (C) In an artist's studio
    (D) In an electronics store

12. Who is the first speaker?
    (A) A teacher
    (B) A mechanic
    (C) A doctor
    (D) A pharmacist

Activity Questions

These questions ask what one or both speakers are doing or are going to do. These questions can be asked in several ways:

- What are they doing?
- What is the man/woman doing?
- What is happening now?
- What is going to happen?
- What is the situation?

Answer choices for these questions are the names of four activities: buying a car, playing cards, eating breakfast, getting a haircut, and so on. There are two or three key vocabulary terms that can be connected with a certain activity. For example, if you hear the words *deck*, *cards*, and *deal*, the answer will be "playing cards."

Sample Item: Activity Question

Man: I haven't seen Brian lately. Isn't he working in the design department anymore?

Woman: Actually, he's in the management training program now.

Man: I didn't know that Brian wanted to be a manager.

What is Brian doing now?

    Ⓐ Designing products
    Ⓑ Working as a manager
    ● Studying management
    Ⓓ Teaching a class

The woman tells the man that Brian is in the management training program, so he is studying management.

Topic Questions

These questions ask about the general subject of the dialog. The subject of the dialog can be a person, a thing, or an activity. Topic questions can be phrased in a variety of ways:

- What/whom are they discussing?
- What are they talking about?
- What are they referring to?
- What is the conversation about?
- What is the topic of the conversation?
- What is the subject of the conversation?

The answer choices will be four plausible topics of conversation. Incorrect answers may include details that are mentioned in the dialog but that are not the main subject of the conversation.

Exercise 3.4

Focus: Answering overview questions dealing with activities and topics.

Directions: Listen to the dialog. Read the question about the dialog and then choose the one answer — (A), (B), (C), or (D) — that best answers the question.

 Now start the audio program.

1. What are they discussing?
    Ⓐ A boat trip
    Ⓑ Fishing
    Ⓒ A ball game
    Ⓓ Medical care

2. What are they doing?
    Ⓐ Buying clothing
    Ⓑ Going through customs
    Ⓒ Going grocery shopping
    Ⓓ Getting their luggage

3. Who are they talking about?
    Ⓐ A sculptor
    Ⓑ A novelist
    Ⓒ A painter
    Ⓓ A gardener

4. What is the second speaker doing?
    Ⓐ Renting a car
    Ⓑ Looking for retail space
    Ⓒ Trying to find an apartment
    Ⓓ Going shopping

5. What is the conversation about?
    Ⓐ A computer
    Ⓑ A photographer's model
    Ⓒ A sports car
    Ⓓ An old photograph

6. What is Mr. Krueger going to do?
    Ⓐ Have his rug cleaned
    Ⓑ Get his car repaired
    Ⓒ Have his lawn mowed
    Ⓓ Get his hair cut

7. What is the subject of the conversation?
    Ⓐ A dangerous intersection
    Ⓑ A new store
    Ⓒ An airline accident
    Ⓓ Outdoor lighting

8. What are they going to do?
    Ⓐ Go horseback riding
    Ⓑ Go skiing
    Ⓒ Go on a plane trip
    Ⓓ Go shopping

9. What is the situation?
    (A) The woman is being interviewed
        for a job.
    (B) The man is trying to sell the woman
        a computer.
    (C) The woman is applying to a college.
    (D) The man is asking the woman if he
        can use her computer.

10. What will they do?
    (A) Go deep-sea fishing
    (B) Examine some documents
    (C) Watch television
    (D) Go out to a movie

B. Detail Questions

Detail questions ask about specific points in the dialog. However, the answer to these questions is generally not found in a single line of the dialog. It's usually necessary to understand the entire conversation. Some of the most common detail questions are given below, but there are other types that are not listed.

Main Types of Detail	Typical Question Words
1. Questions about time	1. When . . . ?
2. Questions about reasons	2. Why . . . ?
3. Questions about plans	3. What . . . do?
4. Questions about problems	4. What's the matter with . . . ?
5. Questions about opinions	5. What . . . think of . . . ?
6. Questions about advice	6. What . . . suggest?

Questions About Time

These questions ask when an event or activity takes place. Some time questions ask about frequency or duration. Time questions can be asked in several ways:
- When . . . ?
- At what time . . . ?
- How often . . . ? (frequency)
- How long . . . ? (duration)

The answer choices are times of day, parts of the day, days of the week, dates, years, and amounts of time, and so on. Often, one or more of the distractors are mentioned in the dialog but do not answer the question. And sometimes the correct answer is not mentioned directly by the speakers.

Sample Item: Time Question

Man: So you're still leaving on Tuesday, Rita?
Woman: No, I'm going to delay my trip for a day.
Man: That's probably a good idea.
When will Rita leave?
    (A) Monday.   ● Wednesday.
    (B) Tuesday.   (D) Thursday.   (A) (B) ● (D)

The woman says that she is not going to leave on Tuesday; she is going to delay her trip for a day. Therefore, she will leave on Wednesday.

Questions About Reasons

These questions ask why someone does something, why someone feels a certain way, why an event occurs, and so on. These are typical reason questions:

- Why did . . . happen?
- Why does the man/woman want to . . . ?
- Why is the man/woman going to . . . ?
- Why is the man/woman upset/happy/puzzled?

Some reason questions are negative questions.

- Why did . . . **not** happen?
- Why does he/she **not** want to . . . ?

Sample Item: Reason Question

Woman: Good morning, National Office Supplies.
Man: Yes, this is Mr. Tupton. I'm calling about an order I just received. There were twenty packages of blue paper, and we ordered white paper.
Woman: I'll connect you with the customer service department, Mr. Tupton.
Why is Mr. Tupton calling?
  Ⓐ To complain about an order.   ● To reassure a customer.
  Ⓑ To discuss a legal problem.   Ⓓ To place an order.

The man received the wrong order, and he is calling to complain about it.

Exercise 3.5

Focus: Answering detail questions dealing with time and reasons.

Directions: Listen to the dialog. Read the question about the dialog and then choose the one answer — (A), (B), (C), or (D) — that best answers the question.

🔲 Now start the audio program.

1. Why is Mr. Maras leaving?
   Ⓐ To talk to a client
   Ⓑ To go to his office
   Ⓒ To board an airplane
   Ⓓ To meet his wife

2. When will the office open again?
   Ⓐ This weekend
   Ⓑ On Monday
   Ⓒ On Tuesday
   Ⓓ On Wednesday

3. At what time will the man see the movie?
   Ⓐ At 7:30
   Ⓑ At 7:40
   Ⓒ At 9:00
   Ⓓ At 9:10

4. Why does Carlos congratulate Eva?
   Ⓐ She'll be making more money.
   Ⓑ She found a better job.
   Ⓒ She's been promoted.
   Ⓓ She likes the region where she'll be working.

5. When did Frank start working here?
   Ⓐ In 1992   Ⓒ In 1994
   Ⓑ In 1993   Ⓓ In 1995

6. When does Patrick want to come in?
   Ⓐ At lunchtime
   Ⓑ This afternoon
   Ⓒ Tomorrow morning
   Ⓓ Tomorrow afternoon

7. Why did the man NOT take the shuttle bus?
   - (A) He wanted to save time.
   - (B) He wanted to impress someone.
   - (C) It was too expensive.
   - (D) It came too early for him.

8. Why is Dan upset?
   - (A) He does not have his coffee mug.
   - (B) He could not attend the conference.
   - (C) He did not get any coffee this morning.
   - (D) He could not find some important papers.

9. How long was Ms. Shearson out of the country?
   - (A) For a few days
   - (B) For a month
   - (C) Exactly a year
   - (D) Just over a year

10. Why is Jim NOT going to the trade fair?
   - (A) The distribution manager will not permit it.
   - (B) He is too busy.
   - (C) The trip is too expensive.
   - (D) He does not want to attend.

Questions About Plans

These questions ask what a person intends to do in the future. They can be phrased in a number of ways:
- What is the man/woman planning to do?
- What plan has been suggested?
- What does the man/woman plan to do next?
- What does the man/woman want to do?

The answer choices are four plausible plans. One or two of the distractors may be discussed in the dialog but are incorrect because the plan or plans are changed or rejected.

Sample Item: Plan Question

Woman: George, have you seen that video about new management techniques?
Man: No, but I intend to. I've heard it's interesting.
Woman: It's more than interesting — it could change your whole management style.

What is George planning to do?
- ● Watch a video
- (B) Talk to the manager
- (C) Change his style
- (D) Read a book

The woman asks the man if he has seen a video, and he responds that he intends to see it.

Questions About Problems

These questions ask about some difficulty that one or both of the speakers experience. There are several ways to phrase these questions:
- What is the problem here?
- What is the man's/woman's problem?
- What is wrong with . . . ?
- What is bothering the man/woman?
- What is the man/woman concerned about?
- What is the man/woman worried about?

The answer choices are four possible problems. One or more of the choices may be mentioned but are not the problem being asked about.

Exercise 3.6

Focus: Answering detail questions that deal with plans or problems.

Directions: Listen to the dialog. Read the question about the dialog and then choose the one answer — (A), (B), (C), or (D) — that best answers the question.

Now start the audio program.

1. What is the problem with the bicycle?
   (A) It is very old.
   (B) There is no key for the lock.
   (C) It has been stolen.
   (D) There is no air in one tire.

2. What is Mr. Neufield's immediate plan?
   (A) To postpone the meeting with Mr. Utsumi
   (B) To meet with the chief engineer
   (C) To talk with Mr. Utsumi
   (D) To make several phone calls

3. What does Mary plan to do?
   (A) Change her field
   (B) Go on vacation
   (C) Start her own business
   (D) Go to graduate school

4. What is the problem here?
   (A) The tape has broken.
   (B) The woman dislikes the music.
   (C) The tape player is out of order.
   (D) The man can't find the tape.

5. What does Mrs. Powers plan to do before hiring Katie?
   (A) Interview her again
   (B) Write her a letter
   (C) Give her a test
   (D) Contact her references

6. What plan does the second speaker suggest?
   (A) Traveling to Manila
   (B) Asking Mr. Quizon to visit
   (C) Changing their place of operations
   (D) Offering Mr. Quizon another position

7. Why is the woman concerned about the documents?
   (A) They have been lost.
   (B) They contain many mistakes.
   (C) They are not in the proper order.
   (D) They have not been read.

8. What is wrong with the apartment?
   (A) It is too big for him.
   (B) It does not have enough rooms.
   (C) It is too expensive.
   (D) It is not in the right location.

9. What is the problem?
   (A) The flowerpot is broken.
   (B) The glass cannot be replaced.
   (C) The table has not been set.
   (D) The tabletop was damaged.

10. What does Mr. Dufour plan to do?
    (A) Become an artist
    (B) Buy some art
    (C) Hire more advisors
    (D) Study art

Questions About Suggestions

These questions ask what advice one speaker gives to another person (usually the other speaker). These questions can be phrased in various ways:

- What is the man's/woman's suggestion?
- What is the man/woman suggesting?
- What suggestion is made?
- What is the man's/woman's advice?
- What does the man/woman advise . . . to do?

Sample Item: Suggestion Question

Woman: So, do you like working here?
Man: Yes, but not as much as I thought I would.
Woman: Give it a chance — you've only been here for a month.
What advice does the woman give?
     ● To stay on the job
     Ⓑ To take a risk
     Ⓒ To apply for another position
     Ⓓ To give someone a present

The man indicates that he doesn't like working there very much. The woman tells him to "give it a chance" — in other words, to stay on the job for now.

Questions About Opinions

These questions ask how a speaker feels about something or someone. These questions can be phrased in a number of ways:

- What is the man's/woman's opinion of . . . ?
- How does the man/woman feel about . . . ?
- What does the man/woman think about . . . ?

Sample Item: Opinion Question

1st man: Have you read that new book by Donald Hobart?
2nd man: I tried to, but I found it hard to follow.
1st man: So did I, but the critics sure seemed to like it.
What do the speakers think of the book?
     Ⓐ It is very enjoyable.
     Ⓑ It is too critical.
     Ⓒ It is difficult to find.
     ● It is too confusing.

The second man says that he found the book "hard to follow" (confusing). The first man agrees.

Exercise 3.7

Focus: Answering detail questions involving suggestions and opinions.

Directions: Listen to the dialog. Read the question about the dialog and then choose the one answer — (A), (B), (C), or (D) — that best answers the question.

Now start the audio program.

1. What is Mr. Lo's advice?
   - (A) That the woman bring her child to the party
   - (B) That the woman contact his wife
   - (C) That his wife take care of the woman's child
   - (D) That the couple stay home

2. What suggestion is made?
   - (A) To cut prices
   - (B) To reduce the number of workers
   - (C) To get some good advice
   - (D) To bring in fewer consultants

3. What did the man think of the play?
   - (A) It was boring.
   - (B) He liked the first half better than the woman did.
   - (C) He did not see it.
   - (D) It was uninteresting.

4. How does the man feel about Arlene's job?
   - (A) It provides many opportunities.
   - (B) It takes up too much of her time.
   - (C) It does not pay well enough.
   - (D) It is interesting work.

5. What does Hans suggest?
   - (A) That she go out for a meal
   - (B) That she work in her room
   - (C) That she have food delivered
   - (D) That she go to sleep now

6. What does she think they should do?
   - (A) Have the copier repaired
   - (B) Buy some antique furniture
   - (C) Replace the copier
   - (D) Get some more copies made

7. What does the first man think of the plan?
   - (A) It will never be adopted.
   - (B) It may save money.
   - (C) It will not impress customers.
   - (D) It is a waste of time.

8. What does she suggest that the man do?
   - (A) Go to a nearby cafe
   - (B) Wait for Ms. Bauer
   - (C) Go to the meeting
   - (D) Come back another day

9. How does Donna feel about the building?
   - (A) It is not warm enough.
   - (B) It has too many windows.
   - (C) It is too stuffy.
   - (D) It is not safe.

10. What does the woman suggest that the man sell?
    - (A) His business
    - (B) His automobile
    - (C) His exercise equipment
    - (D) His health club membership

C. Inference Questions

The answers for inference questions are not directly given in the dialogs. Instead, you have to draw a conclusion — called an **inference** — based on the information that is presented by the speakers. In other words, the answers are only suggested; they are not directly stated.

Inference questions can be phrased in various ways:

- What is the man/woman saying about . . . ?
- What does the man/woman mean?
- What is probably true about . . . ?
- What can be said about . . . ?
- What is known about . . . ?

Exercise 3.8

Focus: Answering inference questions.

Directions: Listen to the dialog. Read the question about the dialog and choose the one answer — (A), (B), (C), or (D) — that best answers the question.

🔲 Now start the audio program.

1. What is known about their situation?
   Ⓐ They are having dinner by candlelight.
   Ⓑ The electricity is not on.
   Ⓒ They are examining something with a flashlight.
   Ⓓ It is the middle of the day.

2. What can be said about the situation?
   Ⓐ They are not at home.
   Ⓑ The sky is seldom clear here.
   Ⓒ The smell is unpleasant.
   Ⓓ They have just walked for miles.

3. What does the woman mean?
   Ⓐ She cannot go sailing tomorrow.
   Ⓑ Her decision depends on the weather.
   Ⓒ There will not be enough wind for sailing.
   Ⓓ She enjoys this kind of weather.

4. What is probably true about Natalie?
   Ⓐ She makes her own clothing at home.
   Ⓑ She does not need any new clothes.
   Ⓒ She has worked there only for a few weeks.
   Ⓓ She no longer works as a clerk.

5. What is the man saying?
   Ⓐ He just started playing the piano.
   Ⓑ He would like to take lessons from the woman.
   Ⓒ He has never taken lessons.
   Ⓓ He does not play as well as the woman.

6. What is known about the security system?
   Ⓐ It is generally turned on in the morning.
   Ⓑ It is an unusual system.
   Ⓒ It was broken when the man arrived.
   Ⓓ It was recently installed.

7. What is true about the climate where they live now?
   Ⓐ It has four seasons.
   Ⓑ It is always warm.
   Ⓒ It is usually cool and brisk.
   Ⓓ It is nicest in the autumn.

8. What is known about these two?
   Ⓐ They do not have to work today.
   Ⓑ They have to attend a meeting.
   Ⓒ They wrote the memo.
   Ⓓ They are not new employees.

More Practice

Directions: Listen to the dialog. Read the question about the dialog and choose the one answer — (A), (B), (C), or (D) — that best answers the question.

🔲 Now start the audio program.

1. When will Ms. Rao pick up her dry cleaning?
   - (A) Thursday morning
   - (B) Thursday afternoon
   - (C) Friday morning
   - (D) Friday afternoon

2. Who will meet the client?
   - (A) The first speaker
   - (B) The second speaker
   - (C) The boss
   - (D) Mr. Saito

3. What does Mark suggest they ask for?
   - (A) A new project
   - (B) More time
   - (C) A new supervisor
   - (D) More money

4. Which of these decreased?
   - (A) Market share
   - (B) Labor costs
   - (C) Profits
   - (D) Taxes

5. How many brothers and sisters does the woman have?
   - (A) None
   - (B) One
   - (C) Two
   - (D) Three

6. What are the people discussing?
   - (A) Sports
   - (B) The unemployment rate
   - (C) Business
   - (D) The newspaper

7. When will the inspection take place?
   - (A) Today
   - (B) Tomorrow
   - (C) The day after tomorrow
   - (D) In three days

8. Where are they?
   - (A) In an airport
   - (B) In a luggage store
   - (C) In a parking lot
   - (D) In a hotel

9. Why does Dennis want to leave?
   - (A) It's too noisy.
   - (B) The service is too slow.
   - (C) The food isn't good.
   - (D) The restaurant is closing.

10. What are they doing now?
    - (A) Going for a drive
    - (B) Eating at a restaurant
    - (C) Taking a hike
    - (D) Painting a scene

11. What is famous?
    - (A) The woman's business
    - (B) The temple
    - (C) The conference
    - (D) The hotel

12. Who is Cynthia?
    - (A) A photographer
    - (B) A clothing designer
    - (C) A painter
    - (D) A fashion model

13. What is she doing?
    Ⓐ Exchanging some merchandise
    Ⓑ Going through customs
    Ⓒ Investigating a crime
    Ⓓ Changing money

14. How will the woman pay?
    Ⓐ With traveler's checks
    Ⓑ With cash
    Ⓒ With a credit card
    Ⓓ With a personal check

15. What can be said about the office tower?
    Ⓐ It was built long ago.
    Ⓑ It is smaller than the neighboring buildings.
    Ⓒ It is like all the buildings on Market Street.
    Ⓓ It is quite modern.

16. Why does the man NOT want to take a September vacation?
    Ⓐ It's too cool then.
    Ⓑ His children can't go then.
    Ⓒ The resorts aren't open then.
    Ⓓ It's too crowded then.

17. What is the man's problem?
    Ⓐ He cannot open the cabinet.
    Ⓑ He lost a file.
    Ⓒ He cannot get into his office.
    Ⓓ There is no more room for files.

18. When is the soonest Mr. Ranglos can get an appointment?
    Ⓐ In a few minutes
    Ⓑ This afternoon
    Ⓒ Tomorrow morning
    Ⓓ Tomorrow afternoon

19. How does the first speaker feel about the flowers?
    Ⓐ They're quite beautiful.
    Ⓑ They should be bought more often.
    Ⓒ They cost too much.
    Ⓓ They're necessary but expensive.

20. What is known about Roy?
    Ⓐ He does not want to work in public relations.
    Ⓑ He is not sure where he will work.
    Ⓒ He was not trained to work in sales.
    Ⓓ He does not have a job right now.

21. What happened to the bid?
    Ⓐ It was accepted.
    Ⓑ It did not arrive in time.
    Ⓒ It was misplaced.
    Ⓓ It was not sent.

22. Where are they?
    Ⓐ At an automobile rental agency
    Ⓑ At a restaurant
    Ⓒ At a hotel
    Ⓓ At a bus station

23. What are they discussing?
    Ⓐ An elevator
    Ⓑ A heater
    Ⓒ An air conditioner
    Ⓓ A computer

24. Who did the man think the woman was?
    Ⓐ Ms. Silverman
    Ⓑ An administrative assistant
    Ⓒ A personnel officer
    Ⓓ A new employee

25. What kind of weather is predicted?
    Ⓐ Sunny
    Ⓑ Cooler
    Ⓒ Snowy
    Ⓓ Warmer

26. Who is the second speaker?
    Ⓐ An electrician
    Ⓑ A carpenter
    Ⓒ A cleaner
    Ⓓ A plumber

27. What is the problem?
    (A) There is no printer paper.
    (B) The instruction manual is missing.
    (C) The printer is broken.
    (D) He does not know how the printer works.

28. What are they planning to do?
    (A) Go camping
    (B) Clean the kitchen
    (C) Stay at a hotel
    (D) Go to the circus

29. What does the man mean?
    (A) The ski season is almost over.
    (B) A lot of snow has fallen.
    (C) He's never been to Winter Star.
    (D) The skiing was better last week.

30. What is the man doing?
    (A) Making a purchase
    (B) Packing some boxes
    (C) Making a delivery
    (D) Planting a crop

Short Talks

 Preview: Lesson Outline

 Part IV **Format**

In Part IV, you hear a number of talks read on the tape. There are two, three, and sometimes four questions based on each talk. The questions are written out in your test booklet. There are four answer choices following each question. You have to choose the best answer to the question based on the information that you hear in the talk. Before each of the questions, there is an introductory statement.

Some examples

Questions 80 to 82 are based on the following announcement:
Questions 93 to 96 refer to the following lecture:

Following each talk, you'll hear instructions to answer particular questions, with ten-second pauses between each of them. (You do *not* have to wait for these announcements to answer the questions.)

Because this part of the test consists of both spoken material on the tape and written questions and answer choices, it tests both listening and reading skills.

1. **The talks:** The talks are all monologs — that is, they are delivered by one speaker. They are fairly short — most are less than one minute long.

2. **The questions:** Three main types of questions are asked about the talks: overview questions, detail questions, and inference questions.
    - **Overview questions** require a general understanding of the lecture or of the situation in which it is given. Overview questions ask about the main idea or

purpose of the lecture, or about the speaker, the audience, or the location where the talk is given. Some typical overview questions:

> Who is speaking?
> What is the purpose of the talk?
> What kind of people would probably be interested in this talk?
> What is happening in this talk?
> Where is this announcement being made?

- **Detail questions** relate to specific points in the talk. They begin with *wh-* words: *who, what, where, why, when, how, how much,* and so on. Some are negative questions; they ask what was *not* mentioned in the talk.

> Which of the following is *not* true about . . .

- **Inference questions** require you to make a conclusion based on the information provided in the talk. These questions often contain the word *probably*.

> What is probably true about . . .

3. **The answer choices:** All the answer choices are plausible answers to the questions. In many cases, the distractors are mentioned in the talk. Just because you hear an answer choice mentioned in the talk does not mean it is the correct answer for a particular question.

Tactics for Part IV

1. Listen carefully to the announcement that is given before each talk. It will tell you what kind of talk you are going to hear (an announcement or a commercial, for example) as well as which questions to look at during that talk.
2. Always look at the questions as the talk is being given on the tape. Do *not* look away or close your eyes in order to concentrate on the spoken material. You must focus on both the talk and the written questions.
3. Because the questions are written out, you can use them to focus your listening for particular information.
4. Do *not* mark your answer sheet while the talk is going on, even if you know the answer. The act of answering a question may cause you to miss the information you need to answer the question or questions that follow. Instead, if you are sure of an answer, make a light pencil mark by the letter of the answer in your answer book; then transfer that answer to your answer sheet after the talk. Be sure to erase these marks later.
5. Do *not* wait for the speaker on the tape to instruct you to answer the questions. In fact, you should ignore those announcements. Begin answering as soon as the talk is over, and answer all the questions related to that talk as soon as you can. If you have a few seconds left before the next talk begins, preview the next few questions in your test booklet.
6. Never continue working on the questions about one talk after another talk has begun.
7. If you are not sure of an answer, eliminate unlikely choices and then guess.
8. Always answer each question. Never leave any blanks.

Sample Test

Directions: During this part of the exam, there are a number of brief talks. These talks are not written out and are spoken only once, so you must listen carefully.

There are two or more questions about each of the talks. Following the questions are four possible answers — (A), (B), (C), and (D). You must decide which of these best answers the question and then mark the correct answer.

1. Which of these is NOT permitted?
   (A) Leaving a vehicle unattended
   (B) Unloading suitcases
   (C) Letting passengers out of a vehicle
   (D) Stopping for a short period

2. Where is long-term parking available?
   (A) In front of the terminal
   (B) In the airport parking structure
   (C) At a parking lot downtown
   (D) At the Jones Road facility

3. What kind of weather is predicted for the weekend?
   (A) Rapidly changing
   (B) Sunny but cooler
   (C) Rainy or snowy
   (D) Warm and sunny

4. During what season is this forecast being given?
   (A) Spring   (C) Autumn
   (B) Summer   (D) Winter

5. Where is the talk probably being given?
   (A) At a pharmacy
   (B) At a sporting event
   (C) At a department store
   (D) At a gas station

6. What has been found?
   (A) A black briefcase
   (B) A piece of paper
   (C) A pair of glasses
   (D) Some medicine

7. Who is Elizabeth Bryce?
   (A) An employee in the shipping department
   (B) A supervisor
   (C) The speaker
   (D) An assistant to the CEO of the corporation

8. Which of the following is NOT true about Elizabeth Bryce?
   (A) Her suggestion may save the company money.
   (B) She can park next to the CEO this month.
   (C) She will get a promotion.
   (D) Her evaluations were very good.

9. What does the employee of the year receive?
   (A) A small bonus
   (B) The CEO's parking place
   (C) Thousands of dollars a year
   (D) A new car

10. Who would be most interested in what is being offered in this talk?
    (A) Business travelers
    (B) University students
    (C) Language teachers
    (D) Foreign tourists

11. Which of these courses is NOT presently available?
    (A) Japanese   (C) Spanish
    (B) English   (D) Russian

12. How many videocassettes are enclosed in each kit?
    (A) One   (C) Four
    (B) Two   (D) Eight

Testing Points and Skill-Building Exercises

The talks that you hear on the tape during Part IV concern many different topics and are given in a variety of situations. However, most of the talks can be classified into one of the categories presented in this section of the lesson.

In each part of this section, a different type of talk and the questions about it are briefly analyzed. Then there are exercises involving four or five talks of that type.

A. Public Announcements

These talks are brief informational messages like those given to groups of people in public places. The most common type is announcements made on board airliners or in airports. Others are given at stores, at sporting events, and in other situations.

Sample Items: Public Announcement

Woman: [Attention, shoppers: someone has just turned in a pair of prescription sunglasses in a black leather case. They were found on the floor of the sporting goods section. If these glasses are yours, please come to the customer service booth to claim them.]

Where is the talk probably being given?

    Ⓐ At a pharmacy   ● At a department store

    Ⓑ At a sporting event   Ⓓ At a gas station

This is an overview question about the location where the talk is given. A number of key words provide clues to the location: *shoppers*, *sporting goods department*, and *customer service booth*. These words point to the conclusion that the talk is given in a department store.

What has been found?

    Ⓐ A black briefcase   ● A pair of glasses

    Ⓑ A piece of paper   Ⓓ Some medicine

The speaker says that the lost item is a pair of prescription sunglasses in a black leather case.

Exercise 4.1

Focus: Understanding and answering questions about public announcements.

Directions: Listen to the talks, and then answer the questions about them by marking the correct choice — (A), (B), (C), or (D).

    Now start the audio program.

1. Where is this announcement being made?
     Ⓐ On an airliner   Ⓒ At an airport
     Ⓑ In Glasgow   Ⓓ On a shuttle bus

2. Why is Mr. Kim being paged?
     Ⓐ There's a message for him.
     Ⓑ His flight has been delayed.
     Ⓒ Someone has found his ticket.
     Ⓓ There is an emergency.

3. Where are the white telephones located?
     Ⓐ On board the aircraft
     Ⓑ At the ticket counter
     Ⓒ All over the airport
     Ⓓ At an information booth

4. Who is the audience for this talk?
     Ⓐ People at a cafeteria
     Ⓑ Shoppers at a grocery store
     Ⓒ Guests at a party
     Ⓓ People who want to go fishing

5. What is being offered at a special price?
   - (A) Meat
   - (B) Charcoal
   - (C) Bread
   - (D) Fish

6. Where is this announcement being made?
   - (A) On an airplane
   - (B) At a shopping center
   - (C) Aboard a ship
   - (D) In a seaside restaurant

7. Who is Nicholas?
   - (A) A lost child
   - (B) Someone's father
   - (C) A waiter
   - (D) The purser

8. What problem is mentioned?
   - (A) High waves
   - (B) Long delays
   - (C) Strong winds
   - (D) High prices

9. What will people see on the tour?
   - (A) A skyscraper
   - (B) A national monument
   - (C) A cavern
   - (D) A factory

10. How long does the tour last?
   - (A) Fifteen minutes
   - (B) Two hours
   - (C) Four hours
   - (D) All day

11. At what age must someone purchase a full-price ticket?
   - (A) Four
   - (B) Six
   - (C) Twelve
   - (D) Thirteen

12. Where must someone go right after purchasing tickets?
   - (A) To the gift shop
   - (B) To the elevators
   - (C) To the top level
   - (D) To the north side

13. What is the destination of this flight?
   - (A) Los Angeles
   - (B) The Grand Canyon
   - (C) Flagstaff
   - (D) Denver

14. When will this plane be landing?
   - (A) In a few minutes
   - (B) In around twenty minutes
   - (C) In about an hour
   - (D) In around nine hours

15. What will probably be served on this flight?
   - (A) Breakfast
   - (B) Lunch
   - (C) Dinner
   - (D) Late-night snack

B. News, Weather, and Public Service Bulletins

These talks are similar to ones you might hear on radio and television, especially on news programs. Questions usually ask what is being reported and about details given in the talk.

Sample Items: Bulletin

Man: [It looks as though our warm, sunny, summer-like weather will continue at least through Saturday and Sunday, so this weekend will be the perfect time to go out to the countryside to view the colorful fall foliage. On Monday, though, it appears we're in for a change. It should be much cooler, and there's a good chance of rain or perhaps even snow flurries.]

What kind of weather is predicted for the weekend?
   - (A) Rapidly changing
   - (B) Sunny but cooler
   - (C) Rainy or snowy
   - ● Warm and sunny

The speaker says that the weather will be warm and sunny through the weekend. Choice (C) refers to the prediction the speaker makes for Monday.

During what season is this talk being given?
   - (A) Spring
   - (B) Summer
   - ● Autumn
   - (D) Winter

The speaker says that the weather will be "summer-like." This indicates that the weather will be warm, as it is in summer. The speaker also forecasts possible snow for Monday, and snow is associated with winter. However, it is clear from the mention of colorful fall foliage (leaves) that this is autumn.

Exercise 4.2

Focus: Understanding and answering questions about news, weather, and public service bulletins.

Directions: Listen to the talks, and then answer the questions about them by marking the correct choice — (A), (B), (C), or (D).

🖭 Now start the audio program.

1. What caused the delay in the launch?
   - (A) Bad weather
   - (B) The failure of the rocket engines
   - (C) Scheduling problems
   - (D) Computer problems

2. How do new-generation space shuttles differ from older shuttles?
   - (A) They have more powerful engines.
   - (B) They can stay in space longer.
   - (C) They are not affected as much by the weather.
   - (D) They have far more advanced computers.

3. When will the shuttle *Pathfinder* be launched?
   - (A) This afternoon
   - (B) Tonight
   - (C) Tomorrow
   - (D) The day after tomorrow

4. What is the purpose of this bulletin?
   - (A) To warn residents of a damaging storm
   - (B) To indicate that there is no danger
   - (C) To report on the destruction
   - (D) To ask for listeners' help

5. Where is the hurricane now moving?
   - (A) Towards the open ocean
   - (B) To the southeast
   - (C) Towards the Eastern Seaboard
   - (D) Over Bermuda

6. How fast were the winds predicted to be?
   - (A) 80 miles an hour
   - (B) 100 miles per hour
   - (C) 120 miles per hour
   - (D) 200 miles per hour

7. What is the purpose of this talk?
   - (A) To sell more balloons
   - (B) To invite parents to a special event
   - (C) To discuss a potential danger
   - (D) To introduce a new type of balloon

8. Which of these may present a danger to children?
   - (A) An inflated balloon
   - (B) The gas inside a balloon
   - (C) The sound of a popping balloon
   - (D) A piece of popped balloon

9. Which of the following would the speaker NOT approve of for safety reasons?
   - (A) Allowing young children to blow up balloons
   - (B) Using balloons at an adult's birthday party
   - (C) Tying strings to balloons
   - (D) Popping balloons with a pin

10. Where is the speaker?
    - (A) In a radio station
    - (B) In a helicopter
    - (C) On the side of the road
    - (D) In a truck

11. How did the truck cause a delay?
- (A) It dropped its cargo.
- (B) It collided with a car.
- (C) It broke down.
- (D) It ran out of fuel.

12. Which of the following does the speaker recommend for northbound drivers?
- (A) Interstate 74
- (B) The Valley Expressway
- (C) Lake Avenue
- (D) Route 8

C. Commercial Messages

These talks resemble the advertisements that you hear on radio or television. They attempt to sell listeners goods or services. Questions about commercial messages often ask what product is being advertised, what kind of people would be interested in the product, and, sometimes, how much the product costs.

Sample Items: Commercial Message

Man: [Are you frustrated because you need to know a language for business reasons but you're just too busy to take classes? Then order a language kit from Translingua. Watch our videocassettes and work on our CD-ROM computer program in the comfort of your home. Learn in a natural way by listening to native speakers in business situations and then responding to them in your own words. Courses now available in English, Spanish, and Japanese. Courses in French and Russian will be available in the next few months. Each kit contains four workbooks, two videocassettes, and one CD-ROM computer disk. Call Translingua today.]

Who would probably be most interested in what is being offered in this talk?
- ● Business travelers
- (B) University students
- (C) Language teachers
- (D) Foreign tourists

The advertisement begins by discussing the problem businesspersons face in learning another language. It also mentions that the course involves "native speakers in business situations." This course would probably be of most interest to business travelers.

Which of these courses is NOT presently available?
- (A) Japanese
- (B) English
- (C) Spanish
- ● Russian

According to the speaker, courses in English, Spanish, and Japanese are currently available. The course in Russian will not be available for a few months.

How many videocassettes are enclosed in each kit?
- (A) One
- ● Two
- (C) Four
- (D) Eight

According to the talk, there are two videocassettes in each language kit.

Exercise 4.3

Focus: Understanding and answering questions about commercial messages.

Directions: Listen to the talks, and then answer the questions about them by marking the correct choice — (A), (B), (C), or (D).

🔲 Now start the audio program.

1. Which of the following is NOT available at the time this talk is being given?
   (A) Water sports
   (B) Golf
   (C) Skiing
   (D) Fishing

2. Which of the following people would be most interested in the festival held in June?
   (A) People who enjoy jazz
   (B) Artists and craftspeople
   (C) Classical music fans
   (D) Beginning skiers

3. How do summer hotel rates compare to winter rates?
   (A) They are twice as high.
   (B) They are slightly higher.
   (C) They are the same.
   (D) They are half as high.

4. Which of these products is especially for international use?
   (A) The radio
   (B) The clock
   (C) The iron
   (D) The briefcase

5. What claim is NOT made for these products?
   (A) They are attractive.
   (B) They are very durable.
   (C) They are lightweight.
   (D) They are inexpensive.

6. What advantage does this magazine have over other business magazines?
   (A) It is more interesting and readable.
   (B) It is available in more locations.
   (C) It offers more up-to-date news. ⌄
   (D) It covers more international business.

7. How often is the magazine published?
   (A) Once a month
   (B) Once a week
   (C) Five times a week ⌄
   (D) Seven times a week

8. What is being offered?
   (A) Message delivery
   (B) Package design
   (C) Coffee products
   (D) Baked goods

9. What claim does the speaker make about the products?
   (A) They can be made to suit special occasions.
   (B) They are sold at discount prices.
   (C) They are available twenty-four hours a day.
   (D) They can be found all over the world.

10. Which of the following is NOT mentioned as an occasion to use these products?
    (A) Retirements
    (B) Weddings
    (C) Birthdays
    (D) Meetings

D. Business Talks

These talks are similar to introductions or remarks made at business meetings, or to announcements made in work settings. Questions about these talks often focus on the location, the speaker, or the audience, as well as on details brought up in the talks.

Sample Items: Business Talk

Man: [And now, ladies and gentlemen, I'd like to present the award for employee of the month to Elizabeth Bryce from the shipping department. She not only received top evaluations from her supervisor; she also submitted a suggestion that could save our company thousands of dollars a year in shipping costs. Besides a small bonus in next week's paycheck, Ms. Bryce gets a reserved parking place for a month — the one right next to the CEO's spot. She also becomes eligible for the employee of the year award, and as you know, the employee of the year wins a new car.]

Who is Elizabeth Bryce?
- ● An employee in the shipping department
- Ⓑ A supervisor
- Ⓒ The speaker
- Ⓓ An assistant to the CEO of the corporation

The speaker is presenting the employee of the month award, and she mentions that Elizabeth Bryce works in the shipping department of this firm.

Which of the following is NOT true about Elizabeth Bryce?
- Ⓐ Her suggestion may save the company money.
- Ⓑ She can park next to the CEO this month.
- ● She will get a promotion.
- Ⓓ Her evaluations were very good.

Only choice (C) is not mentioned.

What does the employee of the year receive?
- Ⓐ A small bonus
- Ⓑ The CEO's parking place
- Ⓒ Thousands of dollars a year
- ● A new car

According to the speaker, the employee of the year is awarded a new car.

Exercise 4.4

Focus: Understanding and answering questions about business talks.

Directions: Listen to the talks, and then answer the questions about them by marking the correct choice — (A), (B), (C), or (D).

🔲 Now start the audio program.

1. When is this talk being given?
   (A) During a party
   (B) Before a sales presentation
   (C) After a celebration
   (D) At a meeting

2. What had the speaker probably told the audience last month?
   (A) That the sales figures had increased
   (B) That a celebration was being planned
   (C) That they should try to increase sales
   (D) That they must prepare an agenda

3. Whose sales figures increased most in the previous month?
   (A) Jane's
   (B) Rob's
   (C) Nina's
   (D) Tom's

4. What is the woman's purpose in giving the talk?
   (A) To request some information about satellites
   (B) To introduce her firm's products
   (C) To thank her colleagues for doing a good job
   (D) To suggest a merger between the two firms

5. What will the woman do next?
   (A) Give a multimedia presentation
   (B) Examine a new product
   (C) Take a short break
   (D) Answer some questions

6. Where are the shots being given?
   (A) In the nurse's office ⌣
   (B) In the lunchroom
   (C) At the health department
   (D) At a clinic

7. How much will the shots cost?
   (A) Nothing ⌣
   (B) Ten dollars
   (C) Twenty-five dollars
   (D) Forty dollars or more

8. Why is the company offering these shots?
   (A) The health department requires it.
   (B) The workers have demanded it.
   (C) The firm doesn't want workers to miss work.
   (D) The flu has been especially severe this year.

9. What is the speaker's purpose?
   (A) To propose changes in a schedule
   (B) To welcome some visitors
   (C) To discuss some technical matters
   (D) To introduce new members of the board

10. What is the occasion of this talk?
    (A) A meeting of the executive board
    (B) A conference in Singapore
    (C) A tour of the facilities
    (D) An informal social gathering

E. Recorded Messages

These talks are similar to the recorded messages you might hear on the telephone and in other situations. Questions about these talks usually concern the situation in which the talk is given, the audience, and details given in the recording.

Sample Items: Recorded Message

Woman: [Your attention please. Stopping momentarily in front of the airport terminal building is permitted only for the unloading of passengers and baggage. Short-term parking is available at the airport parking structure, and long-term parking is available at the facility on Jones Road. Do not leave your vehicle unattended for any reason. Unattended vehicles will be ticketed and towed to the police lot downtown. Your cooperation is appreciated.]

Which of these is NOT permitted?
- ● Leaving a vehicle unattended
- Ⓑ Unloading suitcases
- Ⓒ Letting passengers out of a vehicle
- Ⓓ Stopping for a short period

The speaker says, "Do not leave your vehicle unattended for any reason." The other activities are allowed.

Where is long-term parking available?
- Ⓐ In front of the terminal
- Ⓑ In the airport parking structure
- Ⓒ At a parking lot downtown
- ● At the Jones Road facility

The speaker says that long-term parking facilities are on Jones Road.

Exercise 4.5

Focus: Understanding and answering questions about recorded messages.

Directions: Listen to the talks, and then answer the questions about them by marking the correct choice — (A), (B), (C) or (D).

📼 Now start the audio program.

1. Why is the caller unable to speak to anyone?
    - Ⓐ It is after business hours.
    - Ⓑ The representatives are talking to other people.
    - Ⓒ The airline's phone system is out of order.
    - Ⓓ The airline has gone out of business.

2. What is the caller told to do?
    - Ⓐ Stay on the phone
    - Ⓑ Use another number
    - Ⓒ Call back later
    - Ⓓ Answer a question

3. Who is listening to this announcement?
    - Ⓐ Passengers on an airplane
    - Ⓑ Visitors to an amusement park
    - Ⓒ Passengers on a train
    - Ⓓ Tourists entering a national park

4. What are listeners told to do in an emergency?
    - Ⓐ Wait for assistance
    - Ⓑ Pull up the safety bar
    - Ⓒ Get away quickly
    - Ⓓ Call the park personnel

5. Why is this announcement being given?
   (A) To request assistance
   (B) To warn of an emergency
   (C) To explain a delay
   (D) To provide safety information

6. Which of the following does Woodland Gear probably NOT sell?
   (A) Hiking boots
   (B) Tents and sleeping bags
   (C) Vacation tours
   (D) Outdoor clothing

7. What should a caller press if he or she did not receive goods ordered last month?
   (A) * 1
   (B) * 2
   (C) * 3
   (D) * 4

8. Which of these movies has the latest starting time?
   (A) *Neon Streets*
   (B) *Daisy*
   (C) *Rico's Revenge*
   (D) *Star Voyage*

9. To which of these would someone go to see a family comedy?
   (A) Cinema 1
   (B) Cinema 2
   (C) Cinema 3
   (D) A special showing

10. How much is admission to the first showing of all the movies?
   (A) $2.00
   (B) $3.00
   (C) $4.00
   (D) $7.00

More Practice

Directions: Listen to the talks, and then answer the questions about them by marking the correct choice — (A), (B), (C) or (D).

Now start the audio program.

1. What is one disadvantage of a rowing machine?
   (A) It is not easy to assemble.
   (B) It is extremely expensive.
   (C) It exercises only half of the body.
   (D) It cannot be used by a beginner.

2. What do exercise experts claim?
   (A) Four months is all that is needed to get into shape.
   (B) One should exercise each muscle system separately.
   (C) Exercising only the upper body is dangerous.
   (D) It is best to exercise both body halves at one time.

3. How much will a customer have to pay for the Exersystem per month?
   (A) $100   (C) $300
   (B) $200   (D) $400

4. Why would someone rent a car from this agency?
   (A) To impress someone
   (B) To save time
   (C) To rent the newest models
   (D) To save money

5. Where is the rental agency located?
   (A) At the airport
   (B) On Marshall Boulevard
   (C) At a downtown hotel
   (D) In the Oxford Mall

6. What is the speaker doing?
   (A) Introducing a new topic
   (B) Agreeing to a change in plans
   (C) Disagreeing with another speaker
   (D) Requesting more information

7. With which of these statements would the speaker agree?
   A. The Shannon project should not be completed.
   B. Future projects will be delayed.
   C. Jim's plan will save time and money.
   D. Temporary workers should not be hired.

8. Who is the speaker?
   A. A newspaper journalist
   B. A fire chief
   C. An owner of a warehouse
   D. A television reporter

9. How many people have been reported injured?
   A. None
   B. One
   C. Two
   D. Six

10. When did the fire break out?
    A. In the early morning
    B. Around noon
    C. Late in the afternoon
    D. In the evening

11. What was the cause of the fire?
    A. The owners refuse to say
    B. An electrical explosion
    C. A deliberate act of arson
    D. The cause is still unknown

12. How fast does Mario promise to serve items from the special menu?
    A. In two minutes
    B. In five minutes
    C. In eight minutes
    D. In ten minutes

13. What is the prize in Mario's weekly drawing?
    A. Cash
    B. Two free dinners
    C. A goldfish bowl
    D. A free lunch

14. When will the man return to the office?
    A. In a few minutes
    B. Late in the afternoon
    C. Tomorrow morning
    D. In nine days

15. What does the speaker tell people who want to speak to him today?
    A. To come to his home
    B. To call him later in the day
    C. To leave a message for him
    D. To call him at his partner's office

16. Who is Robin Sitwell?
    A. The man's partner
    B. The person recording the message
    C. The man's assistant
    D. An important client

17. Who is the speaker?
    A. The host of a radio show
    B. A university professor
    C. A guest on a television program
    D. A weather forecaster

18. Why should corn be harvested in the morning?
    A. It contains more vitamin C.
    B. It tastes sweeter.
    C. It contains more water.
    D. It is easier to pick.

19. What will probably be heard right after this talk?
    A. An advertisement for seeds
    B. More information about vitamins
    C. A discussion of plant parasites
    D. Some tips for cooking vegetables

20. At what time of year is this talk given?
    A. Spring
    B. Summer
    C. Autumn
    D. Winter

Guide to Reading Comprehension

This section consists of three sections, each with its own directions and format:

Part V: Sentence Completion .... 40 items
Part VI: Error Identification .... 20 items
Part VII: Short Passages .... 40 items

Although ETS calls this section "Reading," only Part VII actually tests reading skills. Parts V and VI test your knowledge of grammar, usage, and vocabulary.

Timing is an important factor in the second section. Your goal is to finish all the items and leave yourself a few minutes to go back to items that you found difficult.

Part VII is the most time consuming because it takes time to read the passages. You may be able to go through the items in Parts V and VI quickly, but you don't want to go so fast that you make simple mistakes. Remember: You don't get any extra points for answering Part VII questions.

This part of the *Guide* is divided into three lessons, each concerning one part of the test. These lessons familiarize you with the kinds of problems you will encounter on the test and provide exercises to prepare you for each type of problem.

LESSON 5

Sentence Completion

Preview: Lesson Outline

- Part IV Format
- Tactics for Part IV
- Sample Test
- Testing Points and Skill-Building Exercises
  - A. Word Choice
  - B. Word Forms
  - C. Word Choice/Word Forms
  - D. Verb Forms
  - E. Prepositions
  - F. Connecting Words
  - G. Gerunds, Infinitives, and Simple Forms
- More Practice

Part V **Format**

This section consists of thirty sentences, each missing one or more words. Below each sentence are four words or phrases. Your job is to decide which of these four choices produces a complete, grammatical, and logical sentence when it is put into the sentence.

Tactics for Part V

1. Begin by reading each item carefully. Try to guess what word or words are missing. Look for these words or similar words among the answer choices.
2. The most common testing point in Part V involves word choice. You can identify these items because the four answer choices look alike or have similar meanings. Use the context of the sentence to help you choose the answer, and look for any grammar clues that help you eliminate distractors.
3. The second most common type of item in Part V involves word form. You can recognize these because the answer choices are all forms of the same word. Use the endings of the words to determine which choice is correct in the context of the sentence.
4. Verb-form problems are the third most common item type in Part V. The answer choices for these items are four forms of the same verb. Look for time words and other clues.
5. If the correct choice is not obvious, eliminate choices that are clearly incorrect and guess. Put a mark by items that you found difficult so that you can come back to them if you have time. Never leave any items unanswered.
6. Never spend too much time on any one item.
7. As soon as you finish Part V, go on to Part VI.

Sample Test

Directions: This part of the test consists of incomplete sentences. Beneath each sentence, four words or phrases appear. Mark the answer choice — (A), (B), (C), or (D) —that best completes the sentence.

Example

Mr. Morales read over the contract with great _____.

- Ⓐ interesting
- ● interest
- Ⓒ interested
- Ⓓ interestingly

This sentence should correctly read, "Mr. Morales read over the contract with great interest." Therefore the best answer is (B).

1. We did not have _____ questions for the lecturer.
   - Ⓐ none
   - Ⓑ some
   - Ⓒ any
   - Ⓓ no

2. The company could save money if it bought a fleet of more _____ vehicles.
   - Ⓐ economize
   - Ⓑ economic
   - Ⓒ economics
   - Ⓓ economical

3. The cafeteria begins serving lunch at noon and stays open _____ three.
   - Ⓐ to
   - Ⓑ until
   - Ⓒ by
   - Ⓓ within

4. I cannot work at home because there are too many _____ there.
   - Ⓐ attractions
   - Ⓑ detractors
   - Ⓒ distractions
   - Ⓓ contractors

5. Mr. Nakamura was put in charge of the media department, _____ was recently reorganized.
   - Ⓐ who
   - Ⓑ in which
   - Ⓒ which
   - Ⓓ which it

6. The Buckingham Hotel has very reasonable _____ for single rooms.
   - Ⓐ rates
   - Ⓑ fees
   - Ⓒ fares
   - Ⓓ bills

7. Marbelis is looking for a job in _____ advertising or public relations.
   - Ⓐ both
   - Ⓑ or
   - Ⓒ neither
   - Ⓓ either

8. We are planning _____ out to dinner tonight.
   - Ⓐ taking our clients
   - Ⓑ our clients going
   - Ⓒ our clients will go
   - Ⓓ to take our clients

9. Jerry made his children _____ on Saturday.
   - Ⓐ do some chores
   - Ⓑ some chores were done
   - Ⓒ to do some chores
   - Ⓓ they did some chores

10. Anna _____ in this department since January.
    - Ⓐ have been working
    - Ⓑ works
    - Ⓒ has worked
    - Ⓓ has been worked

Testing Points and Skill-Building Exercises

Part V is a test of grammar, usage, and vocabulary. There is a wide range of testing points, and any list of these will be incomplete. However, certain patterns appear again and again. Most Part V items on a given TOEIC fit into one of the six testing-point categories.

A. Word Choice

Word-choice problems are the most common type of item in Part V. Usually, around 40% to 50% of all items involve word choice. This part of the lesson discusses four types of word-choice problems:

- Words with similar forms
- Function words with similar meanings
- Content words with similar meanings
- Problems involving grammar clues

Words with Similar Forms

Answer choices similar in form look alike in some way. For example, they may have the same prefix (*sub*mit, *sub*tract, *sub*side, *sub*sist). They may have the same root (inter*cept*ion, con*cept*, re*cept*ion, ac*cept*ance). They may have the same suffix (subsid*ize*, sanit*ize*, satir*ize*, serial*ize*). The four terms may be linguistically unrelated but have similar spellings (*hearty*, *hardy*, *handy*, *healthy*). Combinations of these are also possible — two choices may have the same prefixes and two the same suffixes, for example.

Sample Item: Words with Similar Forms

I can't work at home because there are too many_____ there.
- Ⓐ attractions
- Ⓑ detractors
- ⬤ distractions
- Ⓓ contractors

Only the word *distractions* — meaning something that takes away attention—completes this sentence in a logical, meaningful way.

Exercise 5.1

Focus: Completing sentences with expressions that are similar in form.

Directions: Decide which of the expressions on the right best completes each sentence on the left, and write the letter of that expression in the blank. For each set of items, there is one expression on the right that will not be used.

1. This fax from Mr. Dubitski was _____ at 11 AM Eastern Standard Time.
2. Ms. Ingram was _____ to the marketing department from the executive office staff.
3. Most food products are _____ by truck.

(a) transplanted
(b) transferred
(c) transported
(d) transmitted

4. The government appointed a labor mediator to act as a _____ in the dispute between the union and the auto industry.
5. The _____ was defeated by a few votes.
6. There was no choice of breaking the deadlock because of both sides' _____ to negotiate.

(a) refusal
(b) referendum
(c) refugee
(d) referee

7. The heat was so _____ that the firefighters had to evacuate the building.
8. When he dropped the bag, the _____ spilled out on the floor.
9. Margaret _____ that she is completely innocent of the charges.

(a) intense
(b) contents
(c) intends
(d) contends

10. I will be happy to provide a _____ for you when you apply for another job.
11. I am going to attend a business _____ in Toronto next week.
12. He always treats his boss with respect and _____.

(a) conference
(b) inference
(c) reference
(d) deference

13. Martha Lyons was elected to the city _____ in the last election.
14. The pilot examined the instruments on his _____.
15. Mr. Aalberg has provided valuable _____ to our firm on matters of international trade.

(a) console
(b) counsel
(c) consul
(d) council

16. This is entirely a work of _____ ; none of the characters is based on an actual person.
17. Only a small _____ of the small businesses that open this year will still be operating in ten years.
18. Lubrication reduces _____ .

(a) faction
(b) fraction
(c) friction
(d) fiction

19. When he was threatened with a lawsuit, he _____ his previous statements.
20. His muscles _____ involuntarily.
21. I finally _____ Mr. Hapsa in Cairo and gave him the message.

(a) retracted
(b) contracted
(c) detracted
(d) contacted

Function Words with Similar Meanings

Some answer choices don't look alike but have related definitions. Usually, all four choices have similar definitions, but sometimes choices have opposite meanings. Sometimes the words involved are function words (words used primarily to show grammatical relationships).

Sample Item: Function Words with Similar Meanings

We did not have _____ questions for the lecturer.

Ⓐ none   ● any
Ⓑ some   Ⓓ no

Choices (A) and (D) are negative words and cannot correctly be used with the negative auxiliary *didn't*. Choice (B), "some" can be used only in affirmative statements and questions.

Certain function words are closely related and often appear in the same items. Following is a list of some of these expressions with sentences that illustrate their use and explanatory notes.

enough	I don't have *enough* money to buy that sweater now. Besides, I don't think it's big *enough* for me.
too	It's *too* expensive to buy right now.
so	The suitcase was *so* heavy that I could barely lift it.
such	It was *such* a heavy suitcase that I could barely lift it.

Enough is used to indicate that there is the correct amount of something needed to accomplish a certain goal. *Too* is used to indicate that there is more than the correct amount. *So* is used before an adjective (*so heavy*); *such* is used before an adjective and a noun (*such a heavy suitcase*).

most	*Most* people enjoy music.
most of the	*Most of the* people at the concert seemed to enjoy it.
almost	*Almost* all the parking spaces were taken.
the most	This is *the most* exciting book I have read in a long time.

Most means "the majority." It is used to speak of a large, generalized group (*most people*). *Most of the* is used to speak of a specific group (*most of the people at the concert*). *Almost* means "nearly." *Almost all the parking spaces* means nearly all of them. *The most* is used with the superlative forms of some adjectives (*the most exciting*).

yet	Has Henrik arrived *yet*?
still	No, he is *still* not here.
anymore	Trisha does not live in that apartment complex *anymore*.
already	She *already* found another place to live.

Yet and *still* both mean "up to now." *Yet* is used chiefly in questions and negative statements, and usually comes at the end of a clause. *Still* is used in all types of sentences: questions, statements, and negative statements. *Anymore* is used to indicate that something is not happening now. It occurs in questions and negative statements, and usually comes at the end of a clause. *Already* is used to indicate that something has happened before now. It is used in statements and questions.

any	Do you have *any* change?
	No, I don't believe I have *any*.
some	Can I have *some* soup?
	Sure, there's *some* in the pot.

Any is used in questions and negative statements. *Some* is used in questions and affirmative statements.

ever	Have you *ever* gone skydiving?
	No, and I do not *ever* plan to go.
never	I have *never* been skydiving either, but I would like to go.

Ever is used in questions and negative statements. *Never* is used in affirmative statements.

no	There was *no* coffee in the pot.
none	There was *none* left.
not	This is *not* coffee — it's tea.
	I do *not* want any tea.

No is used before nouns (*no coffee*) and certain comparative words (*no sooner, no longer*). *None* means "not any" or "not one." *Not* is a function word that makes almost any word or words negative.

after	We will go to dinner *after* the theater.
	We will go to dinner *after* the play is over.
afterwards	We will go to the theater first, and to dinner *afterwards*.

After is used as a preposition before nouns (*the theater*) or as an adverb-clause marker before a clause (*the play is over*). *Afterwards* is an adverb and is usually used at the end of a clause.

| much | Will the trip take *much* time? |
| many | Yes, it will be *many* hours before we arrive. |

| little | There is a *little* money in the wallet. |
| few | There are a *few* dollars. |

| amount | There is a large *amount* of work that has not been done. |
| number | There are a *number* of jobs that must be done. |

The terms *much*, *little*, and *amount* are used with noncount nouns (*time*, *money*, and *work*). The terms *many*, *few*, and *number* are used with countable nouns (*hours*, *dollars*, and *jobs*).

alike	Field hockey and soccer are *alike* in many respects.
like	*Like* soccer, field hockey is a fast-paced game.
	Field hockey, *like* soccer, is a fast-paced game.
	Field hockey is *like* soccer in that both are fast-paced.
similar (to)	Your leather coat and mine are *similar*.
	Your leather coat is *similar to* mine.
the same (as)	Your leather coat and mine are nearly *the same*.
	Your leather coat is *the same* size *as* mine.

Alike is used in the pattern "A and B are alike." *Like* is used in these patterns: "Like A, B. . .," "A, like B, . . . ," and "A is like B. . . ." *Similar* is used in the patterns "A and B are similar" or "A is similar to B." *The same* is used in the patterns "A and B are the same" and "A is the same as B."

| between | Relations *between* the two countries are cordial. |
| among | The man divided his estate *among* his four children. |

Between is used to refer to two entities; *among* is used to refer to more than two.

Exercise 5.2

Focus: Word-choice problems with function words.

Directions: Underline the word in parentheses that best completes each sentence.

1. The bill for lunch was (so/such) high that I decided to put it on my credit card.
2. Mr. Ridgeway decided to invest (any/some) money in hotels in eastern Europe.
3. There was not (enough/too much) tape to seal the package properly.
4. I had (such/so) a bad flight that I (ever/never) intend to fly on that airline again.
5. (Most/Almost) of the rice grown in this country is exported.
6. We have sold (many/much) computer chips to that firm.
7. I intend to see that film, but I have not had a chance to see it (still/yet).
8. (Less/Fewer) people attended the conference this year.
9. Betina does not work here (still/anymore).
10. (Like/Similar to) Miami, Los Angeles has a mild climate.
11. (No/Not) meals are served on this flight.
12. The Malay language and the Indonesian language are (like/alike) in (almost/most) every respect.
13. There are not (some/any) apartments available in that price range.
14. There is (too much/enough) wind today to fly a kite — it feels like a hurricane out there.
15. Large (numbers/amounts) of fertilizer and water are required for high-yield hybrid crops.
16. (Alike/Like) most professionals, doctors work long hours.
17. Mr. Olowu has (already/still) returned to Nigeria.
18. The capital city has (such/so) a large, rapidly growing population that city officials have (no/not) been able to solve the problem of waste disposal there.
19. (Among/Between) (most/the most) impressive buildings in the city of Hanoi is the Opera House.
20. (Little/Few) research has been done in that field (anymore/yet).

Content Words with Similar Meanings

Some items involve not function words but content words — usually nouns, verbs, and adjectives — with similar meanings.

Sample Item: Content Words with Similar Meanings

The Buckingham Hotel has very reasonable _____ for single rooms.
- ● rates
- Ⓑ fees
- Ⓒ fares
- Ⓓ bills

The four answer choices are all nouns with related definitions; they all deal with the idea of payment or cost. *Fees* are payments for certain services. *Fares* are payments for transportation. *Bills* are written statements of charges. *Rates* are used for hotel costs.

Exercise 5.3

Focus: Completing sentences involving content words with similar meanings.

Directions: Decide which of the expressions on the right best completes each sentence on the left, and write the letter of that expression in that blank. For each set of items, there is one expression on the right that will not be used. After you complete the exercise, look up words that you are unfamiliar with in a dictionary.

1. I am going to ____ a vacation in late August.
2. Let's ____ lunch at Alfredo's Restaurant tomorrow.
3. Before you ____ a decision, consider all the facts.

(a) keep   (c) make
(b) take   (d) have

4. How much was the ____ for dinner?
5. You must pay a ____ to go into the national park.
6. My plane ____ to Los Angeles was quite reasonable.

(a) bill   (c) fee
(b) payment (d) fare

7. After twenty-five years with the firm, Mr. Osumi ____.
8. Gary was ____ because he was constantly late for work.
9. The company ____ the salaries of some of its executives in order to cut its expenses.

(a) reduced
(b) dismissed
(c) resigned
(d) fell

10. Ice cream and other frozen foods are located in the next _____.
11. We have to turn left at the next intersection, so you should get in the left _____.
12. I had to stand in ____ for fifteen minutes.

(a) line
(b) row
(c) lane
(d) aisle

13. Sylvie bought a ____ of French bread to make sandwiches.
14. I would like a ____ of butter on my toast.
15. There is just a ____ or two of orange juice left.

(a) loaf
(b) cut
(c) pat
(d) drop

Problems Involving Grammar Clues

In some word choice problems, grammar clues can indicate the correct answer, or at least help you eliminate distractors.

Sample Item: Problems Involving Grammar Clues

The shift manager _____ everyone go home a half-hour early on Friday afternoon.
     Ⓐ allowed   Ⓒ permitted
     ● let   Ⓓ got

The verb *let* has the same meaning as *allowed* and *permitted*. However, only *let* is used with the simple form of the verb (*go*). The verbs *permitted*, *allowed*, and *got* are all followed by a full infinitive (*to go*).

Exercise 5.4

Focus: Using grammar clues to complete word choice problems.

Directions: Underline the form that correctly completes the sentence. (See the Answer Key for an explanation of the grammar clues.)

1. The boss (said/told) that I had to work late.
2. (Visitors/Guests/Tourists) to the site should sign in here.
3. The new computer is (two/twice/double) as fast as the old one.
4. Nelson's uncle (recommended/suggested/advised) him to study management information systems.
5. The (shipment/merchandise/goods) are stored in the warehouse.
6. Suyarat was (looking/seeing) out the window of the plane.
7. Do you want to (pay/purchase/buy) for this with a check?
8. If I (say/tell) you a secret, do you promise not to talk to anyone about it?
9. My new apartment is (close/near/nearby) to the Medical Center.
10. The St. James Hotel has set (standards/models/samples) for excellence in the hospitality industry.
11. He is (regarded/considered) as an expert in the field of biotechnology.
12. Nancy (listened/heard) the governor's speech on the radio.

Exercise 5.5

Focus: Reviewing and practicing all types of word choice problems in the Part V TOEIC format.

Directions: Decide which of the choices — (A), (B), (C), or (D) — best completes the sentence.

1. Investments in genetic engineering firms _____ down slightly last year.
    - (A) went
    - (B) declined
    - (C) reduced
    - (D) jumped

2. Our products are carefully _____ before they are shipped to wholesalers.
    - (A) projected
    - (B) detected
    - (C) inflected
    - (D) inspected

3. The various departments must _____ their activities more carefully.
    - (A) cooperate
    - (B) correlate
    - (C) coordinate
    - (D) coronate

4. Penelope auditioned for a _____ in the play, but she did not get it.
    - (A) role
    - (B) character
    - (C) piece
    - (D) line

5. _____ can understand this manual; it just does not make sense.
    - (A) Somebody
    - (B) No one
    - (C) Anyone
    - (D) Everybody

6. The process _____ about an hour to complete.
    - (A) takes
    - (B) spends
    - (C) has
    - (D) was

7. Smoking is permitted only in specially _____ areas.
    - (A) defined
    - (B) described
    - (C) denied
    - (D) designated

8. You can read about this problem in an _____ edition of the magazine.
    - (A) uprising
    - (B) outgoing
    - (C) outfitting
    - (D) upcoming

9. We lifted the package out of the _____ of the car.
   - (A) trunk
   - (B) track
   - (C) truck
   - (D) trek

10. Ms. Yoosten has _____ finished preparing the financial statement.
   - (A) more or less
   - (B) little or no
   - (C) more and more
   - (D) sooner or later

11. Mr. Hamilton was _____ that Liza was the best person for the job.
   - (A) competent
   - (B) confident
   - (C) consonant
   - (D) consequent

12. The nurse took a blood _____ from Mr. Galindo.
   - (A) sample
   - (B) model
   - (C) example
   - (D) selection

13. What time does the store _____?
   - (A) close
   - (B) finish
   - (C) end
   - (D) complete

14. In order to start the machine, _____ this key to the right.
   - (A) spin
   - (B) cross
   - (C) turn
   - (D) press

15. The president of NFX Computers is a _____ professional soccer player.
   - (A) once
   - (B) previous
   - (C) former
   - (D) past

B. Word Forms

In Section A of this lesson, you looked at problems in which the answer choices consist of four different but related words. In this section, you will see items in which the answer choices consist of four forms of the same base word. In some of these items, each answer choice represents a different part of speech: noun, verb, adjective, or adverb. In other items, there is more than one form of a noun, verb, or adjective.

Sample Item: Word Forms

The company could save money if it bought a fleet of more _____ vehicles.
   - (A) economize
   - (B) economic
   - (C) economics
   - ● economical

All four choices are forms of the same base word. Choice (A) is a verb, choice (C) a noun. Choices (B) and (D) are both adjectives. An adjective is required to modify the noun *vehicles*. The adjective *economic* means "related to an economy;" *economical* means "efficient and inexpensive."

To answer these questions, you should be able to identify the forms that are given as adjectives, nouns, verbs, or adverbs, and to recognize which best fits into the blank in the sentence.

Nouns

Nouns name persons, places, things, and concepts. Concrete nouns refer to physical things while abstract nouns refer to qualities and concepts. Most of the nouns that are tested in this section are abstract nouns.

Some common noun endings:

-tion	information	*-ery*	recovery
-dom	freedom	*-ship*	friendship
-ence	experience	*-tude*	solitude
-ance	acceptance	*-ism*	industrialism
-ity	creativity	*-cracy*	democracy
-hood	brotherhood	*-logy*	biology
-ness	happiness		

Common endings for nouns that refer to persons:

-er	writer	*-ee*	retiree
-or	governor	*-ic*	comic
-ist	psychologist	*-ian*	technician

Verbs

Verbs may be action verbs or linking verbs.
>She *exercises* every day. (action verb)
>They *seem* upset. (linking verb)

Common verb endings:

-ize	sanitize	*-ify*	satisfy
-en	lengthen	*-ate*	incorporate
-er	recover		

Adjectives

Adjectives modify nouns, noun phrases, and pronouns. Most adjectives tested in this section refer to abstract qualities.

- Adjectives are used before nouns.
  >a *prosperous* business   a *common* occurrence
- Adjectives are used after the verb *to be* and other linking verbs.
  >That song is *sad*.
  >She looks *sleepy*.
  >That doesn't seem *important*.

Common adjective endings:

-ate	moderate	*-y*	sunny
-ous	ominous	*-ic*	economic
-al	normal	*-ical*	logical
-ing	interesting	*-ial*	remedial
-ed	bored	*-ory*	sensory
-able	comfortable	*-less*	hopeless
-ible	sensible	*-ive*	competitive
-ish	sluggish	*-ly*	friendly

Adverbs

Most of the adverbs seen in word-form problems are adverbs of manner. These adverbs are formed by adding the suffix *-ly* to an adjective.
>quickly   reasonably   precisely   enthusiastically

- Adverbs are most often used to modify verbs. They may come before or after the main verb, or at the end of the sentence.
    He *eagerly* accepted the challenge.
    Ms. Isgaard spoke *forcefully* to the audience.
    Wilson met his sales quota *quickly*.
- Some adverbs are used to modify adjectives, and occur before those adjectives.
    His mail-order business has been *moderately* successful.
    This bulletin is *slightly* out of date.
- A few adverbs have the same form as adjectives.
    fast   hard   high
- The adverb form of *good* is *well*.

Exercise 5.6

Focus: Completing sentences with the correct word forms.

Directions: Decide which of the expressions on the right best completes each sentence on the left, and write the letter of that expression in the blank. For each set of items, there is one expression on the right that will not be used.

1. What do you ____ me to do?
2. You should ask Paul for some ____.
3. Do you really feel that changing jobs at this time is ____ now?

(a) advice
(b) advise
(c) advisor
(d) advisable

4. What this country needs is some honest ____.
5. I make it a point never to discuss religion or ____ at dinner.
6. Anne Toshira won the election even though she did not have as much ____ experience as her opponent.

(a) politics
(b) political
(c) politicians
(d) politically

7. Is your insurance company going to reimburse you for your ____?
8. When did you ____ your watch?
9. I was unable to retrieve the ____ data.

(a) lost
(b) losing
(c) lose
(d) loss

10. Who is going to ____ for your cat while you are out of town?
11. ____ drivers often cause accidents.
12. Follow the directions ____, or you will make a mistake.

(a) care
(b) carefully
(c) careless
(d) careful

13. You can ____ yourself with this issue by reading these briefing papers.
14. ____ with computers can help you get a job.
15. I am not ____ with that account.

(a) familiar
(b) familiarly
(c) familiarize
(d) familiarity

16. Economists fear that the recession may ____ next year.
17. She was ____ offended by his unkind remark.
18. Divers without their own supply of oxygen can descend to a maximum ____ of around 100 feet.

(a) deep
(b) deepen
(c) depth
(d) deeply

19. My _____ specializes in working on European cars.
20. I cannot fix this machine; I'm not _____ inclined.
21. The train crash was due to human error, not _____ failure.

(a) mechanic
(b) mechanism
(c) mechanical
(d) mechanically

22. I cannot afford a new computer, so I am looking for a good one.
23. On a desert island, money would be _____.
24. _____ of the software will not believe how simple it is to operate.

(a) uses
(b) users
(c) used
(d) useless

Exercise 5.7

Focus: Reviewing and practicing word-form problems in the Part V format.

Directions: Decide which of the choices — (A), (B), (C), or (D) — best completes the sentence.

1. Mr. Uhl will _____ the technical manual into German.
   Ⓐ translate   Ⓒ translator
   Ⓑ translation   Ⓓ translatable

2. The management team encourages everyone to make _____ .
   Ⓐ suggests   Ⓒ suggestible
   Ⓑ suggestions   Ⓓ suggestive

3. This toy requires some _____ at home.
   Ⓐ assemblage   Ⓒ assembler
   Ⓑ assemble   Ⓓ assembly

4. If a product is _____ packaged, it will get consumers' attention.
   Ⓐ attractively   Ⓒ attract
   Ⓑ attraction   Ⓓ attractive

5. There has been a lot of _____ about this new scheme.
   Ⓐ exciting   Ⓒ excitable
   Ⓑ excite   Ⓓ excitement

6. Mr. Hall has a lot of common _____ .
   Ⓐ sensibility   Ⓒ sense
   Ⓑ sensitivity   Ⓓ sensation

7. Boston's Back Bay is a beautiful _____ containing many fine old houses.
   Ⓐ neighborhood   Ⓒ neighboring
   Ⓑ neighbor   Ⓓ neighborly

8. When can we expect _____ of those parts?
   Ⓐ delivery   Ⓒ deliverance
   Ⓑ deliver   Ⓓ deliverer

9. Gomarco Enterprises' environmental problems were revealed by a team of _____ journalists from a local television station.
   Ⓐ investigation   Ⓒ investigators
   Ⓑ investigate   Ⓓ investigative

10. Ms. Drake _____ her point of view very well.
    Ⓐ defensive   Ⓒ defended
    Ⓑ defendant   Ⓓ defense

11. The personnel manager read all the _____ herself.
    Ⓐ applications   Ⓒ applicants
    Ⓑ applies   Ⓓ applicators

12. I went to a wonderful exhibit of _____ art at a gallery on Drew Street.
    Ⓐ photographer   Ⓒ photograph
    Ⓑ photography   Ⓓ photographic

C. Word Choice/Word Forms

Some Part V items are a combination of word-choice problems and word-form problems.

Sample Item: Word Choice/Word Forms

Yusef's work is _____ excellent.
- ● consistently
- Ⓑ constructive
- © consequently
- Ⓓ consistent

This problem requires you to choose between adjective forms (*consistent* and *constructive*) and adverb forms (*consistently* and *consequently*). It also requires you to choose between words with different meanings. In problems where there is one pair of related words (such as *consistent* and *consistently*) and two unrelated words, the correct answer is usually one of the two related words, in this case the adverb *consistently* (A).

Exercise 5.8

Focus: Solving sentence-completion items that are a combination of word-choice and word-form problems.

Directions: Decide which of the choices — (A), (B), (C), or (D) — best completes the sentence.

1. Exercise can help _____ stress.
   - Ⓐ reduction
   - © reduce
   - Ⓑ induce
   - Ⓓ deduction

2. In its year-end report, the corporation reported _____ levels of profit.
   - Ⓐ record
   - Ⓑ recommend
   - © recommendation
   - Ⓓ recording

3. Pacific Rim Travel _____ in arranging trips and tours to Asia.
   - Ⓐ specialties
   - Ⓑ concentrations
   - © focuses
   - Ⓓ specializes

4. We discussed this matter at a _____ early-morning briefing.
   - Ⓐ late
   - Ⓑ recent
   - © lately
   - Ⓓ recently

5. The national air travel system was _____ by a pilots' strike.
   - Ⓐ parallel
   - Ⓑ paralysis
   - © paradox
   - Ⓓ paralyzed

6. Our firm still has an _____ to buy that piece of land.
   - Ⓐ optional
   - Ⓑ optical
   - © optimism
   - Ⓓ option

7. You need a _____ from the Ministry of Forestry to cut down trees in this area.
   - Ⓐ permission
   - Ⓑ remission
   - © permit
   - Ⓓ commit

8. According to this article, Peerless Tools is one of the most _____ firms in the machine-tool industry.
   - Ⓐ competitive
   - Ⓑ contemplative
   - © compatibility
   - Ⓓ competition

9. To make the proper decision, voters must be _____ on the issue.
   - Ⓐ uninformed
   - Ⓑ informed
   - © unformed
   - Ⓓ informal

10. This system allows us to forecast costs with greater _____.
   - Ⓐ precision
   - Ⓑ prediction
   - © procession
   - Ⓓ predictable

11. These new developments may bring about a _____ in the communications industry.

    Ⓐ resolution   Ⓒ resolve
    Ⓑ revolutionary   Ⓓ revolution

12. Zesta Soups is a _____ owned subsidiary of Consolidated Foods.

    Ⓐ wholesome   Ⓒ thoroughly
    Ⓑ fully   Ⓓ wholly

D. Verb Forms

Answer choices of this type of problem consist of four forms of the same verb. The verb forms may be main verbs or auxiliary verbs plus main verbs.

Sample Items: Verb Forms

Anna _____ in this department since January.

    Ⓐ have been working   ● has worked
    Ⓑ works   Ⓓ has been worked

In choice (A), *have* does not agree with the singular subject, *Anna*. Choice (B) incorrectly uses the simple present tense; the phrase *since January* indicates that the present perfect is needed. Choice (D) incorrectly uses the passive form of the verb.

Evening dress _____ at formal functions.

    Ⓐ wearing   Ⓒ is wore
    ● is worn   Ⓓ wears

Choice (A), an *-ing* form used alone, cannot function as a main verb. In choice (C), the past tense (*wore*) is used incorrectly in place of the past participle. Choice (D) is an active form; a passive form is required.

Correct answer choices in this section have the following characteristics:

Correct Tense
Time words in the sentences provide clues as to which tense to choose. In the first sample item, the phrase *since January* indicates that the present perfect should be used. Look at these sentences:

    He _____ to Brazil *a month ago.*
    She _____ ballet *since she was a child.*
    Ali *always* _____ a cup of coffee as soon as he *gets* to work.

In the first sentence, the phrase *a month ago* indicates that a past-tense verb is needed. In the second, the clause *since she was a child* indicates that the present perfect tense is required. In the third, the word *always* and the use of the present tense in the second clause (*gets*) suggest that the simple present tense should be used.

Correct Voice (Active or Passive)
You may have to choose between active and passive verb forms. In the first sample item, choice (D) incorrectly involves the passive because the subject (*Anna*) performs the action rather than receives it. In the second sample item, choice (D) incorrectly uses the active voice; the subject (*Evening dress*) receives the action rather than performs it.

Agreement of Subject and Verb
Singular verbs (*is, has, was, does,* and so on) must be used with singular subjects. Plural verbs (*are, have, were, do,* and so on) must be used with plural subjects. In the first sample item, choice (A) is incorrect because the plural verb *have* does not agree with the subject.

Correct Form of Irregular Verbs

Verb-form problems often involve verbs with irregular forms, especially those with different past tense and past participle forms. In the second sample item, choice (C) is incorrect because the past tense is used after *is*.

In some verb-form problems, infinitives (*to* + the simple form), *-ing* forms, and past participles are incorrect choices because they are used in place of main verbs. Used alone, these forms can never function as main verbs. For example, in the second sample item, choice (A) is incorrect because the *-ing* form cannot serve as a main verb.

Many items require you to choose between simple forms of the verb, *-ing* forms, and past participles. Here are some hints for selecting the correct forms:

- **The simple form follows all modal auxiliaries.**

might be	can stay	should hurry
must know	could take	may sell

  (Certain similar auxiliary verbs require infinitives.)
  ought to go used to play   have to hurry

- **The simple form is used in *that* clauses after certain verbs and adjectives.**
  (This verb form is sometimes called the present subjunctive.)

Verbs		Adjectives	
ask	recommend	better	mandatory
advise	request	essential	necessary
demand	suggest	imperative	vital
insist	urge	important	
propose			

  I insist that Bill *accompany* us.
  It's essential that everyone *work* overtime this week.

  The passive form is *be* + past participle.
  I recommend that Judith *be promoted*.

- **The past participle is used after a form of *have* in all perfect forms of the verb.**

has said	had called	should have gone
have run	will have read	could have decided

- **The *-ing* form is used after a form of *be* in all progressive forms of the verb.**

is sleeping	has been writing	should have been wearing
was studying	had been drawing	will be waiting

- **The past participle is used after a form of *be* in all passive forms of the verb.**

is worn	has been shown
is being considered	had been promised
were told	will have been missed

  would have been lost
  might have been canceled

Exercise 5.9

Focus: Completing sentences with the correct tense or form of the verb.

Directions: Fill in the blanks with the correct form of the verb in parentheses.

1. At this time of year, the sun (rise) _____ at about 5:30 A.M.
2. The game of backgammon (play) _____ for many centuries.
3. I (watch television) _____ last night when, suddenly, the electricity went out.
4. Margot (just return) _____ from Bangkok when she had to leave for Tokyo.
5. I probably (finish) _____ around midnight tomorrow night.
6. Peter may (spend) _____ his vacation in Bali.
7. It (snow) _____ in the mountains last night.
8. Since 1992, David Michaels (own) _____ a financial consulting firm.
9. That memo (write) _____ by Sadashumi yesterday.
10. I suggest that you (discuss) _____ this matter with Inspector Hanson.
11. I should have (take) _____ a vitamin pill this morning.
12. This newspaper (publish) _____ since 1872.
13. Caroline (give) _____ the baby a bath right now — can she call you back in a few minutes?
14. It is important that this product (promote) _____ heavily.
15. You must have (drive) _____ all night in order to get here so soon.

Exercise 5.10

Focus: Completing sentences with the correct forms of irregular verbs.

Directions: Decide which of the expressions on the right best completes each sentence on the left, and write the letter of that expression in the blank. For each set of items, there is one expression on the right that will not be used.

1. This watch was _____ to me by my grandfather.   (a) gave
2. I _____ those files to Marta an hour ago.   (b) gives
3. Karl always _____ his wife a dozen roses for their anniversary.   (c) giving
   (d) given

4. Last year I _____ over 50,000 miles.   (a) flying
5. This fighter plane was _____ on over forty missions during the war.   (b) flown
   (c) flew
6. I will be _____ to Nairobi early next week.   (d) fly

7. I _____ at some wonderful restaurants when I was in New Orleans last spring.   (a) eats
   (b) ate
8. Jean seldom _____ lunch before one-thirty.   (c) eaten
9. I have never _____ frog legs — have you?   (d) eating

10. She _____ skiing in Zermatt, Switzerland, last winter.

11. Mr. Zhang said he might _____ to Los Angeles later this year.

12. Naomi had already _____ by the time I got to the office.

(a) go
(b) went
(c) going
(d) gone

13. I may _____ a new car this year.

14. Joel has _____ a lot of mail.

15. A few years ago, we _____ a lot more foot traffic on this street.

(a) get
(b) got
(c) getting
(d) gotten

Exercise 5.11

Focus: Practicing and reviewing verb-form problems in the Part V format.

Directions: Decide which of the choices — (A), (B), (C), or (D) — best completes the sentence.

1. Portuguese is _____ in Brazil, the largest country in South America.
- Ⓐ speaking
- Ⓒ speak
- Ⓑ spoke
- Ⓓ spoken

2. The plane was _____ its final approach to the airport when it developed a problem with its landing gear.
- Ⓐ made
- Ⓒ make
- Ⓑ making
- Ⓓ makes

3. Tokyo's entertainment district _____ the Ginza.
- Ⓐ is called
- Ⓒ is calling
- Ⓑ calls
- Ⓓ calling

4. Carol Bridwell has _____ a senior partner in the law firm of Mason and Woodford.
- Ⓐ elected
- Ⓒ been elected
- Ⓑ electing
- Ⓓ being elected

5. Matthew _____ the CPA exam last month.
- Ⓐ will pass
- Ⓒ have passed
- Ⓑ passing
- Ⓓ passed

6. It's mandatory that passengers _____ their seat belts.
- Ⓐ fasten
- Ⓒ should fasten
- Ⓑ fastening
- Ⓓ have fastened

7. Right now, day care is not provided at the factory, but a new day care center _____.
- Ⓐ is constructing
- Ⓒ has constructed
- Ⓑ is being built
- Ⓓ building

8. We must _____ faster to keep up with the project schedule.
- Ⓐ to work
- Ⓒ work
- Ⓑ working
- Ⓓ worked

9. The accident victim _____ to the emergency room.
- Ⓐ was taken
- Ⓒ was taking
- Ⓑ took
- Ⓓ taken

10. Mr. O'Dell insisted that the proposal _____ .
- Ⓐ rewrite
- Ⓑ be rewritten
- Ⓒ is rewritten
- Ⓓ rewrote

11. Although people say that seeing is believing, I still cannot believe that what I _____ last night was a UFO.
- Ⓐ seen
- Ⓒ saw
- Ⓑ had seen
- Ⓓ might see

12. Ricardo _____ tennis since he was eight years old.
- Ⓐ has been playing
- Ⓑ playing
- Ⓒ was playing
- Ⓓ had played

13. They are still _____ for an explanation.
- Ⓐ wait
- Ⓒ waited
- Ⓑ waiting
- Ⓓ waits

14. You ought _____ a thank-you note to Ms. Velez.

  (A) send
  (C) have sent
  (B) sending
  (D) to send

15. I am afraid the train will _____ by the time you get to the platform.

  (A) leaving
  (C) left
  (B) have left
  (D) be left

E. Prepositions

Answer choices for this type of problem consist of four prepositions. You must chose the correct one, based on the context of the sentence.

Sample Items: Prepositions

The cafeteria begins serving lunch at noon and stays open _____ three.

  (A) to
  (C) by
  ● until
  (D) within

All four prepositions can be used to express relationships of time, but only (B) indicates that an action ("staying open") continues up to a certain point ("three").

The Mississippi River roughly divides the United States _____ eastern and western halves.

  ● into
  (C) on
  (B) to
  (D) between

After the verb *divide,* both *between* and *into* can be used. *Divide between* is used with two people. ("He divided the money between his two children.") *Divide into* is used with parts ("eastern and western halves").

In some items, the key to choosing the correct preposition is the word that comes before the blank, because certain nouns, adjectives, and verbs are always followed by the same prepositions. (This is true in the first sample item.)

Following are lists of nouns, adjectives/participles, and verbs that are commonly paired with certain prepositions, along with a list of phrasal prepositions, which are prepositions that consist of more than one word.

Nouns + Prepositions	
appointment with	influence on
approach to	interest in
cause of	native of
combination of	part of
contribution to	price of
cure for	probability of
decrease in	problem with
demand for	process of
development of (something)	quality of
development in (a field)	reliance on
effect on (the thing affected)	result of
effect of (something that affects)	rules for (doing something)
example of	rules of (a game)
experience in (a field)	satisfaction with
experience with (something)	solution to
exception to	source of
idea for	supply of
improvement in	variety of
increase in	

Adjectives/Participles + Prepositions

acquainted with	inferior to
accustomed to	made of (material)
afraid of	married to (someone)
angry with (someone)	native to (somewhere)
angry at (something)	necessary for
attached to	next to
aware of	pleased with
based on	polite to
capable of	preferable to
close to	perfect for
dependent on	related to
different from	responsible for (something)
disappointed with/by	responsible for (someone)
eligible for	satisfied with
essential to/for	similar to
familiar with	suitable for
free of (impurities)	superior to
free from (control)	surprised at/by
identical to	

Verbs + Prepositions

account for	invest in
agree to (a plan)	move into (a house or room)
agree with (someone)	move to (a city or country)
approve of	participate in
arrive in (a city or country)	pay for
arrive at (an airport, a train station,	plan on
a building)	prepare for
begin by (doing something)	prohibit from
begin with (something)	recover from
believe in	rely on
cooperate with	replace with
caution against	respond to
consist of	result in
contribute to	succeed in
deal with	subscribe to
decide on	substitute for
depend on	talk about (a topic)
engage in	talk to (an audience or a person)
escape from	talk with (a person)
grow into	wait for (someone or something)
divide into (parts)	wait on (a customer)
divide among (more than two people)	
divide between (two people)	
interfere with	

Phrasal Prepositions

according to	in spite of
ahead of	instead of
along with	on account of
because of	prior to
by means of	regardless of
due to	thanks to
in charge of	together with
in favor of	

Exercise 5.12

Focus: Completing sentences with prepositions that follow nouns, adjectives, and verbs, or are part of phrasal prepositions.

Directions: Complete the following sentences with the correct prepositions. (If you are unsure of the answer, take a guess before you check the lists.)

1. As the quality _____ this product has improved, the demand _____ it has grown.
2. This suit made _____ wool is superior _____ the other one.
3. Diana is planning to move _____ the office next _____ mine.
4. If there are any more problems _____ this design, Ms. Yamada, who is _____ charge _____ the art department, can deal _____ them.
5. The explosion that occurred was the result _____ a combination _____ several factors.
6. This sports car might not be suitable _____ a family, but it is perfect _____ a single person.
7. After he gets his doctoral degree, Li-Ming hopes to contribute _____ the search _____ a cure _____ cancer.
8. The development _____ a good bookkeeping system was essential _____ modern business.
9. Mr. Ewool, a native _____ Ghana, moved _____ the United Kingdom fifteen years ago.
10. There are many rules _____ using prepositions but unfortunately, there are many exceptions _____ the rules.
11. Thanks _____ improvements _____ medical technology, doctors today are capable _____ making much more accurate diagnoses.
12. I made an appointment _____ Mr. Hilbert to talk _____ the upcoming merger.
13. Although you will not be eligible _____ retirement for many years, you should start to prepare _____ it now.
14. According _____ some experts, the long-term effect _____ pollution _____ people's health may be more serious than was once thought.
15. Zaire is the source _____ much of the world's supply _____ cobalt.
16. Together _____ his aides, the chancellor arrived _____ the airport.
17. We have found a solution _____ part _____ the problem.
18. If we intend to compete _____ Rockwood Industries, we must take a new approach _____ distribution and marketing.
19. I agreed _____ George when he said that, before we decide _____ a plan, we need to talk _____ someone who has a lot of experience _____ this area.
20. Instead _____ guessing blindly, you should make an educated guess _____ means _____ the process _____ elimination.

In some items, the key to the correct preposition is the word that follows the blank — the prepositional object — or an overall understanding of the sentence. Some uses of common prepositions are given here:

Using *In*

> *Time*
>
in + century (in the twenty-first century)
in + decade (in the 1940s; in the nineties)
in + year (in 1987)
in + season (in the spring)
in + month (in October)
in + parts of the day (in the morning; in the afternoon; in the evening)

In (or *within*) is also used with amounts of time:
> I'll be home *in* (*within*) an hour.

> *Place*
>
in the world
in + continent (in Africa)
in + body of water (in the Caribbean)
in + country (in Thailand)
in + state/province (in Massachusetts; in Ontario)
in + city (in Munich)
in + building (in the World Trade Center)
in + room (in the kitchen)

> *Other*
>
in + clothing (in a gray suit)
in + language (in Japanese)
in + book (in *The Complete Guide to TOEIC*)
in + newspaper (in the *International Herald-Tribune*)
in + magazine (in *Asia Week*)
in + department (in the legal department)
in + field (in computer science; in architecture)
in + a person's opinion (in my opinion)
in the past/future
in a car/taxi
in trouble
in danger (of)
in part (= partially)
in front of
in the middle of
in back of
in the rear
in the market (for) (= trying to buy something)
in line

Using *On*

> *Time*
>
on + date (on May 23)   on + day (on Friday)

Place
on the earth/the planet/the globe   on + street (on Wall Street)
on + coast (on the East Coast)   on + floor (on the 42nd floor)

Other
on a vehicle (on a bus; on a train; on a plane)
on foot
on the cover (of)
on a trip
on sale (= for sale at a reduced price)
on the market (= for sale)
on schedule
on + musical instrument (on the guitar)
on time (for)
on television/radio
on the phone
on a farm
on a map
on the other hand
on purpose (= intentionally)

Using *At*

Time
at + time of day (at 9:20; at midnight)
at night

Place
at + address (at 634 Sutter Street)
at + building (at the Prado Museum)
at home

(Note: Both *in* and *at* can be used with buildings. *In* emphasizes that someone or something is inside the building.)

Other
at present   at times (= sometimes)
at the moment   at once (= immediately)
at first/last   at a high/low price
at most/least   (not) at all

Using *By*

By is used before a point of time to indicate the latest possible time. *By*, in this case, means "before" or "at."
    I will be home *by* noon.

By can mean "next to."
    She's standing *by* her friend.

By is used after passive verbs to identify the agent (the "doer") of the action.
    This report was written *by* Paco.

By is used with means of transportation and communication.
　　by car　　　by plane　　　by letter

(Note: Both *by* and *in/on* are used before means of transportation or communication. *By* is used only before singular nouns without articles or other determiners. If the noun is plural, or if it is preceded by a determiner, *in* or *on* is used.)
　　in my car　　　on the plane　　　in letters

> *Other*
> by chance　　　　　　　　　　by hand
> by far　　　　　　　　　　　　by check/credit card

Using *For*

For is used with a period of time to show the duration of an action.
　　Smythe has been living abroad *for* six months.

Note: *Since* is used with points of time to show a similar relationship.
　　Smythe has been living abroad *since* January.

For is used to show purpose.
　　He went to the store *for* milk and bread.

For can mean "in place of" or "on behalf of."
　　I asked Sally to work *for* me on Saturday.

> *Other*
> for free　　　　　　　　　　for sale (= on the market)
> for rent　　　　　　　　　　for good (= permanently)

Using *During*

During is used with periods of time.
　　It snows a lot in Montreal *during* the winter.
　　His company grew rapidly *during* the 1980s.

During is *not* used with dates or days of the week.

Using *With*

With is used to express the idea of accompaniment or ownership.
　　I went to the restaurant *with* Andrea.
　　The man *with* the briefcase is the vice-president.

With is also used to indicate the tool or instrument used to accomplish something.
　　He opened the door *with* his key.
　　He paid for the bill *with* a credit card.

Using *Until*

Until is used with points of time to indicate that an action continues up to that point.
　　Helen practiced the piano *until* noon.
　　They won't arrive *until* tomorrow.

Using *From . . . To* and *Between . . . And*

These phrases are used with starting points and ending points.
> *From* 1990 *to* 1993, Mr. Nolan was in charge of the sales division.
> *Between* 1990 *and* 1993, Mr. Nolan was in charge of the sales division.
> Interstate Highway 90 runs *from* Boston *to* Seattle.
> Interstate Highway 90 runs *between* Boston *and* Seattle.

Exercise 5.13

Focus: Completing sentences with prepositions that precede certain prepositional objects.

Directions: Fill in the blanks with the correct prepositions.

1. I met my friend Howard _____ chance _____ the lobby of the Raffles Hotel _____ Singapore.
2. There's a phone number _____ the newspaper that we can call _____ more information.
3. _____ Korea, it is considered bad luck to sign your name _____ a red-ink pen.
4. The plumber promised me he would be here _____ least _____ three, but he didn't arrive _____ five.
5. Intersystem's international sales increased _____ 21% _____ 1990 and 1995.
6. Mr. Poernomo asked me to meet him _____ his office _____ the third floor _____ two-thirty, so I need to leave _____ a few minutes.
7. Deborah got _____ trouble _____ her boss for illegally copying software.
8. I always shower _____ the morning, but my roommate showers _____ night.
9. Ms. Vu has been living _____ that apartment building _____ 2460 Vine Street _____ September, but her sister has been there _____ several years.
10. The oil industry is _____ far the most important industry _____ Saudi Arabia.
11. Mr. Demmings bought some property _____ the West Coast _____ the early 1980s.
12. _____ January, all of the office furniture at Office Works will be _____ sale _____ greatly reduced prices.
13. I will arrive _____ Orly Airport _____ Paris _____ around nine o'clock.
14. _____ present, there are no job openings _____ the design department, but there may be an opening _____ a month or two.
15. Some of the most fashionable and expensive stores _____ the United States are _____ Rodeo Drive _____ Los Angeles.
16. Textiles were made _____ hand _____ the invention of the power loom _____ the nineteenth century.
17. Her photo appeared _____ the cover of *Business Watch,* and there was a story about her _____ the magazine as well.
18. I commute to work _____ the city _____ train, but my friend always travels there _____ his own car.
19. Every year, people _____ Mexico celebrate their independence from Spain _____ September 16.
20. _____ 1985 to 1988, he lived _____ a small farm _____ Vermont.

Exercise 5.14

Focus: Reviewing and practicing preposition choice problems in a format similar to that of Part V of TOEIC.

Directions: Decide which of the choices — (A), (B), (C), or (D) — best completes the sentence.

1. Botswana is famous _____ its diamond mines.
    (A) for
    (B) of
    (C) with
    (D) by

2. Padang food is a style of Indonesian food that is eaten _____ one's fingers.
    (A) by
    (B) with
    (C) in
    (D) to

3. This package must be in Wellington at least _____ noon Tuesday.
    (A) on
    (B) at
    (C) for
    (D) by

4. Ms. Chadwick was disappointed _____ the results of the advertising campaign.
    (A) for
    (B) of
    (C) on
    (D) with

5. The cheapest way to move goods overseas is _____, but that is also the slowest way.
    (A) by ships
    (B) on ship
    (C) by ship
    (D) to ships

6. _____ the next few months, we hope to arrange a joint venture with a company in the Czech Republic.
    (A) Within
    (B) With
    (C) Since
    (D) At

7. Choudhuri was hired because he is familiar _____ the latest developments in biotechnology.
    (A) to
    (B) with
    (C) in
    (D) about

8. Most of the delegates arrived _____ taxis.
    (A) at
    (B) on
    (C) in
    (D) by

9. The store is open _____ nine to six.
    (A) from
    (B) at
    (C) by
    (D) between

10. Bonnie has been married _____ Steve for two years.
    (A) with
    (B) at
    (C) by
    (D) to

11. If Mr. Tyler had cooperated _____ us, we could have finished in a couple of hours.
    (A) to
    (B) of
    (C) with
    (D) from

12. This novel is based _____ part on a true story.
    (A) in
    (B) on
    (C) by
    (D) at

F. Connecting Words

Expressions that join words, phrases, and clauses sometimes appear as answers in Part V.

Marbelis is looking for a job in _____ advertising or public relations.

    Ⓐ both   Ⓒ neither

    Ⓑ or   ● either

The correct pattern is *either A or B.*

_____ I knew she had worked in an insurance agency for a year, I did not realize that she was so knowledgeable about health insurance.

    Ⓐ However   Ⓒ Despite

    ● Although   Ⓓ Even

Only the adverb-clause marker *although* correctly completes the sentence. (The marker *even though* would also be correct.)

This town is not on the map _____ I have.

    Ⓐ this   Ⓒ where

    Ⓑ whom   ● that

The adjective-clause marker *that* must be used to refer to a thing (*map*).

This part of the lesson discusses the following types of joining words:

1.	Coordinate conjunctions	4.	Adjective-clause markers
2.	Correlative conjunctions	5.	Adverb-clause markers
3.	Noun-clause markers	6.	Prepositional expressions

Coordinate conjunctions

These one-word conjunctions are used to join words, phrases, and independent clauses:

Coordinate Conjunction	Use	Example
and	Used for addition.	He wore a red *and* white tie. Mr. Iachini works at home *and* at his office.
or	Used for alternatives.	Do you want a sandwich *or* some soup?
but	Used for contrast.	The house is large *but* in poor condition.
nor	Used for negative alternatives.	Kent doesn't own a boat, *nor* does he intend to buy one.
so	Used for effect/cause; means "for this reason."	Ramona did a great job, *so* she was given a raise.

Correlative Conjunctions

These two-word conjunctions are also used to join words, phrases, and independent clauses.

Correlative Conjunction	Use	Example
both . . . and	Used for addition.	There are vacancies at *both* the Imperial *and* the Sherman hotels.
not only . . . but also	Used for addition.	She *not only* has a real estate license *but also* owns a real estate company.
either . . . or	Used for alternatives.	You can go *either* by car *or* by bus.
neither . . . nor	Used for negative alternatives	He had *neither* strong financial backing *nor* a sound business plan.

Exercise 5.15

Focus: Completing sentences with coordinate and correlative conjunctions.

Directions: Decide which of the expressions on the right best completes each sentence on the left, and write the letter of that expression in the blank. For each set of items, there is one expression on the right that will not be used.

1. My desk is usually cluttered with papers, _____ my office mate's desk is always neat and clean.
2. I do not think we should discuss the proposal now, _____ do I think we should vote on it.
3. You can use the front door _____ the side door.
4. We ran out of copy paper, _____ we had to borrow some from another department.

(a) nor
(b) and
(c) or
(d) but
(e) so

5. The fax machine is not working, _____ is the telephone.
6. Are you looking for a new car _____ a used one?
7. My parents understand a little English, _____ they cannot speak it very well.
8. The brakes on your bicycle are not working very well, _____ you had better be careful.

(a) so
(b) nor
(c) or
(d) and
(e) but

9. Ellen plans to buy _____ a minivan or a small truck.
10. Nicolai studied English not only in the United States _____ in the United Kingdom.
11. I visited _____ Houston and Dallas to see clients and make some new contacts.
12. Neither a tennis court _____ a racquetball court was available for Saturday morning.

(a) both
(b) either
(c) but also
(d) nor
(e) or

13. Gloria's report was _____ precise but also well-organized.
14. We would like the walls in the boardroom painted a neutral tone — either cream-colored _____ light tan.
15. Despite his improved performance, Frank was _____ promoted nor given a raise.
16. E-mail is both a fast _____ convenient means of communication.

(a) neither
(b) not only
(c) and
(d) or

Noun-Clause Markers
These words are used to join noun clauses to main clauses.

Noun-Clause Marker	Use	Example
that	Used when the noun clause is formed from a statement.	*Original sentence:* Mr. Kee's office is down the hall. *Sentence with noun clause:* I know *that* Mr. Kee's office is down the hall.

if/whether	Either of these words can be used when the noun clause is formed from a yes/no question.	*Original sentence:* Is Mr. Kee's office down the hall? *Sentence with noun clause:* Do you know *if* (or *whether*) Mr. Kee's office is down the hall?
wh- words (what, when, why, where, what size, and so on).	Used when the noun clause is formed from an information (*wh-*) question.	*Original sentences:* Where is Mr. Kee's office? What floor is Mr. Kee's office on? *Sentences with noun clauses:* I wonder *where* Mr. Mr. Kee's office is? Could you tell me *what floor* Mr. Kee's office is on?

Adjective-Clause Markers

These words join adjective clauses (also called relative clauses) to main clauses. They are sometimes called relative words.

Adjective-Clause Marker	Use	Example
who	Used as the subject of an adjective clause; refers to people.	The employees *who* were hired last month have completed their training program.
whom	Used as the object of a verb or a preposition in an adjective clause; refers to people.	The woman *whom* you met is an executive secretary. You should speak to the man to *whom* the package was sent.
whose	Used to show possession; usually refers to people.	The woman *whose* jewelry was stolen called the police.
which	Used to refer to things or concepts.	Goods *which* last for more than four months are called durable goods. The computers *which* we bought last month are much faster than the old ones. This is one process *by which* steel can be made.
that	Used in certain adjective clauses in place of *who* or *which*; refers to both people and things.	The family *that* lives next door to us will be moving soon. The jewelry *that* was stolen was recovered the following week.
when	Used to refer to time.	This is the time of day *when* I often feel a little sleepy.
where	Used to refer to places.	That's the site *where* the company plans to build a new storage facility.

Note: In TOEIC problems, you will not be asked to decide whether *whom* is used correctly in place of *who*, or whether *that* is used correctly in place of *which* or *who*.

Focus: Completing sentences with noun-clause markers or adjective-clause markers.

Directions: Decide which of the expressions on the right best completes each sentence on the left, and write the letter of that expression in that blank. For each set of items, there is one expression on the right that will not be used.

1. I am lost; can you tell me _____ I can get back to the Palace Hotel from here?
2. Did you know _____ Donna was once a golf pro?
3. I am not sure _____ Paul quit, but he must have had a good reason.
4. I cannot decide _____ I should buy a car or lease one.

    (a) how
    (b) where
    (c) whether
    (d) that
    (e) why

5. Do you know _____ Jean-Marc is in his hotel room?
6. I am not sure _____ people were actually at the reception, but over 200 had been invited.
7. Angel told me _____ I would find the folder.
8. Did you see _____ that magician just did?

    (a) if
    (b) how much
    (c) where
    (d) what
    (e) how many

9. The woman _____ is standing by the water cooler has just started working in the finance department.
10. The friendships _____ I made in college are some of the most valuable ones I have ever made.
11. We are going to spend our vacation in a small town in France _____ my wife once lived.
12. The artist _____ paintings are on the walls of the office building has won several awards for her work.

    (a) which
    (b) who
    (c) where
    (d) when
    (e) whose

13. I believe it was around July 1 _____ the buy-out took place.
14. The sales agent with _____ you will be training is named Tony Covello.
15. Anyone _____ car is parked in a red zone will get a parking ticket.
16. This is the part of the factory _____ the actual production work takes place.

    (a) whom
    (b) which
    (c) whose
    (d) when
    (e) where

Adverb-Clause Markers

These words are used to join adverb clauses (also called subordinate clauses) to main clauses. These words are also called subordinate conjunctions. The adverb clause can either precede the main clause or follow it; if the adverb clause comes first, it is set off by a comma.

Adverb-Clause Markers (Time)	Use	Example
before	Means "earlier than the time that."	The game started *before* I got to the stadium.
after	Means "later than the time that."	You can read this memo *after* I have read it.
since	Means "from a time in the past until now."	I have not seen Kevin *since* he returned from Europe.
until	Means "up to the time that."	Freida watched television *until* her roommate came home.
once	Used to indicate that when one action occurs, another takes place.	*Once* Gustav arrives, we will start the meeting.
as soon as	Used to indicate that when one action occurs, another takes place.	*As soon as* we have had lunch, we will resume the discussion.
as	Means "at the same time that."	Martha arrived at the party just *as* we were leaving.
when	Means "at the same time that."	*When* I arrived at the office, there was an important message for me.
while	Means "at the same time that." Used when the action of the verb has duration (when it takes some time to complete).	*While* Belinda was talking on the phone, I waited outside her office.

Other Adverb-Clause Markers	Use	Example
because since	Used for cause/effect.	Mikos joined a health club *because* (or *since*) he wanted to get in shape.
although even though though while	Used to show contrast or opposition.	*Although* (or *Though* or *Even though* or *While*) he was late, he didn't miss his plane.
if	Used to introduce a conditional clause; the condition may be possible or impossible (contrary to fact).	*Possible condition:* *If* Sam and Janet invite us, we will go to their party. *Impossible condition:* *If* Juan were here, he would be upset.
unless	Used to indicate a negative condition; means "if . . . not."	*Unless* we hurry, we will be late.

Prepositional Expressions

These expressions have the same meaning as certain adverb clause markers, but are used before noun phrases rather than before clauses.

Prepositional Expressions	Use	Example
because of due to	These expressions have the same meaning as *because*.	*Because of* (or *Due to*) the bad weather, the garden party was canceled.
in spite of despite	These expressions have the same meaning as *although*.	*Despite* (or *In spite of*) their loss, the team is still in first place.

Exercise 5.17

Focus: Completing sentences with conjunctive adverbs, adverb-clause markers, and prepositional expressions.

Directions: Decide which of the expressions on the right best completes each sentence on the left, and write the letter of that expression in the blank. For each set of items, there is one expression on the right that will not be used.

1. Neil is familiar with Malaysia _____ he lived there as a child.
2. _____ the attractive offer Drummund Industries made him, he decided not to accept the job.
3. _____ temperatures are quite high here at this time of year, the ocean breezes make it seem cooler than it actually is.
4. _____ the heavy fog, flights out of Seattle have been canceled.

   (a) because of
   (b) although
   (c) despite
   (d) if
   (e) because

5. The pilot inspected the plane just _____ he took off.
6. _____ you begin working full time, you will have less time for your hobbies.
7. Nancy has been acting differently _____ she became the manager.
8. I cannot go to the beach _____ I have finished this work.

   (a) since
   (b) once
   (c) while
   (d) until
   (e) before

9. _____ their best efforts, the firefighters were unable to save the building.
10. _____ the weather was cool, he was wearing only a thin summer shirt.
11. _____ our continued growth and success, our firm will be hiring a number of new employees in the near future.
12. _____ we had to respond to so many people, we used a form letter.

   (a) despite
   (b) since
   (c) even though
   (d) unless
   (e) because of

13. _____ you want to spend a fortune, I wouldn't eat dinner at Chez Michel's.
14. He was not elected _____ the scandal he had been involved in.
15. _____ the risk, he loves racing his motorcycle.
16. _____ I were you, I would get a lawyer's advice on this matter.

(a) because of
(b) until
(c) despite
(d) if
(e) unless

Exercise 5.18

Focus: Reviewing and practicing all types of connecting-word problems in the Part V format.

Directions: Decide which of the choices — (A), (B), (C), or (D) — best completes the sentence.

1. _____ you return from Istanbul, you'll have to fill out a trip report.
   (A) So that
   (B) Once
   (C) Since
   (D) The sooner

2. Write down _____ your home phone number and your number at your office.
   (A) either
   (B) not only
   (C) both
   (D) neither

3. When did you realize _____ you had made a mistake?
   (A) that
   (B) if
   (C) because
   (D) so

4. In this light, I cannot tell if this suit is dark blue _____ black.
   (A) either
   (B) and
   (C) both
   (D) or

5. Architecture is a profession _____ has always interested me.
   (A) which
   (B) who
   (C) in which
   (D) whose

6. A preliminary investigation indicates that the accident occurred _____ pilot fatigue.
   (A) because
   (B) due
   (C) because of
   (D) since

7. _____ you have any problems with this product, please contact our customer service representative.
   (A) If
   (B) Unless
   (C) Would
   (D) That

8. This is the village _____ Gunther was born.
   (A) which
   (B) where
   (C) which in
   (D) in that

9. David wanted to know _____ he had not been invited.
   (A) because
   (B) why
   (C) who
   (D) due to

10. That author _____ books you enjoy so much is going to be on a talk show on television tomorrow.
    (A) whose
    (B) his
    (C) who
    (D) who his

11. The CEO has not decided _____ of the two strategies he should adopt.
    (A) what
    (B) that
    (C) which
    (D) who

12. The magazine has attracted many new readers _____ Marilyn Bixby became the managing editor.
    (A) while
    (B) since
    (C) once
    (D) if

13. _____ its conservative appearance, this car has plenty of power and handles almost like a sports car.
- Ⓐ Despite
- Ⓑ Although
- Ⓒ In spite
- Ⓓ Even

14. Some corporations realize the importance of golf to business, _____ they sponsor golf tournaments.
- Ⓐ so
- Ⓑ due to
- Ⓒ since
- Ⓓ because of

15. No one in the theater group is a professional actor, _____ their performances are always first-rate.
- Ⓐ moreover
- Ⓑ or
- Ⓒ unless
- Ⓓ but

16. Mr. McCormick has _____ a master's degree nor a bachelor's degree in business.
- Ⓐ either
- Ⓑ not only
- Ⓒ neither
- Ⓓ both

G. Gerunds, Infinitives, and Simple Forms

Correct answers to these problems are gerunds (-*ing* forms), infinitives (*to* + simple forms), or simple forms of the verb. Distractors often include one or both of the other two forms and full clauses (subjects + verbs).

Sample Items: Gerunds, Infinitives, and Simple Forms

We are planning _____ out to dinner tonight.
- Ⓐ taking our clients
- Ⓑ our clients going
- Ⓒ our clients will go
- ● to take our clients

The verb *are planning* is followed by an infinitive, not by a gerund, as in choices (A) and (B), or by a clause, as in choice (C).

He succeeded by _____ hard.
- Ⓐ work
- ● working
- Ⓒ he worked hard
- Ⓓ to work

After a preposition (*by*), a noun or a gerund must be used. Choice (A), *work*, might be a noun, but then the sentence would have to read *by hard work*. A preposition cannot be followed by a clause (C) or an infinitive (D).

Jerry made his children _____ on Saturday.
- ● do some chores
- Ⓑ some chores were done
- Ⓒ to do some chores
- Ⓓ they did some chores

The verb *made* is followed by an object and a simple form ("made someone do something"). *Made* cannot be followed by an infinitive (C) or by clauses (B) and (D).

Gerunds are verbal nouns. Gerunds may be the subjects of verbs, the objects of prepositions, or the objects of certain verbs. (See list, page 121.)

Swimming is good exercise. (Gerund as subject)

John gets his exercise by *jogging*. (Gerund as object of preposition)

I enjoy *playing* tennis. (Gerund as object of verb)

Infinitives can also be used as verbal nouns. Infinitives can be the subjects of verbs or the objects of certain verbs. (See list.) Infinitives *cannot* be used as the objects of prepositions.

To fly a small plane must be exciting. (Infinitive as subject)

My brother wants *to get* a pilot's license. (Infinitive as object of verb)

After certain verbs, a noun or pronoun object must be used before the infinitive.

My father advised *my brother* to wait.

Infinitives have quite a few other uses.

- To show purpose (why something happens):

    She went to the bank *to deposit* the day's receipts.

    He took lessons *to learn* how to sing.

- After certain adjectives:

    I'm anxious *to learn*.

    It's nice *to see* you again.

- After nouns:

    The next person *to walk* through that door will win a prize.

    That's not a common sight *to see*.

Simple forms (sometimes called "bare infinitives") are used after a few verbs. (See list.)

The office manager let Bill *move* to another desk.

Verbs Followed by Gerunds	Verbs Followed by Infinitives	Verbs Followed by Objects + Infinitives	Verbs Followed by Simple Forms
admit	afford	allow	have[3]
anticipate	agree	ask	let
appreciate	aim	cause	make[3]
avoid	arrange	choose	would rather
can't help	ask	convince	
delay	choose	get[3]	
deny	decide	instruct	
discuss	deserve	invite	
dislike	know (how)	permit	
enjoy	learn (how)	persuade	
finish	seem	prepare	
go[1]	stop[2]	need	
justify	would like	remind	
keep	vote	require	
mind		teach (how)	
miss		tell	
practice		use	
recommend		warn	
risk		would like	
stop[2]			
suggest			

Notes:

1. The verb *go* is followed by the *-ing* form of many "activity verbs": *go shopping, dancing, go skiing, go bowling,* and others.

2. The verb *stop* is followed by either a gerund or an infinitive, depending on meaning.

    I stopped *smoking*. (means "I no longer smoke.")

    He stopped *to light* his pipe. (means "He stopped doing something else in order to light his pipe.")

3. The verbs *get, have,* and *make* are known as causative verbs because they indicate that one person causes another person to do something. They are used in the following patterns:

   We got Bob *to help* us.
   We had Bob *help* us.
   We made Bob *help* us.

Get and *have* can also be followed by past participles:

   I got my car *washed*.
   I had my car *washed*.

Some verbs (which are not listed) can take either infinitive or gerund objects.

   I like *to eat* ice cream.
   I like *eating* ice cream.

Since both answers are correct, these verbs will seldom be tested on TOEIC.

In addition to the listed verbs, all two- and three-word verbs are followed by gerunds rather than by infinitive objects.

   Are you thinking of *moving*?
   Don't count on *seeing* Mr. Thomas.

Gerunds are used even when the verb phrase contains the word *to*, as in *look forward to, object to, devote to,* or *be opposed to.*

   He devotes much of his time to *planning* for the future.

Some verbs on the list that are followed by infinitives are often used in passive patterns:

   This tool is used *to open* cardboard boxes.
   He was asked *to join* the committee.

Exercise 5.19

Focus: Completing sentences with gerunds, infinitives, or simple forms.

Directions: Complete the sentences with the gerund, infinitive, or simple form of the verb in parentheses.

1. By (sign) _____ this contract, you are agreeing (deliver) _____ these goods to us by the end of the month, or you risk (pay) _____ a penalty.
2. The president of Pioneer Avionics decided (implement) _____ new cost-control measures.
3. I enjoy (cook) _____, but I dislike (clean up) _____.
4. These boots are perfect for (hike) _____.
5. A sudden noise made the golfer (miss) _____ his shot.
6. I need (practice) _____ (speak) _____ Spanish before I travel to Venezuela.
7. It is important (be) _____ on time for your interview.
8. Kim invited me (go) _____ (shop) _____ with him when I return to Seoul.
9. The clerk denied (take) _____ the money, but he could not convince the store manager (drop) _____ the charges against him.

10. When I have the mechanic (fix) _____ my brakes, I am going to get him (change) _____ my oil as well.
11. Gwendolyn's doctor told her (stop) _____ (drink) _____ so much coffee.
12. I do not have enough money (pay) _____ all my bills.
13. My boss lets me (work) _____ at home whenever possible, and she allows me (arrange) _____ my own schedule.
14. I am really looking forward to (go) _____ to Mexico next month.
15. I would rather (go) _____ (hike) _____ than (stay) _____ home today.

Exercise 5.20

Focus: Reviewing and practicing problems involving gerunds, infinitives, or simple forms in the Part V format.

Directions: Decide which of the choices — (A), (B), (C), or (D) — best completes the sentence.

1. I enjoy _____ a walk in the park after lunch whenever I have time.
   (A) taking
   (B) go for
   (C) take
   (D) to have

2. The health department requires the operators of restaurants _____ sanitary conditions.
   (A) maintenance
   (B) maintaining
   (C) to maintain
   (D) maintain

3. The latest economic statistics seem _____ an upturn in the economy.
   (A) pointing to
   (B) a prediction
   (C) to indicate
   (D) demonstrating

4. Animal rights groups are opposed _____ health and beauty products on animals.
   (A) to test
   (B) testing
   (C) tests of
   (D) to testing

5. My father taught _____ skeptical of claims made by advertisers.
   (A) me to be
   (B) to be
   (C) my being
   (D) for me to be

6. _____ here is not permitted.
   (A) Park
   (B) You can park
   (C) Having parked
   (D) Parking

7. Did you have your assistant _____ this report?
   (A) edit
   (B) editing
   (C) an edition
   (D) to edit

8. I intend to stop _____ after January 1.
   (A) to smoke
   (B) smoking
   (C) smoke
   (D) smokes

9. I watched the man _____ the sign.
   (A) paint
   (B) to paint
   (C) painted
   (D) was painted

10. Atsuko is going to Vancouver _____ some of her clients.
    (A) for to visit
    (B) visiting
    (C) to visit
    (D) visit

11. Please complete the paperwork before _____ in line.
    (A) to stand
    (B) be
    (C) wait
    (D) getting

12. Did you get someone _____ your car?
    (A) wash
    (B) washed
    (C) washing
    (D) to wash

More Practice

Directions: Decide which of the choices — (A), (B), (C), or (D) — best completes the sentence.

1. Some people have a _____ to overwork.
   - (A) tension
   - (B) tendency
   - (C) tending
   - (D) tendon

2. When Lubis was in college, he was a very _____ person.
   - (A) student
   - (B) study
   - (C) studies
   - (D) studious

3. _____ the warning, they failed to evacuate the area.
   - (A) Despite of
   - (B) Although
   - (C) Even so
   - (D) In spite of

4. Aston Industries offers not only a generous base salary _____ an excellent benefits package.
   - (A) and
   - (B) but also
   - (C) as well
   - (D) or else

5. Bubble gum was first _____ in 1928.
   - (A) markets
   - (B) in the market
   - (C) marketing
   - (D) marketed

6. We are sorry to _____ you.
   - (A) convenient
   - (B) inconvenience
   - (C) convenience
   - (D) inconvenient

7. Ten countries _____ the trade agreement.
   - (A) ratified
   - (B) registered
   - (C) assigned
   - (D) notified

8. I do not mind taking a business trip now and then, but I dislike _____ too much time away from home.
   - (A) to spend
   - (B) that I spend
   - (C) spent
   - (D) spending

9. Current liabilities are debts that must be paid _____ a year.
   - (A) by
   - (B) within
   - (C) with
   - (D) until

10. I did not see _____ of my friends at the party.
    - (A) any
    - (B) someone
    - (C) none
    - (D) anybody

11. A number of automobile _____ agencies are located on the lower level of the airport.
    - (A) renting
    - (B) rents
    - (C) rental
    - (D) rented

12. Although I was angry, I could not help _____ at his excuse.
    - (A) to laugh
    - (B) laughter
    - (C) laughing
    - (D) I laughed

13. It was _____ nice photograph that she had it framed and hung it on her wall.
    - (A) so
    - (B) too
    - (C) enough of a
    - (D) such a

14. We have been working on the balance sheet _____ two days now.
    - (A) since
    - (B) for
    - (C) in
    - (D) until

15. I am not sure how _____ it is from here to the capital.
    - (A) far
    - (B) much
    - (C) long
    - (D) distance

16. Will you _____ me to your associates?
    - (A) introduction
    - (B) introduce
    - (C) introductory
    - (D) introducing

17. The unemployment rate has _____ in recent months.
   Ⓐ fallen
   Ⓒ falling
   Ⓑ fell
   Ⓓ fall

18. The Matsuno Corporation manufactures small kitchen _____ such as electric food processors, mixers, and knife sharpeners.
   Ⓐ applicants
   Ⓒ aptitudes
   Ⓑ appliances
   Ⓓ amplifiers

19. He is convinced that the team from his country _____ the next World Cup.
   Ⓐ has won
   Ⓒ will win
   Ⓑ will have won
   Ⓓ would win

20. This device can detect the _____ of even small amounts of carbon monoxide gas.
   Ⓐ presents
   Ⓒ presence
   Ⓑ presentations
   Ⓓ pretext

21. Put your carry-on luggage under the seat in front of you or in the overhead _____.
   Ⓐ apartment
   Ⓒ appointment
   Ⓑ department
   Ⓓ compartment

22. Job descriptions allow both prospective and current employees _____ what is expected of them.
   Ⓐ to know
   Ⓒ knowledge of
   Ⓑ and know
   Ⓓ knowing

23. Obtaining a patent for an invention can be _____ process.
   Ⓐ a retracted
   Ⓒ a lengthened
   Ⓑ an extensive
   Ⓓ a prolonged

24. This dish _____ better if you use fresh herbs and garlic.
   Ⓐ will be tasting
   Ⓑ tastes
   Ⓒ would have tasted
   Ⓓ tasted

25. A nearly _____ diamond is more valuable than one with imperfections.
   Ⓐ flawed
   Ⓒ perfectly
   Ⓑ imperfect
   Ⓓ flawless

26. _____ most people in his department, he has a degree in engineering.
   Ⓐ Unlikely
   Ⓒ Similar from
   Ⓑ Different from
   Ⓓ Like

27. The _____ of transducers should arrive later today.
   Ⓐ ship
   Ⓒ shipment
   Ⓑ shipping
   Ⓓ shipshape

28. I am completely _____ as to who wins the local election.
   Ⓐ different
   Ⓒ indifferent
   Ⓑ uncaring
   Ⓓ rigid

29. It was uncomfortably cold in the boardroom because someone had set the air conditioner _____ low.
   Ⓐ such
   Ⓒ far
   Ⓑ too
   Ⓓ much

30. This sports car is equipped with a _____ eight-cylinder engine.
   Ⓐ powerful
   Ⓒ power
   Ⓑ powering
   Ⓓ powerfully

31. I do not know _____ he can make enough money by working only ten hours a week.
   Ⓐ why
   Ⓒ that if
   Ⓑ how much
   Ⓓ how

32. Prices on the stock exchange have been _____ wildly all week.
   Ⓐ vibrating
   Ⓒ intensifying
   Ⓑ wavering
   Ⓓ fluctuating

33. Many _____ entrepreneurs are self-taught in the field of business.
   (A) successful   (C) success
   (B) succeed   (D) successfully

34. The tour _____ about an hour to complete.
   (A) makes   (C) has
   (B) takes   (D) spends

35. A buyer's market is a market _____ sellers are so eager to sell that they offer very favorable terms to buyers.
   (A) which in   (C) in which
   (B) where in   (D) which

36. The water treatment plant _____ by the flood.
   (A) damaged   (C) damaging
   (B) was damaged   (D) has damaged

37. I first visited New Delhi fifteen years _____.
   (A) ago   (C) prior
   (B) previous   (D) early

38. When I take a trip, I like to get an early _____.
   (A) beginning   (C) go
   (B) start   (D) leaving

39. Are you planning to talk to Ms. Petrov on the phone or meet with her _____ person?
   (A) on   (C) by
   (B) to   (D) in

40. We have been looking for a suitable location for a branch office in Yokohama, but we _____ have not found one.
   (A) yet   (C) anymore
   (B) still   (D) already

LESSON

6 Error Identification

Preview: Lesson Outline
- Part VI Format
- Tactics for Part VI
- Sample Test
- Testing Points and Skill-Building Exercises
    - A. Verb Errors
    - B. Word-Choice Errors
    - C. Word-Form Errors
    - D. Preposition Errors
    - E. Errors with Gerunds, Infinitives, and Simple Forms
    - F. Errors with Pronouns
    - G. Errors with Singular and Plural Nouns
    - H. Errors with Comparative and Superlative Forms of Adjectives
    - I. Errors with Articles
    - J. Word-Order Errors
    - K. Errors with Connecting Words
    - L. Errors with Participial Adjectives
- More Practice

Part VI **Format**

Section VI of TOEIC tests your ability to recognize mistakes in grammar or usage in written sentences. It consists of twenty items. In each item, four expressions — usually one or two words each — are underlined. You have to examine all four items and decide which one must be rewritten (it can't simply be omitted) to form a correct sentence. In other words, you need to find the underlined expression that contains a mistake.

Tactics for Part VI

1. Read each item word for word. Don't just look at the underlined portion of the sentences because the error is often incorrect only because of the context of the sentence.
2. Don't read too quickly. If you do, your eyes may skip over errors, especially those involving "small words" (prepositions, pronouns, articles). Try to pronounce each word in your mind as you read. This will help you catch errors that "sound wrong."
3. If you are unable to find an error after the first reading, look at the verbs in the sentence to see if they are used correctly, since verb errors are the most common errors in Part VI. Check the verb's tense, form, and agreement with the subject.
4. If the verb seems to be used correctly, check for other common errors: word choice, word form, preposition use, and so on.
5. If you still cannot find an error, eliminate choices that seem to be correct. If more than one choice remains, make a guess. Put a mark on your answer sheet next to items that you are not sure of so that you can come back to these items if you have

time at the end of Section 2. (Be sure to erase all these marks before the end of the test.)

6. Never spend too much time on any one item.
7. Never leave any blank answers. Always guess.
8. As soon as you finish Part VI, go on to Part VII. Keep in mind that Part VII (Reading Comprehension) takes more time to complete than either Part V or Part VI.

Sample Test

Directions: In each sentence in this section, four words or phrases are underlined and marked (A), (B), (C), and (D). You must choose the *one* underlined expression that must be rewritten in order to form a correct sentence. Then mark the correct answer.

> **Example**

Every <u>workers</u> in <u>this</u> department <u>will receive</u> a bonus <u>in</u> September.
     A   B   C   D

●   Ⓑ   Ⓒ   Ⓓ

Choice (A), "workers," is incorrectly used in this sentence. The correct sentence should read, "Every worker in this department will receive a bonus in September." You should mark letter (A).

As soon as you are ready, you can begin the Sample Test Section.

1. <u>Of the</u> three cars <u>that</u> we took for a test drive, the Italian one <u>was</u> the <u>faster</u>.
    A   B   C   D

Ⓐ   Ⓑ   Ⓒ   Ⓓ

2. Tagalog is Florinda's <u>first</u> language, <u>but</u> she also <u>speaks</u> Spanish and English

                           A   B   C

<u>fluency</u>.
 D

Ⓐ   Ⓑ   Ⓒ   Ⓓ

3. I have hardly <u>never</u> had the <u>opportunity</u> <u>to fly</u> <u>in a</u> helicopter.
             A   B   C   D

Ⓐ   Ⓑ   Ⓒ   Ⓓ

4. Today, <u>most</u> companies get the <u>opinion</u> of focus groups before marketing <u>its</u>
         A   B   C

products on a <u>large scale</u>.
            D

Ⓐ   Ⓑ   Ⓒ   Ⓓ

5. <u>Sales</u> personnel <u>must understand</u> <u>psychology human</u> in order <u>to be</u> successful.
   A   B   C   D

Ⓐ   Ⓑ   Ⓒ   Ⓓ

6. I had just <u>hang</u> up the phone after <u>speaking</u> with you <u>when</u> it <u>rang</u> again.
           A   B   C   D

Ⓐ   Ⓑ   Ⓒ   Ⓓ

7. <u>In the</u> Chapter 1 of the manual, the author <u>primarily</u> defines <u>some</u> important <u>terms</u>.
   A   B   C   D

Ⓐ   Ⓑ   Ⓒ   Ⓓ

8. <u>Because of</u> the flood, we will <u>have to</u> drink <u>bottling</u> water <u>instead of</u> tap water.
     A   B   C   D

Ⓐ   Ⓑ   Ⓒ   Ⓓ

9. I <u>prefer not</u> to take <u>a lot</u> of <u>luggages</u> with me on a <u>business trip</u>.
       A   B   C   D

Ⓐ   Ⓑ   Ⓒ   Ⓓ

10. I hope <u>taking</u> a course <u>in</u> information <u>systems</u> at the community college <u>next fall</u>.
          A   B   C   D

Ⓐ   Ⓑ   Ⓒ   Ⓓ

11. You <u>should keep</u> <u>your</u> immigration control card <u>attached with</u> your passport
           A   B   C

<u>at all times</u>.
   D

Ⓐ   Ⓑ   Ⓒ   Ⓓ

12. <u>The</u> proposal <u>whom</u> Mr. Seong <u>made</u> was eventually <u>adopted</u>.
    A   B   C   D

Ⓐ   Ⓑ   Ⓒ   Ⓓ

Testing Points and Skill-Building Exercises

As in Part V, the range of testing points in Part VI is quite large. However, a large majority of the item types fit into the categories of errors discussed in this section.

Because many of the testing points are the same as those in Part V, you will sometimes be referred back to Lesson 5 for more information. You should review this information before completing the exercises for these sections.

A. Verb Errors

(For more information about verbs, see Lesson 5, Section D, pages 101-102.)

Verb errors are the most common type of error in Part VI. Whenever a verb or verb phrase is underlined in a sentence, you should check for verb errors. There are three main types of verb errors:

Errors in Subject/Verb Agreement

A singular verb must be used with a singular subject, a plural verb with a plural subject.

Sample Item: Verb Agreement Error

A picture of <u>some</u> mountains <u>were</u> hanging on <u>the wall</u> <u>behind</u> his desk.
           A   B   C   D

Ⓐ   ●   Ⓒ   Ⓓ

A singular verb, *was*, should be used to agree with the singular subject. (The subject is *picture*, not *mountains*.)

In some sentences, the subject of the verb is separated from the verb, and other nouns may come between the subject and the verb. This is true in the sentence above, where the singular subject *picture* is separated from the verb by a prepositional phrase (*of some mountains*). If you are not careful, you may assume that the plural verb is correct because the phrase *mountains were* seems correct. To spot the error, you need to identify the real subject and decide if it is singular or plural.

There are also some specific rules for subject/verb agreement that you should be aware of:

- Two singular subjects joined by *and* take a plural verb.

  The manager and her assistant *were* . . .
- Singular subjects followed by phrases such as *together with, along with, accompanied by, in addition to, such as,* and *as well as* are used with singular verbs.

  Mr. Lee, along with his family, *lives* . . .

  The president, accompanied by his advisors, *was* . . .
- Irregular plurals (such as *people, women, men, children, feet,* and *teeth*) do not end in -*s* but are used with plural verbs.

  The people *have* . . .

  His teeth *are* . . .
- Some nouns end in -*s* but are singular and take singular verbs. These words include the names of many fields (such as *physics, mathematics,* and *economics*). The word *news* is another word of this type.

  Economics *is* . . .

  The good news *was* . . .
- When the word *there* introduces a sentence, the verb may be either singular or plural, depending on the grammatical subject (the noun that follows the verb).

  There *was* a meeting . . .

  There *were* two police officers . . .
- In adjective clauses, either a singular or plural verb can be used, depending on the noun that the clause modifies.

  The houses which *are* . . .

  I spoke to the man who *was* . . .
- Phrases beginning with "a number of" are used with a plural verb; phrases beginning with "the number of" are used with a singular verb.

  A number of his friends *are* . . .

  The number of incidents *has* . . .
- Phrases beginning with the words *each, every,* and *one* take singular verbs. So do compound words beginning with *every,* such as *everyone* or *everything.*

  Every one of the players *was* . . .

  Each of the towns *is* . . .

  Each one of the towns *is* . . .

  Every player *was* . . .

  Every one of the players *was* . . .

  Everything *has* . . .

  One of the books *was* . . .
- Plural names of organizations take singular verbs.

  The United Nations *is* . . .
- Amounts of time, money, or distance used as subjects take a singular verb.

  A hundred dollars *is* . . .

  Three months *has* . . .
- Some adjectives are used with the word *the* to mean "people who are ..." These take a plural verb.

  The wealthy *do* not . . .

  The British *are* . . .

Exercise 6.1

Focus: Identifying errors involving subject-verb agreement.

Directions: Decide if the underlined word or phrase is used correctly. If so, mark it "C" for "Correct." If not, mark the sentence "X" and rewrite the underlined expression, correcting the mistake.

_____ 1. The car and the truck <u>was</u> illegally parked in the fire lane. _____

_____ 2. Each of the three main divisions of the corporation <u>has</u> its own accounting department. _____

_____ 3. The Japanese <u>has</u> some unique methods of arranging flowers. _____

_____ 4. I think that Italian <u>is</u> a beautiful language to listen to. _____

_____ 5. A number of problems <u>have</u> come up in recent weeks. _____

_____ 6. A black and white television set <u>are</u> less expensive than a color television set. _____

_____ 7. Every one of the stores in this town <u>seems</u> to carry the same postcards. _____

_____ 8. Aerobics <u>are</u> a vigorous form of exercise. _____

_____ 9. The children in this school <u>are</u> getting a wonderful education. _____

_____ 10. The news of the earthquake <u>was</u> shocking. _____

_____ 11. A good set of encyclopedias <u>are</u> quite expensive. _____

_____ 12. Even thirty liters of gasoline <u>were</u> not enough to fill my tank. _____

_____ 13. The number of units produced last year <u>were</u> up by fifteen percent. _____

_____ 14. In the nineteenth century, the poor <u>were</u> often thrown in prison if they were unable to pay their debts. _____

_____ 15. The people who <u>attends</u> the ceremony will never forget it. _____

_____ 16. Everything <u>is</u> going smoothly this week. _____

_____ 17. One of my best friends <u>is</u> coming to visit me. _____

_____ 18. General Motors <u>have</u> its corporate headquarters in Michigan. _____

_____ 19. Elizabeth, along with two of her colleagues, <u>is</u> going to work for a year in Budapest. _____

_____ 20. There <u>is</u> several decisions that need to be made at this meeting. _____

Incorrect Choice of Tense

This error involves the use of one tense when another tense is appropriate. Sentences with this type of error usually have time words that indicate which tense is correct.

Sample Item: Verb Tense Error

Mr. Cho <u>has gone</u> to a <u>meeting</u> <u>in</u> Singapore three <u>days</u> ago.
       A   B   C   D

● Ⓑ Ⓒ Ⓓ

The phrase *three days ago* indicates the need for the simple past tense. *Went* should be used in place of *has gone*.

Exercise 6.2

Focus: Identifying errors involving incorrect choice of verb tense.

Directions: Decide if the underlined word or phrase is used correctly. If so, mark it "C" for "Correct." If not, mark the sentence "X" and rewrite the underlined expression, correcting the mistake.

_____ 1. In recent years, recreational vehicles <u>became</u> an increasingly popular activity. _____

_____ 2. I am afraid that this product <u>has had</u> too much negative publicity in the last few months to ever become very popular. _____

_____ 3. When we were in London, I <u>was taking</u> a picture of my friend in front of the House of Parliament. _____

_____ 4. Mr. Peng <u>has been staying</u> at the Continental Hotel all this week. _____

_____ 5. I will not call you until I <u>will have</u> a definite answer for you. _____

_____ 6. When Philip tried to read the technical manual, he <u>is not</u> able to understand all of it. _____

_____ 7. They <u>had</u> dinner at the Nutmeg House restaurant last night. _____

_____ 8. I <u>have been visiting</u> Dubai several times in the last few years. _____

_____ 9. The passengers <u>have just boarded</u> the plane when the pilot announced that they would have to return to the terminal. _____

_____ 10. The firm will not borrow more funds until it <u>will pay off</u> some of its current debts. _____

_____ 11. So far, we <u>had not had</u> any offers for the used office furniture. _____

_____ 12. A few years ago, I <u>have worked</u> at a publishing company. _____

_____ 13. Probably by the time you get this postcard, I <u>will already return</u> from my vacation. _____

_____ 14. I <u>was walking</u> down the street yesterday when I ran into an old friend of mine. _____

_____ 15. I <u>am liking</u> the proposal submitted by Evergreen, Incorporated very much. _____

Errors in Verb Form

This type of error involves the incorrect choice of simple form, *-ing* form, past participle, or past tense form as part of a verb phrase or when used alone.

Sample Item: Verb Form Error

I had just <u>hang</u> up the phone after <u>speaking</u> with you <u>when</u> it <u>rang</u> again.
      A   B   C   D

● Ⓑ Ⓒ Ⓓ

The past participle *hung* should be used in place of the simple form *hang*.

Exercise 6.3

Focus: Identifying errors involving verb forms.

Directions: Decide if the underlined word or phrase is used correctly. If so, mark it "C" for "Correct." If not, mark the sentence "X" and rewrite the underlined expression, correcting the mistake.

_____ 1. Items of that type have not been <u>producing</u> here for years. _____
_____ 2. When I saw Melody, she was <u>jog</u> along the path by the river. _____
_____ 3. I recommend that he <u>reads</u> the company policy manual more carefully. _____
_____ 4. This mark can only be <u>seeing</u> in ultraviolet light. _____
_____ 5. The training film was <u>directed</u> by Mark Graham. _____
_____ 6. Security measures are being <u>strengthen</u> because of an increase in industrial espionage. _____
_____ 7. She must have <u>decided</u> not to attend the seminar. _____
_____ 8. After five years, this pair of boots is almost <u>wore</u> out. _____
_____ 9. As we <u>flown</u> out of San Francisco, we could see the Golden Gate Bridge. _____
_____ 10. Since Steve had <u>drunk</u> the last cup of coffee, he made another pot. _____
_____ 11. According to the recent census, the population of this town has <u>grow</u> by over 25% in the last ten years. _____
_____ 12. They have <u>chosen</u> Kenji to be the new coordinator. _____
_____ 13. She <u>sung</u> the song with great emotion. _____
_____ 14. We have been <u>driven</u> this car for over six hours now. _____
_____ 15. Our plans had to be <u>changing</u>. _____

B. Word-Choice Errors

(For more information about word choice, see Lesson 5, Section A, pages 89-96.)
This error involves the use of words that are not correct given the context of the sentence. The words that are used incorrectly are in some way related to the correct words. In general, these are words that non-native speakers of English (and, in some cases, native speakers!) sometimes confuse.
There are two categories of word-choice problems: those involving function words and those involving content words.

Incorrect Choice of Function Words

Function words, as explained in the previous lesson, are words that are primarily used to express grammatical relationships. Words such as *too, very, such,* and *so* are examples of function words. For a list of function words that are commonly tested on TOEIC, see pages 91-92.

Exercise 6.4

Focus: Identifying errors in word-choice problems involving function words.

Directions: Decide if the underlined word or phrase is used correctly. If so, mark it "C" for "Correct." If not, mark the sentence "X" and rewrite the underlined expression, correcting the mistake.

_____ 1. One of my four brothers is a doctor, and <u>another</u> is a medical student. _____

_____ 2. There was <u>so many</u> furniture in their living room that it was hard to walk around. _____

_____ 3. Maria was <u>very</u> tired to go to the movies this evening. _____

_____ 4. <u>Almost</u> all of the workers here work full-time, but a few have part-time jobs. _____

_____ 5. <u>Afterwards</u> we go to Copenhagen, we will have to return to New York. _____

_____ 6. There is only <u>a little</u> coffee left in the can. _____

_____ 7. It was <u>such</u> cold today that I didn't even want to go out. _____

_____ 8. They play that song on the radio <u>too often</u> that I am getting tired of it. _____

_____ 9. <u>As</u> his father, Georgio studied chemical engineering at the university. _____

_____ 10. Meals are <u>not longer</u> served on this flight. _____

_____ 11. The two accounts of the situation are not very much <u>alike</u>. _____

_____ 12. My friend Roger sat down <u>besides</u> me. _____

_____ 13. There is hardly <u>any</u> air left in this tire. _____

_____ 14. The River Rhine forms the border <u>among</u> Germany and France. _____

Incorrect Choice of Content Words

Other word-choice problems involve content words. Some of these words are similar in form — they "look alike" in some way (*accept* and *except*, for example). In other cases, the words are similar in meaning but not in form (*grow up* and *raise*, for example). Some are similar in both meaning and form (*lay* and *lie*, for example).

The following is a partial list of content words that may be confused in Part VI. (Note: **Intransitive verbs** are verbs that cannot take direct object; **transitive verbs** are ones that do take direct objects.)

accept (verb): agree to; believe
except (preposition): all but; excluding

age (noun): length of existence; lifetime (at the age of thirty)
old (adjective): having existed for a specific length of time (thirty years old)

anonymous (adjective): unknown; nameless
unanimous (adjective): agreed on by everyone

assurance (noun): something that gives confidence
insurance (noun): a policy that protects against loss

borrow (verb): receive money from someone as a loan
lend (verb): give money to someone as a loan

cloth (noun): a material (such as silk or cotton)
clothes (noun): clothing

common (adjective): occurring often; usual
popular (adjective): well-liked by people

costume (noun): special clothes
custom (noun): habit, tradition
customs (noun): procedure for inspecting goods and baggage coming into a country

feel (felt, felt) (verb): experience an emotion or a sensation
fall (fell, fallen) (verb): drop, go down

find (found, found) (verb): locate
found (founded, founded) (verb): establish

grow (intransitive verb): get bigger; mature
       (transitive verb): nurture, take care of (said of plants)
grow up (intransitive verb): get older; mature (said of children)
raise (transitive verb): **1.** nurture (said of plants, animals, and children)
                      2. to cause to go up
      (noun): an increase in salary
rise (rose, risen) (intransitive verb): to go up

hard (adjective): **1.** difficult
2. not soft
(adverb): not easy
hardly (adverb): almost not at all

late (adjective, adverb): not early; not on time
lately (adverb): recently

lay (laid, laid) (transitive verb): put down
lie (lay, lain) (intransitive verb): rest, recline

loose (adjective): not tight
lose (lost, lost) (verb) not be able to find

major (adjective): important
majority (noun, adjective): more than fifty percent

near (preposition): close to
nearly (adverb): almost

owe (verb): have a debt
own (verb): possess

remember (verb): think of someone or something in the past
remind (verb): make someone remember

rob (verb): take illegally (used of people and places)
steal (verb): take illegally (used of money or objects)

safe (adjective): not in danger
save (verb): rescue, salvage

say (verb): to express in words (not used with an indirect object)
"He said that . . . "
tell (verb): to express in words (used with an indirect object)
"He told me that . . . "

The verbs *make* and *do* are also commonly confused. The word *make* means to build, to construct, to create. The verb *do* means to act or perform. These words are also used in many set expressions.

Expressions with *Make*	
make an error, mistake	make an offer
make a meal (lunch, dinner)	make a choice
make a discovery	make a decision
make a profit	make a deal
make an investment	make a prediction
Expressions with *Do*	
do work	do one's best
do research	do one's duty
do an experiment	do a favor
do business (with)	do an errand, a job
do damage	do wrong
do an assignment	

Exercise 6.5

Focus: Identifying errors in word-choice problems involving content words.

Directions: Decide if the underlined word or phrase is used correctly. If so, mark it "C" for "Correct." If not, mark the sentence "X" and rewrite the underlined expression, correcting the mistake.

_____   1. Can you <u>borrow</u> me twenty dollars until next week? _____

_____   2. Will you <u>make</u> me a favor? _____

_____   3. Accidents are more <u>popular</u> at home than anywhere else. _____

_____   4. Before the nineteenth century, most textiles were <u>done</u> at home. _____

_____   5. Market Street is a <u>majority</u> thoroughfare in this town. _____

_____   6. The measure was <u>anonymously</u> approved. _____

_____   7. I started working here when I was twenty-years <u>age</u>. _____

_____   8. I am going to <u>lay</u> down until my headache goes away. _____

_____   9. The pharmaceutical company <u>raised</u> its prices. _____

_____   10. Do not come <u>lately</u> for the appointment. _____

_____   11. Our firm's costs for raw material went up by <u>near</u> fifteen percent. _____

_____   12. Chen was born in Hong Kong, but he was <u>grown up</u> in Vancouver.

_____   13. Because of jet lag, I <u>fell</u> a little sleepy all day. _____

_____   14. I still <u>own</u> about $1,200 on my automobile loan. _____

_____   15. He is afraid that he <u>did</u> the wrong decision. _____

_____   16. A man in a ski mask <u>stole</u> the bank. _____

_____   17. The <u>costumes</u> inspector asked me to open my briefcase. _____

_____   18. The company <u>did</u> a considerable profit in the last quarter. _____

_____   19. The police officer <u>told</u> me to slow down. _____

_____   20. I cannot <u>except</u> Yukio's explanation. _____

C. Word-Form Errors

(For more information about word forms, see Lesson 5, Section B, pages 96-99.)
In this type of problem, one of the underlined words is an incorrect form of the base word, given the context of the sentence.

The two most common types of word-form problems are the use of adverbs in place of adjectives or adjectives in place of adverbs, as in the first sample item. Many other errors are possible: a noun in place of an adverb, as in the second sample, an adjective in place of a noun, a noun in place of a verb, and so on.

One noun form may be used incorrectly in place of another noun form. For example, a "person who . . ." noun may be used in place of a noun that names a field, as in the third sample.

A gerund (a verbal noun ending in *-ing*) may be used in place of an ordinary noun, as in the fourth sample.

Exercise 6.6

Focus: Identifying errors in word-form problems involving adjectives and adverbs.

Directions: Decide if the underlined word or phrase is used correctly. If so, mark it "C" for "Correct." If not, mark the sentence "X" and rewrite the underlined expression, correcting the mistake.

_____   **1.** We voted on that issue at a <u>recently</u> meeting. _____

_____   **2.** The people in my office dress more <u>informally</u> now than they did a few years ago. _____

_____   **3.** Inflation last year was not <u>particular</u> severe. _____

_____   **4.** Henry's dog is friendly and <u>loyally</u>. _____

_____ 5. The fabric doesn't feel as <u>smoothly</u> as real silk. _____

_____ 6. Airlines have to pay <u>annually</u> fees to lease gates at the airport. _____

_____ 7. Much of this province was once covered by <u>densely</u> forest, but today it is mainly farmland. _____

_____ 8. The hotel was <u>seriously</u> damaged in the tropical storm. _____

_____ 9. There was a <u>suddenly</u> increase in new orders last month. _____

_____ 10. Tomatoes grow <u>good</u> in the soil in my garden. _____

Exercise 6.7

Focus: Identifying errors involving a variety of word forms.

Directions: Decide if the underlined word or phrase is used correctly. If so, mark it "C" for "Correct." If not, mark the sentence "X" and rewrite the underlined expression, correcting the mistake.

_____ 1. Mr. Richards is going to take off a few months because of problems with his <u>healthy</u>. _____

_____ 2. Ms. Yoo's job is to <u>analysis</u> commercial loan applications. _____

_____ 3. I enjoy music and <u>dramatic</u>. _____

_____ 4. The leader of the trade delegation gave an interesting <u>speak</u> after dinner. _____

_____ 5. Mr. Dubois is one entrepreneur who is not afraid to take a <u>risk</u>. _____

_____ 6. Air bags and seat belts provide a greater degree of <u>safely</u> than seat belts used alone. _____

_____ 7. Every morning the hotel staff <u>deliveries</u> a newspaper to my door. _____

_____ 8. You and I have completely <u>different</u> opinions of this policy. _____

_____ 9. <u>Pay</u> for the items may be in the form of check, money order, or credit card. _____

_____ 10. Years ago, my first boss gave me some wonderful <u>advise</u>. _____

_____ 11. Our clients have a lot of <u>confident</u> in our services. _____

_____ 12. I cannot wait to get home and take a <u>warmth</u> bath. _____

_____ 13. Christina likes to take long <u>walkings</u> after dinner. _____

_____ 14. <u>Tourist</u> is becoming increasingly important to the economy of this region. _____

_____ 15. Mr. Kang imports Swiss watches and <u>France</u> wines. _____

_____ 16. Three <u>fill</u> bottles for the water cooler were delivered today. _____

_____ 17. This event may <u>proof</u> to be very significant. _____

_____ 18. His <u>flight</u> is due to land at the Nairobi Airport in an hour. _____

_____ 19. Aspirin provides <u>relieve</u> for headaches. _____

_____ 20. Samuel is a natural <u>leadership</u>. _____

Error Identification **139**

Exercise 6.8

Focus: Reviewing and practicing error-identification problems involving verb forms, word choice, and word forms.

Directions: Choose the *one* underlined expression that must be rewritten in order to form a correct sentence. Then mark the correct answer.

1. The editor has gave encouragement to
              A   B
   many young, promising writers.
    C   D
   Ⓐ   Ⓑ   Ⓒ   Ⓓ

2. Miguel threw the ball so hardly that I could
           A   B C
   not catch it.
       D
   Ⓐ   Ⓑ   Ⓒ   Ⓓ

3. Flu is more popular in the winter than at
           A   B
   any other time of year.
    C D
   Ⓐ   Ⓑ   Ⓒ   Ⓓ

4. The director had not idea who had written
           A B   C
   him the anonymous note.
        D
   Ⓐ   Ⓑ   Ⓒ   Ⓓ

5. By this time next year, sales have increased
        A   B   C
   considerably.
      D
   Ⓐ   Ⓑ   Ⓒ   Ⓓ

6. A good golfer careful chooses which club
       A   B   C
   to use.
   D
   Ⓐ   Ⓑ   Ⓒ   Ⓓ

7. The traditional dancers worn bright and
       A   B
   colorful costumes.
    C   D
   Ⓐ   Ⓑ   Ⓒ   Ⓓ

8. You can save some money at the grocery
        A
   store if you make a listing of the items you
           B   C   D
   need.
   Ⓐ   Ⓑ   Ⓒ   Ⓓ

9. Suzanna Hampton will become
                     A
   vice-president in charge of marketing
             B   C
   John Wagner will retire.
            D
   Ⓐ   Ⓑ   Ⓒ   Ⓓ

10. There is several people in the meeting
         A   B
    room waiting for the meeting to begin.
          C   D
    Ⓐ   Ⓑ   Ⓒ   Ⓓ

11. Typically, more trade fairs are hold in Paris
     A   B
    during March than during any other
             C   D
    month.
    Ⓐ   Ⓑ   Ⓒ   Ⓓ

12. The sun setting through the palm trees was
          A
    so beautiful sight that I photographed it.
    B   C   D
    Ⓐ   Ⓑ   Ⓒ   Ⓓ

13. In generally, I enjoy traveling, but there are
       A   B   C
    some places I would rather not go.
                        D
    Ⓐ   Ⓑ   Ⓒ   Ⓓ

14. You can look at the menu on the computer
         A
    screen and choice whatever program
             B   C
    you want.
       D
    Ⓐ   Ⓑ   Ⓒ   Ⓓ

15. The important of this invention will not
       A   B
    be known for at least several years.
     C   D
    Ⓐ   Ⓑ   Ⓒ   Ⓓ

16. After working most of the night, I felt
        A   B   C
    asleep at about five in the morning.
           D
    Ⓐ   Ⓑ   Ⓒ   Ⓓ

17. Deer are sometimes seeing in the hills
            A   B
    north of town.
     C D
    Ⓐ   Ⓑ   Ⓒ   Ⓓ

18. The scientists made many experiments to
              A   B
    prove that the drug was effective.
    C   D
    Ⓐ   Ⓑ   Ⓒ   Ⓓ

19. Who <u>said</u> you <u>that</u> you should <u>deliver</u>
      A   B   C
those <u>goods</u> here?
      D

   Ⓐ   Ⓑ   ©   Ⓓ

20. At our company, <u>raises</u> and <u>promotions</u> <u>are</u>
                        A   B   C
based on performance, not on <u>senior</u>.
                                D

   Ⓐ   Ⓑ   ©   Ⓓ

D. Preposition Errors
(For more information about prepositions, see Lesson 5, Section E, pages 105-112.)

There are two types of preposition errors that appear in the underlined portions of Part VI sentences. These involve preposition choice and the inclusion/omission of prepositions.

Incorrect Preposition Choice
This type of error involves the use of one preposition when another is required, given the context of the sentence.

Sample Items: Preposition Errors

You <u>should keep</u> <u>your</u> immigration control card <u>attached with</u> your passport <u>at all times</u>.
     A   B   C   D

   Ⓐ   Ⓑ   ●   Ⓓ

The participle *attached* is correctly followed by the preposition *to*.

<u>On</u> my opinion, the Allegro Cafe is one of <u>the</u> best <u>restaurants</u> <u>in the</u> city.
A   B   C   D

       ●   Ⓑ   ©   Ⓓ

Before the word *opinion*, the preposition *in* is needed.

Preposition choice depends either on the noun, adjective/participle, or verb that comes before the preposition (as in the first sample item) or on the object that follows the preposition (as in the second sample item).

Exercise 6.9

Focus: Identifying errors involving preposition choice.

Directions: Decide if the underlined word or phrase is used correctly. If so, mark it "C" for "Correct." If not, mark the sentence "X" and rewrite the underlined expression, correcting the mistake.

_____   1. The film starts <u>on</u> seven o'clock. _____
_____   2. Tomiko comes from a town in Japan that is famous <u>of</u> its beautiful pottery. _____
_____   3. Annie has lived in Amsterdam <u>since</u> all her life. _____
_____   4. There will be a meeting of department heads <u>during</u> Wednesday. _____
_____   5. Payday is a week <u>for</u> now. _____
_____   6. The market <u>for</u> this product is still growing. _____
_____   7. The only way you can get to the island is <u>on</u> boat. _____
_____   8. Ben played a lovely melody <u>in</u> his flute. _____

_____ 9. We won't arrive <u>to</u> Bangkok until eleven o'clock. _____

_____ 10. I need to finish this project at least <u>on</u> Friday. _____

_____ 11. The directions for using the tools were printed <u>on</u> four languages. _____

_____ 12. Several business leaders said that they were afraid <u>of</u> a trade war between the two countries. _____

_____ 13. I was satisfied <u>from</u> the performance review I received. _____

_____ 14. Mona grew up <u>in</u> a farm, I believe. _____

_____ 15. Thanks <u>for</u> my neighbor, I was able to get my car started this morning. _____

Inclusion or Omission of Prepositions

Some preposition errors involve the omission or inclusion of prepositions. In other words, a preposition is used when it should not be, or is not used when it should be.

Sample Item: Preposition Omission Errors

Katie <u>is charge</u> of <u>ordering supplies</u> for <u>the office</u>.
     A   B   C   D

    Ⓐ Ⓑ ● Ⓓ

The preposition *in* has been omitted from the phrase *in charge of*.

Exercise 6.10

Focus: Identifying errors involving inclusion or exclusion of prepositions.

Directions: Decide if the underlined word or phrase is used correctly. If so, mark it "C" for "Correct." If not, mark the sentence "X" and rewrite the underlined expression, correcting the mistake.

_____ 1. Next month, Mr. Stewart is traveling <u>to overseas</u> for an international sales conference. _____

_____ 2. I will meet you for lunch <u>on next Friday</u>. _____

_____ 3. The reporter <u>asked me</u> a lot of questions. _____

_____ 4. In <u>spite the problems</u>, I enjoyed the trip. _____

_____ 5. This is the book <u>in which</u> I was telling you about. _____

_____ 6. I think that hat <u>belongs Patty</u>. _____

_____ 7. <u>Most the</u> money is in the vault. _____

_____ 8. Sally <u>went upstairs</u> to get some papers that she had forgotten. _____

_____ 9. <u>Hundreds people</u> gathered in the square. _____

_____ 10. Please <u>contact to one</u> of our sales representatives if you have any further questions. _____

_____ 11. My seat was <u>in the rear the</u> plane. _____

_____ 12. The schedule was <u>approved the director</u>. _____

E. Errors with Gerunds, Infinitives, and Simple Forms

(For more information about gerunds, infinitives, and simple forms, see Lesson 5, Section G, pages 120-123.)

Sample Items: Gerund/Infinitive/Simple Form Errors

I hope <u>taking</u> a course <u>in</u> information <u>systems</u> at the community college <u>next fall</u>.
       A   B   C   D

● Ⓑ Ⓒ Ⓓ

After the verb *hope*, an infinitive (*to take*) is needed.

The Canadian <u>corporation</u> Holiday Hosts plans <u>to opening</u> a chain of <u>low-cost</u> hotels <u>in</u> Asia.
                A   B   C   D

Ⓐ ● Ⓒ Ⓓ

The correct form of the infinitive is *to open*.

There are two main types of errors involving gerunds, infinitives and simple forms:

Use of One of These Three Forms When Another Is Needed
In this type of error, a gerund is used in place of an infinitive, an infinitive in place of a simple form, and so on.

Incorrect Form of the Infinitive
Expressions such as *for to do*, and *to doing* are incorrect forms of the infinitive.

Exercise 6.11

Focus: Identifying errors involving gerunds, infinitives, and simple forms.

Directions: Decide if the underlined word or phrase is used correctly. If so, mark it "C" for "Correct." If not, mark the sentence "X" and rewrite the underlined expression, correcting the mistake.

_____   **1.** Brady was not willing <u>risk</u> his money on that scheme. _____

_____   **2.** I stopped <u>to get</u> a newspaper every morning because I just do not have time to read it. _____

_____   **3.** It is important <u>to following</u> all these directions carefully. _____

_____   **4.** I want to stay home tonight, but my roommate would rather <u>go out</u>. _____

_____   **5.** During my free time, I enjoy <u>acting</u> in amateur theatrical productions. _____

_____   **6.** She had the doorman <u>to get</u> her a taxi. _____

_____   **7.** <u>Commuting</u> to work is much easier now because of the new light-rail system. _____

_____   **8.** Kazuo was able <u>for to record</u> the entire scene on his camcorder. _____

_____   **9.** My friends are looking forward <u>to meeting</u> you. _____

_____   **10.** The boss made me <u>to work</u> late again last night. _____

_____ **11.** It is forbidden <u>importing</u> goods derived from animals on the endangered species list. _____

_____ **12.** I appreciate your <u>help</u> us. _____

_____ **13.** Have you arranged for someone <u>picking</u> you up at the airport? _____

_____ **14.** Ms. Preswick was hired <u>to replace</u> Mr. Clarkson, who is retiring next month. _____

_____ **15.** His financial situation made it necessary for him <u>to work</u> two jobs. _____

F. Errors with Pronouns

(Note: For the purpose of this lesson, possessive adjectives such as *his* or *her* are considered pronouns. Relative pronouns are not discussed in this chapter; they are discussed in Section K, "Errors with Connecting Words.")

Three main types of errors involving pronouns are possible in Part VI sentences: problems involving agreement, form, and inclusion.

Incorrect Agreement of Pronouns and Nouns

A singular pronoun must be used to refer to a singular noun, a plural pronoun to a plural noun. Similarly, a masculine pronoun must be used to refer to a masculine noun, a feminine pronoun to a feminine noun, and a neuter pronoun to a neuter noun.

Sample Items: Pronoun Agreement Errors

Today, <u>most</u> companies get the <u>opinion</u> of focus groups before marketing <u>its</u> products
     A   B   C
on a <u>large scale</u>.
     D

Ⓐ Ⓑ ● Ⓓ

The plural possessive *their* must be used to refer to the plural noun *companies*.

Gardening <u>is</u> a good way <u>to relax</u>, and <u>he</u> can provide fresh vegetables <u>as well</u>.
     A   B   C   D

Ⓐ Ⓑ ● Ⓓ

The neuter pronoun *it* should be used to refer to *gardening*.

Incorrect Form of Pronouns

This error involves the use of incorrect grammatical forms of pronouns.

Sample Item: Pronoun Form Errors

Management at <u>this</u> firm <u>always</u> awards employees for <u>them</u> achievements and hard <u>work</u>.
                 A   B   C   D

Ⓐ Ⓑ ● Ⓓ

The possessive form *their* is needed in place of the object form *them*.

Incorrect Inclusion of Pronouns

This error involves the unnecessary inclusion of a pronoun. In a main clause, a subject pronoun is unnecessary if there is already a subject noun. In an adjective clause, a pronoun is unnecessary if the relative pronoun takes the place of the personal pronoun.

Sample Items: Pronoun Inclusion Errors

<u>That</u> bridge, which was <u>built</u> back <u>in the</u> 1920s, <u>it needs</u> to be replaced.
  A   B   C   D

     Ⓐ Ⓑ Ⓒ ●

The pronoun *it* is unnecessary because there is a noun-phrase subject (*that bridge*).

The telephone system, <u>which it</u> was just <u>installed</u>, <u>still</u> has <u>a few</u> problems.
                         A   B   C   D

    ● Ⓑ Ⓒ Ⓓ

The pronoun *it* is used unnecessarily because *which* is the subject of the adjective clause.

Exercise 6.12

Focus: Identifying errors involving pronouns.

Directions: Decide if the underlined word or phrase is used correctly. If so, mark it "C" for "Correct." If not, mark the sentence "X" and rewrite the underlined expression, correcting the mistake.

_____   1. The client wanted to talk to Mr. Kwang <u>and</u> I alone. _____

_____   2. I heard the news, but I couldn't believe <u>they</u> could be true. _____

_____   3. <u>Yours</u> work on this project impressed the manager. _____

_____   4. <u>This</u> topics were thoroughly discussed at a recent business luncheon. _____

_____   5. Ms. O'Donnel, <u>whose her</u> clothes were lost by the hotel laundry, was understandably upset. _____

_____   6. I hope all of you enjoyed <u>yourself</u> at the company picnic. _____

_____   7. The company raised <u>its</u> prices again. _____

_____   8. Nancy bought her nephew a compact disc for <u>her</u> birthday. _____

_____   9. They left some of <u>theirs</u> papers in the taxi. _____

_____ 10. In <u>that</u> age of e-mail, fax machines, and cellular telephones, business executives can communicate quickly and easily. _____

_____ 11. <u>Bill and I</u> plan to take a vacation in the Bahamas. _____

_____ 12. He cannot remember the names of all the people <u>whom he</u> met at the gathering. _____

_____ 13. That is the same car that <u>we saw it</u> parked here yesterday. _____

_____ 14. This is my briefcase, and that one is <u>yours</u>. _____

_____ 15. I took vitamin C for my cold, but <u>they</u> didn't seem to help. _____

_____ **16.** The waitress burned <u>himself</u> on the hot dish. _____

_____ **17.** I wonder what <u>hers</u> opinion of this issue is. _____

_____ **18.** That man whom I was talking <u>to him</u> at the party last night is my accountant. _____

_____ **19.** We took a lot of pictures at the zoo, but we have not had <u>their</u> developed yet. _____

_____ **20.** This book, which was written by the president of a major corporation, <u>it offers</u> some very practical advice for all managers. _____

G. Errors with Singular and Plural Nouns

There are a number of errors involving singular and plural nouns.

A Singular Noun Used When a Plural Noun Is Required, or a Plural Noun Used When a Singular Noun Is Needed

Sample Items: Singular/Plural Errors

Mr. Devons <u>purchased</u> several small <u>parcel</u> of land <u>on the edge</u> of <u>town</u>.
             A   B   C   D
Ⓐ   ●   Ⓒ   Ⓓ

The plural noun *parcels* should be used. The word *several* indicates the need for a plural noun.

The <u>notebooks</u> <u>on the</u> conference <u>table</u> belongs <u>to</u> Kenji.
       A   B   C   D
●   Ⓑ   Ⓒ   Ⓓ

The singular verb *belongs* indicates that the subject should be singular (*notebook*).

Noncount Nouns Incorrectly Pluralized

As the name indicates, a noncount noun represents something that cannot be counted. Mass nouns (*air, butter, furniture*), abstract nouns (*glory, sincerity, patriotism*), and fields of study (*chemistry, engineering, management*) are all noncount nouns.

Sample Item: Plural Noncount Nouns

I <u>prefer not</u> to take <u>a lot</u> of <u>luggages</u> with me on a <u>business trip</u>.
   A   B   C   D
Ⓐ   Ⓑ   ●   Ⓓ

The noncount noun *luggage* should not be pluralized.

Some determiners (words used before nouns) indicate whether a noun is a singular noun, a plural noun, or a noncount noun, as shown in the following chart:

Determiners Used with Singular Nouns	Determiners Used with Plural Nouns	Determiners Used with Noncount Nouns
a/an one a single each every this that	two, three, four, etc. dozens of, hundreds of, thousands of, etc. a few (of) many (of) a number of the number of a couple of every one of each one of each of one of these those	much little a great deal of an amount of

Incorrect Use of Plural Nouns in Compound Nouns

A compound noun consists of two nouns used together to express a single concept. Only the second noun of a compound noun is pluralized.

    house plants   vegetable gardens
    diamond rings   factory gates

Sample Item: Singular/Plural Errors with Compound Nouns

Today, <u>groceries</u> stores carry many <u>goods</u> that are not <u>considered</u> <u>food</u> items.
        A   B   C   D

● Ⓑ Ⓒ Ⓓ

The first noun of the compound noun should not be pluralized. (The correct phrase is *grocery stores*.)

Errors in Numbers + Nouns

This error involves measurements and other words that are used with numbers. When a number + noun is used before another noun, the first noun is not pluralized and the phrase is hyphenated. When a number + noun is used alone, the noun is pluralized and the expression is not hyphenated.

    a ten-kilometer race   a race of ten kilometers
    a six-year-old girl   a girl who is six years old

Sample Item: Singular/Plural Errors with Number + Noun

This company <u>offers</u> a <u>two-weeks</u> vacation to <u>employees</u> after their first <u>year</u> of employment.
          A   B   C   D

Ⓐ ● Ⓒ Ⓓ

The phrase should read *two-week vacation*.

Errors in Numbers Used Indefinitely

When used indefinitely, numbers such as *dozens*, *hundreds*, and *thousands* are pluralized.

three hundred people	hundreds of people
ten thousand dollars	thousands of dollars

Sample Item: Singular/Plural Errors with Numbers Used Indefinitely

There <u>are</u> probably <u>dozen</u> of ways <u>in which</u> this problem can <u>be solved</u>.
    A   B   C   D

   Ⓐ ● Ⓒ Ⓓ

The word *dozen* should be pluralized.

Errors with Irregular Plurals

Most nouns in English are pluralized by adding the letter *-s* or the letters *-es*, but a few nouns have irregular plurals. Only the most common of these are tested on TOEIC.

Common Irregular Plurals	
Singular	**Plural**
child	children
man	men
woman	women
foot	feet
tooth	teeth

Sample Item: Singular/Plural Errors with Irregular Plurals

<u>Both</u> of her <u>childrens</u> are <u>in</u> high school <u>now</u>.
  A   B   C   D

   Ⓐ ● Ⓒ Ⓓ

The correct plural form of the noun *child* is *children*.

Exercise 6.13

Focus: Identifying errors involving singular and plural nouns.

Directions: Decide if the underlined word or phrase is used correctly. If so, mark it "C" for "Correct." If not, mark the sentence "X" and rewrite the underlined expression, correcting the mistake.

_____ 1. When you go to the store, will you get two <u>pounds of coffees</u>? _____
_____ 2. <u>Hundreds</u> of applications were submitted. _____
_____ 3. Although it looks new, that car is over <u>ten-year old</u>. _____
_____ 4. Many of the most important <u>discovery</u> were made by accident. _____
_____ 5. We rented a <u>two-rooms suite</u> at the Empire Hotel. _____
_____ 6. We tested every one of the <u>components</u>. _____
_____ 7. Your <u>advices</u> on this matter would be appreciated. _____

_____ 8. All of the new <u>employees</u> must attend a meeting at four. _____
_____ 9. His <u>foots</u> hurt after the hike. _____
_____ 10. This solvent is only available in <u>five-liter</u> containers. _____
_____ 11. Can we wait for another few <u>minute</u>? _____
_____ 12. Each <u>department</u> sent a representative. _____
_____ 13. Amy likes to drive her car on twisting <u>mountains roads</u>. _____
_____ 14. Each of the <u>participant</u> will receive a small gift. _____
_____ 15. I have called Ms. Olsson several times, but she has never returned my <u>calls</u>. _____
_____ 16. Alexandria invited a number of <u>the woman</u> that she works with to lunch at her house. _____
_____ 17. There is going to be a gathering of <u>coins collectors</u> at this hotel next weekend. _____
_____ 18. Rafael and Inez have an <u>eight-months-old</u> baby. _____
_____ 19. This store sells simple but elegant <u>jewelries</u>. _____
_____ 20. Several people won <u>door prizes</u>. _____

Exercise 6.14

Focus: Reviewing and practicing problems involving errors with prepositions, gerunds/infinitives/simple forms, pronouns, and singular/plural nouns.

Directions: Choose the *one* underlined expression that must be rewritten in order to form a correct sentence. Then mark the correct answer.

1. <u>You</u> will need a visa <u>in</u> order <u>for to enter</u>
     A   B   C
   <u>that</u> country.
    D
     Ⓐ   Ⓑ   Ⓒ   Ⓓ

2. The assembly-line <u>workers</u> will be more
                  A
   <u>productive</u> when the company <u>installs</u> the
     B   C
   new <u>equipments</u>.
        D
     Ⓐ   Ⓑ   Ⓒ   Ⓓ

3. Skylights allow <u>a lot</u> of <u>light</u> <u>entering</u> a
              A   B   C
   <u>room</u>.
    D
     Ⓐ   Ⓑ   Ⓒ   Ⓓ

4. Antonio is <u>going</u> <u>to abroad</u> <u>to sign</u> an
             A   B   C
   <u>important</u> agreement.
    D
    Ⓐ   Ⓑ   Ⓒ   Ⓓ

5. <u>Thousand</u> of <u>new products</u> become <u>available</u>
      A   B   C
   <u>every</u> year.
    D
     Ⓐ   Ⓑ   Ⓒ   Ⓓ

6. I had to stand <u>on line</u> <u>at the</u> supermarket
                   A   B
   <u>for</u> more than fifteen <u>minutes</u>.
    C   D
     Ⓐ   Ⓑ   Ⓒ   Ⓓ

7. <u>Their</u> negotiations <u>with</u> that company have
     A   B
   <u>led</u> the <u>formation of</u> a joint venture.
    C   D
     Ⓐ   Ⓑ   Ⓒ   Ⓓ

8. The building <u>across</u> the square is one of
             A
   finest <u>example</u> of colonial <u>architecture</u> I
         B   C
   have <u>ever</u> seen.
       D
     Ⓐ   Ⓑ   Ⓒ   Ⓓ

9. Let's <u>meeting for lunch</u> tomorrow <u>to discuss</u>
      A   B   C
<u>your</u> idea.
 D

   Ⓐ   Ⓑ   ©   Ⓓ

10. After <u>finishing</u> college, James and Rick <u>hope</u>
        A   B
<u>to become</u> <u>professionals</u> golfers.
  C   D

   Ⓐ   Ⓑ   ©   Ⓓ

11. A <u>small</u> business often confines <u>theirs</u>
    A   B
operations <u>to</u> a single <u>neighborhood</u>.
        C   D

   Ⓐ   Ⓑ   ©   Ⓓ

12. The <u>dentist</u> put a crown <u>on</u> one of <u>my</u> <u>tooths</u>.
     A   B   C D

   Ⓐ   Ⓑ   ©   Ⓓ

13. <u>As</u> foreigners, <u>I</u> do not <u>understand</u> all the
  A   B   C
<u>customs</u> here.
  D

   Ⓐ   Ⓑ   ©   Ⓓ

14. I have missed <u>to see</u> my sister <u>since</u> <u>she</u>
            A   B C
moved <u>to</u> Toronto.
    D

   Ⓐ   Ⓑ   ©   Ⓓ

15. Executives <u>who accept</u> other positions
             A
should inform <u>their</u> employers at least three
              B
<u>week</u> before <u>leaving</u>.
 C   D

   Ⓐ   Ⓑ   ©   Ⓓ

16. <u>In a</u> recent <u>book</u>, the actress described <u>his</u>
  A   B   C
thirty-five <u>years</u> in the London theater.
         D

   Ⓐ   Ⓑ   ©   Ⓓ

17. <u>There is</u> an <u>apartment</u> <u>on rent</u> in the
  A   B   C
complex where <u>I live</u>.
          D

   Ⓐ   Ⓑ   ©   Ⓓ

18. We <u>attended at</u> several <u>classical</u> music
     A   B
<u>concerts</u> <u>in</u> December.
 C   D

   Ⓐ   Ⓑ   ©   Ⓓ

19. The computer terminal <u>which</u> I was <u>using it</u>
                  A   B
was <u>not</u> attached <u>to</u> the network.
    C   D

   Ⓐ   Ⓑ   ©   Ⓓ

20. Every one <u>of the</u> airline's <u>plane</u> is <u>serviced</u>
          A   B   C
<u>regularly</u>.
 D

   Ⓐ   Ⓑ   ©   Ⓓ

H. Errors with Comparative and Superlative Forms of Adjectives

There are three forms of most adjectives: the absolute (basic) form, the comparative form, and the superlative form. The comparative is used to describe someone or something that has more of a certain quality than someone or something else. The superlative is used to show that someone or something has the most of a quality in a group of three or more. The basic rules for forming comparatives and superlatives are given in the chart.

	Absolute Form	Comparative Form	Superlative Form
One-syllable adjective	long	longer than	the longest
Two-syllable adjectives ending in -y	funny	funnier than	the funniest
Two-syllable adjectives not ending in -y	common	more common than	the most common
Adjectives of three or more syllables	important	more important than	the most important

A few adjectives have irregular forms:

many/much	more than	the most
little/few	less than	the least
good	better than	the best
bad	worse than	the worst
far	farther than (*or* further than)	the farthest (*or* the furthest)

Note: There are two comparative and superlative forms of *far*; the distinction between the two forms will not be tested on TOEIC.

There are two common errors involving the comparative and superlative forms of adjectives:

One Form Used in Place of Another
In this type of problem, an absolute form is used in place of a comparative form, a comparative in place of a superlative, and so on.

Sample Comparative/Superlative Error: Incorrect Choice

<u>Of the</u> three cars <u>that</u> we took for a test drive, the Italian one <u>was</u> the <u>faster</u>.
  A   B   C   D

Ⓐ Ⓑ Ⓒ ⬤

The sentence refers to a group of three cars, so the superlative must be used in place of the comparative.

Comparatives and Superlatives Incorrectly Formed
Expressions such as *more warmer, more dark, most sunniest,* and *beautifulest* are examples of this error.

Sample Comparative/Superlative Error: Incorrect Form

Mexico City <u>is</u> one of the <u>most largest</u> <u>cities</u> in <u>the world</u>.
               A   B   C   D

Ⓐ ⬤ Ⓒ Ⓓ

The expression should correctly read *largest*.

Exercise 6.15

Focus: Identifying errors involving comparative and superlative forms of adjectives.

Directions: Decide if the underlined word or phrase is used correctly. If so, mark it "C" for "Correct." If not, mark the sentence "X" and rewrite the underlined expression, correcting the mistake.

_____   **1.** That was <u>the most serious</u> accident I have ever seen. _____

_____   **2.** It is much <u>more hot</u> in this room than it is in my office. _____

_____   **3.** Of all the firms that make electrical components, I find Cooper Electronics <u>the more reliable</u>. _____

_____   **4.** This is one of the <u>worse</u> movies I have seen in a long time. _____

_____   **5.** My new apartment is <u>closer</u> to my office than my old one was. _____

6. Mount Fuji is the <u>most highest</u> mountain in Japan. _____

7. I think there was <u>least</u> snow this year than there was last year. _____

8. You have been selected to work on one of the <u>importantest</u> projects this firm has ever taken on. _____

9. Clark has <u>more free time</u> than I do. _____

10. Over there is the newest computer we own, and only the mainframe computer downstairs is <u>fastest</u>. _____

I. Errors with Articles

These errors involve the definite article *the* and the indefinite articles *a* and *an*. The basic uses of articles are given in the chart.

Indefinite Articles *A* and *An*	Definite Article *The*	No Article

A or *an* is used before singular nouns when one does not have a specific person, place, thing, or concept in mind:
    an apple
    a suitcase
	The is used before singular, plural, and noncount nouns when one does have a specific person, place, thing, or concept in mind:
	    the apple
	    the apples
	    the fruit
	    the suitcase
	    the suitcases
	    the luggage
		No article is used before noncount nouns or plural nouns when one does not have specific persons, places, concepts, or things in mind:
		    apples
		    fruit
		    suitcases
		    luggage

The indefinite article *a* is used before words that begin with a consonant sound (*a suitcase, a book*); *an* is used before words that begin with a vowel sound (*an apple, an ocean liner*). Before words that begin with the letters *h-* and *u-*, either *a* or *an* can be used, depending on the pronunciation of the words.

Vowel Sounds	Consonant Sounds
an hour an umbrella	a horse a uniform

There are also some specific rules for using (or not using) articles that you should be aware of:

- An indefinite article can be used to mean "one." It is also used to mean "per."
      a half (one half)
      a mile a minute (one mile per minute)
      an apple a day (one apple per day)

- A definite article is used when there is only one example of the thing or person, or when the identity of the thing or person is clear.
      The sun went behind some clouds. (There's only one sun.)
      Please close *the window.* (You know which window I mean.)

- A definite article is usually used before these expressions of time and position:

the morning	the past	the front	the beginning
the afternoon	the present	the back	the end
the evening*	the future	the middle	
		the top	
		the bottom	

  *No article is used in the expression "at night."

- A definite article come before a singular noun that is used as a representative of an entire class of things. This is especially common with the names of plants, animals, inventions, musical instruments, and parts of the body.

  The elephant is a huge creature.
  My favorite tree is *the oak*.
  Cathy can play *the piano* very well.
  Who invented *the typewriter*?
  The brain is marvelously complex.

- A definite article is used before expressions with an ordinal number. No article is used before expressions with cardinal numbers.

The First World War	World War I
the tenth day	day ten

- A definite article is used before decades and centuries.

the 1960s	the 1800s
the nineties	the twenty-first century

- A definite article is used before superlative forms of adjectives.

the worst mistake	the most interesting idea

- A definite article is used in quantity expressions in this pattern: quantity expression + *of* + *the* + noun.

many of the offices	not much of the paper
some of the water	most of the commercials

These expressions can also be used without the phrase *of the*.

many offices	not much water
some water	most commercials

- A definite article is used before the name of a group of people or a nationality. No article is used before the name of a language.

  The Swedish are proud of their ancestors, *the Vikings*.
  She learned to speak *Swedish* when she lived in Stockholm.

- A definite article is used before the "formal" name of a place (usually containing the word *of*). No article is used before the "informal" name.

the Republic of Indonesia	Indonesia
the city of Athens	Athens

- A definite article is used before a noncount noun or a plural noun when it is followed by a modifier. No article is used when these nouns appear alone.

  The rice that I bought today is in the bag.

Rice is a staple in many countries.
Trees provide shade.
The trees in this park are mostly evergreens.

- A definite article is used before the name of a field of study followed by an *of* phrase. If a field is used alone, or is preceded by an adjective, no article is used.

the art of Japan   Japanese art
the history of the   history
twentieth century

In Part VI, there are two main types of errors involving articles.

Incorrect Article Choice
This may involve the use of *a* for *an* or vice versa. It may also involve the use of *the* in place of *a/an* or vice versa.

Sample Article Error: Incorrect Choice

<u>Before</u> Chul-Ho <u>accepted</u> a <u>management</u> position, he had been <u>a engineer</u>.
  A   B   C   D

Ⓐ   Ⓑ   Ⓒ   ●

The article *an* should be used because the noun *engineer* begins with a vowel sound.

Incorrect Omission or Inclusion of an Article
Sometimes an article is used when one is not needed, or one is not used when it is needed.

Sample Article Errors: Omission/Inclusion

I <u>generally</u> <u>take</u> a <u>vacation</u> once <u>year</u>.   Ⓐ   Ⓑ   Ⓒ   ●
   A   B   C   D
The article *a* has been omitted before the word *year.*

<u>In the</u> Chapter One of the manual, the author <u>primarily</u> defines <u>some</u> important <u>terms</u>.
  A   B   C   D

The article *the* should be omitted.   ●   Ⓑ   Ⓒ   Ⓓ

Exercise 6.16

Focus: Identifying errors involving articles.

Directions: Decide if the underlined word or phrase is used correctly. If so, mark it "C" for "Correct." If not, mark the sentence "X" and rewrite the underlined expression, correcting the mistake.

_____ 1. That was one of <u>the best</u> novels I have ever read. _____
_____ 2. I can't find <u>the Volume</u> Three of the encyclopedia. _____
_____ 3. You can see <u>the stars</u> more clearly from the country than from the city. _____
_____ 4. How do I get to <u>airport</u> from here? _____
_____ 5. Tom has <u>a idea</u> he wants to tell you about. _____

_____   6. The invention of <u>the elevator</u> made skyscrapers possible. _____
_____   7. <u>The water</u> is necessary for all life. _____
_____   8. Some of <u>photographs</u> are overexposed. _____
_____   9. There is a radio antenna on <u>a roof</u> of this building. _____
_____   10. Larry works here only three days <u>the week</u>. _____
_____   11. About <u>the third</u> of my country is very mountainous. _____
_____   12. You can expect a package to be delivered to you in <u>a near future</u>. _____
_____   13. He attended <u>an university</u> in California. _____
_____   14. <u>A first</u> time I went to Japan was about ten years ago. _____
_____   15. I think <u>humor</u> is an important quality in anyone. _____
_____   16. <u>Water</u> in the tea kettle is boiling. _____
_____   17. The receptionist said I would have to wait a half hour to see Dr. Bingham, but I actually had to wait <u>a hour</u>. _____
_____   18. You can find vegetarian restaurants in <u>the most</u> big cities. _____
_____   19. Do you speak <u>French</u> very well? _____
_____   20. He studied <u>the business administration</u>. _____

J. Word-Order Errors

Most word-order problems in Part VI involve the incorrect inversion of two words. In other words, if the correct word order is A + B, the underlined words appear as B + A.

Sample Word-Order Item

<u>Sales</u> personnel <u>must understand</u> <u>psychology human</u> in order <u>to be</u> successful.
    A   B   C   D

Ⓐ Ⓑ ● Ⓓ

The correct word order is *human psychology*.

Word-order errors occur in a number of grammatical situations. Some common ones are given in the chart:

Word-Order Error	Example	Correction
noun + adjective	house blue	blue house
incorrect order of nouns in a compound adjective	agent travel	travel agent
subject + verb in a direct question	Where the memo is?	Where is the memo?
verb + subject in an indirect question	Tell me where is the memo.	Tell me where the memo is.
adjective + adverb	an expensive extremely hotel	an extremely expensive hotel
participle + adverb	a read widely magazine	a widely read magazine
relative pronoun + preposition	the taxi which in he arrived	the taxi in which he arrived
enough + adjective	enough warm	warm enough
adverb + *almost*	completely almost	almost completely

Exercise 6.17

Focus: Identifying errors involving word order.

Directions: Decide if the underlined word or phrase is used correctly. If so, mark it "C" for "Correct." If not, mark the sentence "X" and rewrite the underlined expression, correcting the mistake.

_____   1. I'm not sure if the trunk of my car is <u>enough big</u> to hold all this luggage. _____

_____   2. A <u>grown fully</u> Saint Bernard dog may weigh as much as 70 kilograms. _____

_____   3. I don't know what <u>means that</u>. _____

_____   4. Before you begin your job search, ask yourself this question: "What kind of a job <u>am I</u> trying to find?" _____

_____   5. This is the room <u>which in</u> the reception will be held. _____

_____   6. I don't have <u>enough time</u> to talk to him right now. _____

_____   7. Today the discussion will concern air pollution and other <u>problems environmental</u>. _____

_____   8. The hotel is on a beach that is ten <u>long miles</u>. _____

_____   9. The immigration official asked <u>to show us</u> him our passports. _____

_____   10. The porter asked us how many suitcases <u>were there</u>. _____

_____   11. The document consisted <u>entirely almost</u> of mathematical formulas. _____

_____   12. He was <u>too much</u> tired to go out tonight. _____

K. Errors with Connecting Words

(For more information on connecting words, see Lesson 5, Section F, page 121-120.)

A number of problems involving connecting words may appear in underlined portions of Part VI sentences.

Incorrect Forms of Correlative Conjunctions

These errors involve the two-part conjunctions: *either . . . or, neither . . . nor, both . . . and, not only . . . but also.* The error is usually an incorrect matching of the first word and the second.

Sample Item: Connecting Word Error — Correlative Conjunction

<u>There</u> is neither a stoplight <u>or</u> a stop sign at <u>that</u> <u>corner</u>.
  A   B   C   D

     Ⓐ ● Ⓒ Ⓓ

The correct pattern is *neither . . . nor.*

Incorrect Choice of a Noun-Clause Marker

This error involves the incorrect use of *that, if/whether,* or one of the *wh-* words: *what, how, when,* and so on.

Sample Item: Connecting Word Error — Noun-Clause Marker

<u>Please</u> tell <u>them</u> <u>how</u> you want <u>for</u> dinner.
  A   B   C   D
  Ⓐ   Ⓑ   ●   Ⓓ

The noun-clause marker *what* should be used in place of *how*.

Incorrect Choice of Adjective-Clause Marker

This error involves the use of one relative word in place of another. Often, *who* is used in place of *which* to refer to things, ideas, or organizations, or *which* is used in place of *who* to refer to persons.

Sample Item: Connecting Word Error — Adjective-Clause Marker

<u>The</u> proposal <u>whom</u> Mr. Seong <u>made</u> was eventually <u>adopted</u>.
  A   B   C   D
  Ⓐ   ●   Ⓒ   Ⓓ

The relative word *which* (or *that*) must be used in place of *whom* to refer to the noun *proposal*.

Prepositional Expression in Place of an Adverb-Clause Marker, or Vice Versa

This error consists of using expressions such as *although* or *because* before noun phrases, or expressions such as *despite* or *because of* before clauses.

Sample Item: Connecting Word Error — Adverb-Clause Marker/Prepositional Expression

<u>Despite</u> it is old, <u>the house</u> is <u>in</u> good <u>condition</u>.
  A   B   C   D
  ●   Ⓑ   Ⓒ   Ⓓ

Although should be used in place of *despite* before a clause.

Exercise 6.18

Focus: Identifying errors involving connecting words.

Directions: Decide if the underlined word or phrase is used correctly. If so, mark it "C" for "Correct." If not, mark the sentence "X" and rewrite the underlined expression, correcting the mistake.

_____ 1. <u>Because</u> the stress of his job, Mr. Reardon decided to take a long vacation. _____

_____ 2. I wonder <u>how</u> Elaine's opinion of this matter is. _____

_____ 3. There was a cut on his left hand <u>who</u> later became infected. _____

_____ 4. Do you know <u>if that</u> Ms. Vega has finished yet? _____

_____ 5. <u>In spite of</u> his sore ankle, he was able to participate in the dance contest. _____

_____ 6. Those <u>which</u> have not purchased tickets yet should stand in the line on the left. _____

_____ 7. The old cabin had <u>either</u> electricity nor running water. _____
_____ 8. We are still not sure <u>what</u> caused this machine to malfunction. _____
_____ 9. Being in the earthquake was a terrifying experience <u>whom</u> I will never forget. _____
_____ 10. <u>If</u> she was a child, she wanted to be a doctor. _____
_____ 11. He promised the boss <u>whether</u> he wouldn't be late again. _____
_____ 12. The plant is not only expanding its operations <u>and also</u> hiring new workers. _____

L. Errors with Participial Adjectives

This error involves the use of a present participle (an -*ing* form) when a past participle (an -*ed* or an irregular form) is needed, or a past participle when a present participle is needed. A present participle is used to express an active idea. In other words, it is used to describe a person or thing that performs an action.

> This is a *surprising* development.
> This development is *surprising*.

In each of these two sentences, the development surprises people. The noun performs the action of the verb, so the present participle is used.

> Naoki rented a *furnished* apartment.
> The apartment that Naoki rented was *furnished*.

In both sentences, the noun *apartment* receives rather than performs the action. Someone furnishes (provides furniture for) the apartment. Therefore the past participle is used.

Sample Items: Participial Adjective Errors

<u>Because of</u> the flood, we will <u>have to</u> drink <u>bottling</u> water <u>instead of</u> tap water.
    A   B   C   D
        Ⓐ   Ⓑ   ●   Ⓓ

A past participle (*bottled*) is needed because the noun *water* receives the action. In other words, someone bottles the water.

I <u>thought</u> the <u>promotional</u> film <u>that</u> we saw was quite <u>bored</u>.
  A   B   C   D
    Ⓐ   Ⓑ   Ⓒ   ●

The film performs the action. (It bored me.) The present participle *boring* should be used.

Exercise 6.19

Focus: Identifying errors involving participial adjectives.

Directions: Decide if the underlined word or phrase is used correctly. If so, mark it "C" for "Correct." If not, mark the sentence "X" and rewrite the underlined expression, correcting the mistake.

_____ 1. This offer is available for a <u>limiting</u> time only. _____
_____ 2. The president had some <u>disappointed</u> news for the board of directors. _____
_____ 3. A long delay on the phone can be very <u>frustrated</u> to someone who has a lot to do. _____

_____ 4. What are we going to do with five boxes of <u>broken</u> glasses? _____
_____ 5. We had an oral agreement rather than a <u>writing</u> contract. _____
_____ 6. We were all <u>amazing</u> at the revelation. _____
_____ 7. <u>Experienced</u> workers require less training than workers who have no experience. _____
_____ 8. I could hear the <u>approaching</u> train long before I could see it. _____
_____ 9. The film critic found the new movie <u>disgusted</u>. _____
_____ 10. The man was charged with the possession of <u>stealing</u> goods. _____

Exercise 6.20

Focus: Practicing and reviewing errors involving comparative and superlative forms of adjectives, articles, word order, connecting words, and participial adjectives.

Directions: Choose the *one* underlined expression that must be rewritten in order to form a correct sentence. Then mark the correct answer.

1. Chinese New Year <u>is celebrated</u> in
   A
   Hong Kong <u>with</u> <u>an huge</u> fireworks
   B   C
   display <u>over</u> the harbor.
   D
   Ⓐ Ⓑ Ⓒ Ⓓ

2. <u>Freezing</u> foods are the <u>fastest</u> <u>growing</u>
   A   B   C
   segment of the food <u>industry</u>.
   D
   Ⓐ Ⓑ Ⓒ Ⓓ

3. <u>The automobile</u> was <u>developed</u> <u>near end</u>
   A   B   C
   of <u>the nineteenth</u> century.
   D
   Ⓐ Ⓑ Ⓒ Ⓓ

4. Mr. Rhee <u>did well</u> on the job <u>because</u> his
   A   B
   strong <u>background</u> in <u>economics</u>.
   C   D
   Ⓐ Ⓑ Ⓒ Ⓓ

5. The <u>boiling point</u> is the temperature
   A
   <u>which</u> at <u>water</u> begins <u>to bubble</u> and turn
   B   C   D
   to steam.
   Ⓐ Ⓑ Ⓒ Ⓓ

6. I <u>saw</u> the machine, <u>but</u> I didn't know <u>how</u>
   A   B   C
   its <u>purpose was</u>.
   D
   Ⓐ Ⓑ Ⓒ Ⓓ

7. We can either <u>take</u> a <u>shuttle bus</u> <u>and</u> a taxi
   A   B   C
   to <u>the airport</u>.
   D
   Ⓐ Ⓑ Ⓒ Ⓓ

8. Tom said that <u>the</u> shift manager
   A
   <u>reprimanded</u> <u>him</u> for <u>too slow working</u>.
   B   C   D
   Ⓐ Ⓑ Ⓒ Ⓓ

9. <u>That</u> was Vicki's <u>brother</u> <u>whose</u> was
   A   B   C
   playing <u>the guitar</u>.
   D
   Ⓐ Ⓑ Ⓒ Ⓓ

10. It <u>is</u> not <u>enough warm</u> for us <u>to go</u> to the
    A   B   C
    beach <u>this morning</u>.
    D
    Ⓐ Ⓑ Ⓒ Ⓓ

11. The <u>animals</u> in <u>the circus</u> <u>performed</u> some
    A   B   C
    <u>amused</u> tricks.
    D
    Ⓐ Ⓑ Ⓒ Ⓓ

12. <u>Of the</u> two <u>examples</u>, <u>the second</u> one is the
    A   B   C
    <u>clearest</u>.
    D
    Ⓐ Ⓑ Ⓒ Ⓓ

13. That was <u>a most</u> <u>delicious pastry</u> <u>that</u> I
            A   B   C
 have <u>ever tasted</u>.
       D
 Ⓐ   Ⓑ   Ⓒ   Ⓓ

14. Do you <u>believe</u> <u>that</u> there is <u>a life</u> on <u>other</u>
          A   B   C   D
 planets?
 Ⓐ   Ⓑ   Ⓒ   Ⓓ

15. <u>An</u> ice cream <u>that</u> we bought at the store
  A   B
 had almost <u>completely melted</u> <u>before</u>
               C   D
 we got home.
 Ⓐ   Ⓑ   Ⓒ   Ⓓ

16. A dialect of <u>German</u> is <u>the most</u>
            A   B
 <u>spoken widely</u> language <u>in</u> Switzerland.
    C   D
 Ⓐ   Ⓑ   Ⓒ   Ⓓ

17. Continental Motors <u>is developing</u> a
                   A
 <u>new generation</u> of automobiles
     B
 <u>that operate</u> on <u>the electricity</u>.
    C   D
 Ⓐ   Ⓑ   Ⓒ   Ⓓ

18. <u>In the early</u> hours of morning, I saw a
     A
 <u>speeding car</u> race <u>through</u> the
     B   C
 <u>deserting</u> streets.
    D
 Ⓐ   Ⓑ   Ⓒ   Ⓓ

19. <u>Because this</u> side of the building faces
    A
 south, <u>it is</u> <u>more warmer</u> than <u>the other</u>
       B   C   D
 side.
 Ⓐ   Ⓑ   Ⓒ   Ⓓ

20. <u>Do you</u> know <u>what kind</u> of <u>factory</u> <u>is this</u>?
    A   B   C   D
 Ⓐ   Ⓑ   Ⓒ   Ⓓ

More Practice

Directions: Choose the *one* underlined expression that must be rewritten in order to form a correct sentence. Then mark the correct answer.

1. Nutritionists recommend that everyone
 <u>eat</u> from three <u>to</u> five <u>serving</u> of vegetables
  A   B   C
 <u>a day</u>.
  D
 Ⓐ   Ⓑ   Ⓒ   Ⓓ

2. Without <u>operating</u> funds, <u>a firm</u> cannot
       A   B
 <u>continue</u> to <u>make</u> business.
    C   D
 Ⓐ   Ⓑ   Ⓒ   Ⓓ

3. I had <u>already</u> <u>meet</u> Ms. Shim several <u>times</u>
      A   B   C
 before <u>tonight</u>.
     D
 Ⓐ   Ⓑ   Ⓒ   Ⓓ

4. Mr. Klein <u>has</u> decided <u>opening</u> his <u>own</u>
         A   B   C
 international <u>consulting</u> company.
           D
 Ⓐ   Ⓑ   Ⓒ   Ⓓ

5. Henry bought <u>a oak</u> desk <u>that</u> was <u>made</u>
             A   B   C
 over one hundred <u>years ago</u>.
              D
 Ⓐ   Ⓑ   Ⓒ   Ⓓ

6. One of <u>the most</u> popular <u>form</u> of <u>music</u> in
       A   B   C
 the world today is reggae, <u>which</u>
                 D
 originated in Jamaica.
 Ⓐ   Ⓑ   Ⓒ   Ⓓ

7. The company intends <u>for to relocate</u> <u>its</u>
               A   B
 <u>global</u> headquarters to <u>either</u> Australia or
   C   D
 New Zealand.
 Ⓐ   Ⓑ   Ⓒ   Ⓓ

8. We are <u>leaving</u> <u>at the</u> morning on a
       A   B
 <u>three-week</u> trip <u>to</u> South America.
    C   D
 Ⓐ   Ⓑ   Ⓒ   Ⓓ

9. The layout of the <u>streets</u> in the <u>old part</u>
                                 A   B
   of town <u>is</u> very <u>confused</u> to me.
            C   D
   Ⓐ   Ⓑ   Ⓒ   Ⓓ

10. Single proprietorship, <u>partnership</u>,
                                      A

    corporation: <u>this</u> are the <u>main types</u> of
                      B   C

    business <u>organization</u>.
                   D
    Ⓐ   Ⓑ   Ⓒ   Ⓓ

11. The <u>owner</u> of the restaurant is going
           A

    <u>to install</u> a <u>fifty-gallons</u> aquarium in the
        B   C

    <u>dining room</u>.
        D
    Ⓐ   Ⓑ   Ⓒ   Ⓓ

12. This machine needs <u>to be</u> serviced <u>monthly</u>
                            A   B
    under <u>ordinarily</u> <u>conditions</u>.
               C   D
    Ⓐ   Ⓑ   Ⓒ   Ⓓ

13. Demetrios <u>has</u> two <u>brothers</u>, both of <u>which</u>
                   A   B   C
    are <u>airline</u> pilots.
         D
    Ⓐ   Ⓑ   Ⓒ   Ⓓ

14. <u>Alike</u> his <u>father</u>, Rodney is <u>an</u>
     A   B   B
    <u>accomplished</u> jazz <u>musician</u>.
         C   D
    Ⓐ   Ⓑ   Ⓒ   Ⓓ

15. <u>It is</u> much <u>more easy</u> <u>to edit</u> documents on
     A   B   C
    a word processor <u>than it is</u> on a typewriter.
                          D
    Ⓐ   Ⓑ   Ⓒ   Ⓓ

16. <u>Despite</u> Ms. Pardini is one of <u>our</u> top sales
     A   B
    <u>representatives</u>, she hardly ever calls on
         C
    customers <u>in person</u>.
                   D
    Ⓐ   Ⓑ   Ⓒ   Ⓓ

17. I <u>asked</u> Randy <u>to remember</u> me of <u>today's</u>
       A   B   C
    budget <u>meeting</u>.
               D
    Ⓐ   Ⓑ   Ⓒ   Ⓓ

18. Visitors <u>who</u> tour <u>the factory</u> often
              A   B
    comment on <u>how</u> clean and spacious <u>is it</u>.
                   C   D
    Ⓐ   Ⓑ   Ⓒ   Ⓓ

19. Large <u>flocks</u> of birds can <u>be</u> very <u>dangers</u>
               A   B   C
    to jetliners <u>during</u> take-offs and landings.
                      D
    Ⓐ   Ⓑ   Ⓒ   Ⓓ

20. The position <u>that</u> Mr. Ihori was offered
                      A
    sounded <u>quite</u> <u>challenged</u> <u>to</u> him.
                 B   C   D
    Ⓐ   Ⓑ   Ⓒ   Ⓓ

LESSON 7

Short Readings

 Preview: Lesson Outline

- Part VII Format
- Tactics for Part VII
- Sample Test
- Types of Reading and Practice Exercises
    - A. Articles
    - B. Business Correspondence
    - C. Advertisements
    - D. Announcements
    - E. Non-Prose Readings
- More Practice

 Part VII **Format**

Part VII is the longest part of TOEIC. It's also the last part, so you may be starting to get tired. However, you need to stay focused on the test for a little longer.

Part VII consists of short reading passages followed by questions about the passages. There are four possible answer choices for each question. You must pick the best answer choice based on the information in the passage and then mark that answer on your answer sheet.

The Passages　　There are about fifteen passages. Most are quite short. Some consist of only three or four sentences; the longest have around 125 words. The passages deal with a wide variety of topics and involve many different types of written materials.

The Questions　　There is a total of 50 questions in Part VII. They include these three types:

1. Overview questions
2. Detail questions
3. Inference questions

- **Overview questions** occur after most of the passages. To answer overview questions correctly, you need a "global" (overall) understanding of the passage. The most common overview question asks about the purpose or the main topic of the passage:

    > What does this article mainly discuss?
    > What is the purpose of this letter?
    > Why was this notice written?

    Some ask about the best title or heading of a passage:

    > What is the best heading for this announcement?
    > Which of the following is the best title for the article?

    Other overview questions ask about the writer of the passage, the readers of the passage, or the place of publication:

    > In what business is the writer of the passage?
    > What is the author's opinion of _____ ?
    > Who would be most interested in the information in this announcement?
    > For whom is this advertisement intended?
    > Where was this article probably published?

- **Detail questions**, the most common type of Part VII question, ask about specific points in the passage. You will usually have to scan the passage to find and identify the information. Sometimes the answer and the information in the passage do not look the same. For example, a sentence in a passage may read "This process is not as simple as it once was." The correct answer may be "The process is now more complex."

  Some detail questions are negative questions. These always include the words NOT or EXCEPT, which are printed in uppercase (capital) letters.

  > All of the following are mentioned in the passage EXCEPT . . . .
  > Based on the information in the passage, which of the following is NOT true?

  Negative questions often take the longest to answer.

- A few questions in Part VII are **inference questions**. The answers to these questions are not directly stated in the passage. Instead, you must draw a conclusion about the information that is given. Some typical inference questions:

  > Which of these statements is most likely true?
  > What is probably true about . . . ?

Answer Choices   All are believable answers to the questions. Incorrect choices often contain information that is presented somewhere in the passage but does not correctly answer the question.

A Note About Vocabulary   Most of the vocabulary in the passages consists of relatively common English words and phrases, but there will certainly be expressions that you do not know. However, you can understand most of a reading and answer most of the questions even if you don't know the meaning of all the words. Also, you can guess the meaning of many unfamiliar words in the passages through context. In other words, you can use the familiar words in the sentence in which an unfamiliar word appears to get an idea of what the unfamiliar word means.

Tactics for Part VII

1. First, just look at the passage quickly to get an idea of what it is about.
2. Next, read the questions about the passage. You should *not* read the answer choices at this time. Try to keep these questions in the back of your mind as you read the passage.
3. Read the passage. Try to read quickly, but read every word; don't just skim the passage. Look for answers to the questions that you read in Step 2.
4. Answer the questions. For detail and inference questions, you will probably have to refer back to the passage. Use the eraser-end of your pencil as a pointer to focus your attention as you look for the information needed to answer the question.
5. If you are unsure of the answer, eliminate answer choices that are clearly wrong, and guess. Mark items that you guessed at in your test booklet so that you can come back to these questions later if you have time.
6. Don't spend too much time on any item. If you find a question or even an entire passage confusing, guess at the answer or answers and come back to these items later if you have time.
7. If you have not answered all the questions and only a few minutes are left, read the remaining questions without reading the passages, and choose the answers that seem most logical.

Sample Test

Directions: Questions in this part of the test are based on a wide range of reading materials, including articles, letters, advertisements, and notices. After reading the passage, decide which of the four choices — (A), (B), (C), or (D) — best answers the question and mark your answer. All answers should be based on what is stated in or on what can be inferred from the readings.

Now read the following example

La Plata Dinner Theater announces the opening of *Life on the River*, a musical play based on a book by Mark Twain. Dinner is served from 6:30 to 8:00, and the performance begins at 8:30 every evening.

What is opening?
- Ⓐ A bookstore
- Ⓑ An art exhibit
- ● A musical play
- Ⓓ A new restaurant

The reading states that *Life on the River* is a musical play that is opening at La Plata Dinner Theater. You should choose (C).

Questions 1 to 3 refer to the following article:

Go ahead, have a cheeseburger, France's Constitutional Council said recently.

The agency that monitors the constitutionality of laws wasn't ruling on nutrition but on linguistics. Its decision substantially weakens a recent law meant to stop the invasion of foreign words into the French language. That law banned the use of English in broadcasting, advertising, and science. The law would have, for instance, forced restaurateurs to advertise "hamburgers au fromage" instead of cheeseburgers.

However, the Council ruled that the law encroached on "the fundamental liberty of thought and expression" guaranteed by the French constitution.

1. What is this article mainly about?
   - Ⓐ The passage of a new bill
   - Ⓑ A breakthrough in research
   - Ⓒ An invasion of foreigners
   - Ⓓ The weakening of a recent law

2. The members of the Council are probably experts in which of these fields?
   - Ⓐ Nutrition
   - Ⓑ Advertising
   - Ⓒ Law
   - Ⓓ Linguistics

3. How will the owners of restaurants in France be affected by this ruling?
   - Ⓐ They can now serve hamburgers with cheese.
   - Ⓑ They must now use only French words on menus.
   - Ⓒ They may now use English words in advertisements.
   - Ⓓ They can now advertise wherever they want.

Questions 4 to 6 are based on the following chart:

METRO LODGING REPORT: JULY

Location	Room Nights		Occupancy Percentage	Average Room Cost
	Occupied	Available		
AIRPORT	89,649	104,847	85.5%	$68.28
NORTH SUBURBAN	29,686	35,065	84.7%	$53.75
WEST SUBURBAN	46,279	50,950	90.8%	$57.78
MIDTOWN	29,681	37,851	78.0%	$49.70
DOWNTOWN	62,620	77,271	81.0%	$79.61

4. What does this report concern?
   A Apartment buildings
   B Hotels
   C Parking lots
   D Office buildings

5. Which area had the highest rate of occupancy in July?
   A North Suburban
   B Midtown
   C West Suburban
   D Downtown

6. What information does the chart provide about Downtown?
   A On the average, it had the most expensive rooms.
   B It had fewer empty rooms in July than Midtown did.
   C It had more rooms than any other area.
   D There were more rooms per building than in other areas.

Questions 7 and 8 refer to the following advertisement:

Owning a franchise can be magical!

The expanding children's service market offers an excellent return on your investment — and puts a little magic into your summer. Summer Magic Day Camps franchises provide door-to-door pick-up services for children (ages 6–13) and a wide variety of activities in parks and other locations. No need to invest in expensive camp facilities, as all activities are held off-premises. You can operate the business part-time and from home. We provide all the know-how and direction needed for start-up and day-to-day operations. Very reasonable franchise fees.

7. For whom is this advertisement intended?
   A People who want to operate their own business
   B Parents of young children
   C People who own summer camps
   D People who want to work as camp counselors

8. The company placing this advertisement would probably NOT provide information on which of the following?
   A Where to hold activities
   B What kind of activities to provide
   C How to attract campers
   D How to choose a site for the camp

Questions 9 and 10 are based on the following letter:

The Richmond Hotel
Chicago, Illinois

Warren Purcell, Convention Chair
American Association of Photoengravers
North Central District
Suite 28
621 Plum Street
Detroit, Michigan 48201

Dear Mr. Purcell:

Mr. Scarlotti, our general manager, passed on your letter to him requesting information regarding our convention facilities and asked me to respond. I am happy to comply.

As you can see from our brochure, we offer large meeting rooms for plenary sessions and display areas, and an ample number of small "breakdown" rooms for workshops and concurrent meetings. Banquet facilities are also available. Our centralized location is convenient to other hotels, fine restaurants, and all the sights of downtown Chicago, as you can see from the map I've sent. I'm also enclosing a list of special room rates for convention attendees.

I think you will find the Richmond Hotel the perfect host for your convention. Our experienced and courteous staff really knows what it takes to make a convention run smoothly.

Please let me know if there is any other information or help I can provide.

Sincerely,

Diana Lockhurst, Convention and Banquet Manager

Encl: (3)

DL/pw

---

9. What is the main purpose of this letter?
    A To ask for further information
    B To respond to a request
    C To confirm a reservation
    D To explain the general manager's opinion

10. Which of the following is NOT enclosed?
    A A schedule of events
    B A publicity brochure
    C A map of downtown Chicago
    D A list of room rates

Questions 11 and 12 are based on the following announcement:

"American Impressionism and Realism: The Paintings of Modern Life, 1885-1915." This display features more than 80 paintings that contrast two important turn-of-the-century schools of art. Featured artists include impressionists John Singer Sargent and Mary Cassatt and realists Robert Henri, John Sloan, and William Blackins. At the Los Angeles Museum of Art through May 24.

11. What is the main theme of this display?
  (A) The range of contemporary painting in Los Angeles
  (B) The contrast between today's art and turn-of-the-century art
  (C) Paintings produced by students from two universities
  (D) Differences between two important styles of art

12. Which of the following artists is NOT considered a realist?
  (A) John Sloan
  (B) Mary Cassatt
  (C) William Blackins
  (D) Robert Henri

Types of Reading and Practice Exercises

The readings in Part VII cover a wide range of topics and represent many types of materials. Many fit into the four categories described in this part of the lesson. Each section of this part describes a type of reading, presents an analysis of an example for that type, and offers an exercise in answering questions about that type of reading.

A. Articles

Readings of this type resemble brief articles or parts of articles such as the ones found in newspapers or magazines. Some concern business topics. Another common type is a report on a survey or study. You will probably see from two to four articles per test. Overview questions about articles ask about the main point of the article. They may also ask you about the author's opinion or background. Some ask what type of reader would be interested in this article or where the article was probably published.

Detail and negative questions deal with specific points made in the article. Some questions ask you to interpret numbers that appear in the article.

Sample Items: Questions About Articles

Go ahead, have a cheeseburger, France's Constitutional Council said recently.
The agency that monitors the constitutionality of laws wasn't ruling on nutrition but on linguistics. Its decision substantially weakens a recent law meant to stop the invasion of foreign words into the French language. That law banned the use of English in broadcasting, advertising, and science. The law would have, for instance, forced restaurateurs to advertise "hamburgers au fromage" instead of cheeseburgers?
However, the Council ruled that the law encroached on "the fundamental liberty of thought and expression" guaranteed by the French constitution.

What is this article mainly about?
    Ⓐ The passage of a new bill
    Ⓑ A breakthrough in research
    Ⓒ An invasion of foreigners
    ● The weakening of a recent law

The article is primarily about a ruling of the French Constitutional Council that "substantially weakens a recent law."

The members of the Council are probably experts in which of these fields?
    Ⓐ Nutrition   ● Law
    Ⓑ Advertising Ⓓ Linguistics

This is an inference question since the information is not directly provided in the passage. However, it is logical that members of the French Constitutional Council are experts in law.

How will the owners of restaurants in France be affected by this ruling?
    Ⓐ   They can now serve hamburgers with cheese.
    Ⓑ   They must now use only French words on menus.
    ●   They may now use English words in advertisements.
    Ⓓ   They can now advertise wherever they want.

The ruling weakened the law that would have forced advertisers to use only French terms, such as "hamburger au fromage." Therefore, owners are now able to advertise their products using English expressions such as "cheeseburger."

Exercise 7.1

Focus: Understanding and answering questions about articles.

Directions: Read the passages, and then mark the best answers to the questions about them based on the information in the passages.

Questions 1 to 4 are based on the following article:

Every year, about 240 million tires — an average of one tire for every person in the United States — are discarded. Currently, U.S. automobile manufacturers are turning 18 million pounds of tires each year into car parts — seals, air deflectors, and other parts not visible to consumers.

Now, a new process that grinds tires into fine powder and magnetically removes steel belting promises to broaden the range of recycled products. The end product, a mixture of rubber and plastic, can be molded into vehicle parts, and they look new. The first product, a brake-pedal pad, is being field tested on fleets of police cars, rental cars, and taxicabs. They could end up on production vehicles next year. Each recycled tire can produce 250 brake-pedal pads.

1. What is the best title for this article?
   - Ⓐ "Making Tires from Recycled Materials"
   - Ⓑ "A New Use for Old Tires"
   - Ⓒ "Process Makes Old Cars Look New"
   - Ⓓ "New Brakes Make Cars Safer"

2. Which of the following best describes the order of steps in the new process?
   - Ⓐ Magnetize steel, mix rubber and plastic, make parts
   - Ⓑ Powder tires, belt with steel, melt parts
   - Ⓒ Grind tires, remove steel, mold into parts
   - Ⓓ Melt tires, broaden belt, install parts

3. What advantage of parts made by this process is mentioned by the author?
   - Ⓐ They are extremely safe.
   - Ⓑ They last a long time.
   - Ⓒ They are inexpensive.
   - Ⓓ They look new.

4. All of the following are being used to field test brake-pedal pads EXCEPT
   - Ⓐ Police cars
   - Ⓑ Production vehicles
   - Ⓒ Taxicabs
   - Ⓓ Rental cars

Questions 5 and 6 refer to the following passage:

According to a survey taken this year, some 260, or 52%, of the Fortune 500 companies in the United States had at least one woman on their corporate board of directors. That's up from 243, or 49%, last year. Last year's survey was the first such study done since the original one in 1977. At that time, only 46 women held seats on the boards of top U.S. corporations.

5. How many companies had one or more women on their boards of directors this year?
   - Ⓐ 46
   - Ⓑ 243
   - Ⓒ 260
   - Ⓓ 500

6. How many surveys regarding women as members of boards of directors have been done BEFORE this year?
   - Ⓐ None
   - Ⓑ One
   - Ⓒ Two
   - Ⓓ Three

Questions 7 to 10 refer to the following article:

The British Crown Jewels were given a new home in March 1994. The collection includes some 20,000 gems, among which is the world's largest diamond. It had been housed in an underground bunker at the Tower of London which could not accommodate the 2 million visitors a year who wanted to view the jewels. The Crown Jeweler himself, the only person allowed to handle the jewels, packed up the collection for the move to the 10-million-pound Jewel House in Waterloo Barracks, just above the old bunker. The Crown Jewels have been at the Tower since 1327; they have been moved only twice since 1867, the last time to the bunker in 1967. The new premises feature a moving walkway which carries visitors past the displays, preventing the crush that so often occurred in the old site.

7. What claim is NOT made in the article about the Crown Jewels?
   (A) It is the largest jewelry collection in history.
   (B) It is visited by 2 million people a year.
   (C) It contains the world's largest diamond.
   (D) It consists of more than 20,000 jewels.

8. When was the collection moved to the underground bunker?
   (A) In 1327   (C) In 1967
   (B) In 1867   (D) In 1994

9. What was the Crown Jeweler's responsibility during the move?
   (A) To assess the value of the collection
   (B) To locate a new site for the display
   (C) To examine the jewelry for defects
   (D) To pack up the jewelry on his own

10. According to the article, which of the following is one of the advantages of the new site?
    (A) It is in a more convenient location.
    (B) It will seem less crowded.
    (C) It can accommodate more jewels.
    (D) It has a better security system.

Questions 11 and 12 refer to the following passage:

Critics of communities that pass smoke-free restaurant laws warn that business will suffer. But a seven-year study of 30 California communities showed that smoke-free restaurants do not lose business. The study, done by researchers from the University of California at San Francisco, involved fifteen towns that passed smoke-free period and fifteen towns that did not. Smoke-free laws had no effect on restaurant sales, said researchers.

11. The main conclusion of the study is that
    (A) businesses suffer if they restrict smoking
    (B) smoke-free restaurants had higher sales than restaurants that permitted smoking
    (C) criticism of smoke-free restaurant laws is increasing
    (D) restaurant sales were unaffected by smoke-free laws

12. How long did the study last?
    (A) 1 year   (C) 15 years
    (B) 7 years   (D) 30 years

Questions 13 and 14 are based on the following article:

Golf has become increasingly popular in Thailand. The country now boasts more than 50 golf courses. Over half are in Bangkok's suburbs on what until recently were rice paddies, while others have been built at seaside and mountain resorts. A Thai developer stated that the number of golfers in Thailand has tripled to 60,000 in the last five years.

13. Where are most of Thailand's golf courses located?
    (A) In central Bangkok
    (B) At mountain resorts
    (C) In suburban Bangkok
    (D) At the seaside

14. Approximately how many Thai golfers were there five years ago?
    (A) 15,000   (C) 30,000
    (B) 20,000   (D) 60,000

Questions 15 to 17 are based on the following article:

How much money do fliers leave behind on airlines? One international carrier took in $75,000 last year, which it donated to charities. That's an average of $.18 a passenger. If that figure holds true for all 320 million people who fly on the hundreds of international airlines, it amounts to $58 million per year.

Much less is found on domestic U.S. flights. A cleaning crew in Chicago reported finding less than $.10 per flight. An executive of one international airline suggested that on international flights passengers disposed of unwanted coins from the countries they were departing by leaving the coins in their seats or in the seat pockets in front of them.

15. Which is the best headline for this article?
    Ⓐ "Saving Money on International Travel"
    Ⓑ "The Changing Face of Air Travel"
    Ⓒ "How to Hold on to Your Money"
    Ⓓ "Loose Change Found on Planes"

16. What is the figure of $58 million mentioned in the first paragraph based on?
    Ⓐ Data from hundreds of airlines
    Ⓑ Interviews with numerous cleaning crews
    Ⓒ Information provided by one airline
    Ⓓ Estimates made by airline executives

17. What explanation is offered for the greater amount of money left on international flights than on U.S. domestic flights?
    Ⓐ International passengers discard unwanted coins.
    Ⓑ U.S. cleaning crews are keeping the money.
    Ⓒ International airlines are more interested in charity.
    Ⓓ U.S. passengers have fewer pockets.

B. Business Correspondence

This type of reading involves any type of communication sent to or from a business. You will usually see two to three business communications in Part VII per test. Most are business letters. You may also see interoffice memos, which are business communications between two or more employees at the same company. These also have many purposes: to schedule a meeting, to ask for a report, to discuss a problem, to thank someone for a job well done, to request help or information. You may also see faxes (short for *facsimile transmissions*), which are usually sent when it is important that someone view a document as quickly as possible.

Overview questions about business correspondence usually ask about the purpose of the communication. This is generally stated in the first paragraph — usually the first few lines — of the body of the communication.

Answers to detail questions are usually found in the body of the communication but may also be found in the heading or opening.

Sample Items: Questions About Business Communications

The Richmond Hotel
Chicago, Illinois

Warren Purcell, Convention Chair
American Association of Photoengravers
North Central District
Suite 28
621 Plum Street
Detroit, Michigan 48201

Dear Mr. Purcell:

Mr. Scarlotti, our general manager, passed on your letter to him requesting information regarding our convention facilities and asked me to respond. I am happy to comply.

As you can see from our brochure, we offer large meeting rooms for plenary sessions and display areas, and an ample number of small "breakdown" rooms for workshops and concurrent meetings. Banquet facilities are also available. Our centralized location is convenient to other hotels, fine restaurants, and all the sights of downtown Chicago, as you can see from the map I've sent. I'm also enclosing a list of special room rates for convention attendees.

I think you will find the Richmond Hotel the perfect host for your convention. Our experienced and courteous staff really knows what it takes to make a convention run smoothly.

Please let me know if there is any other information or help I can provide.

Sincerely,

Diana Lockhurst

Diana Lockhurst, Convention and Banquet Manager

Encl: (3)

DL/pw

What is the main purpose of this letter?
- Ⓐ To ask for further information
- ● To respond to a request
- Ⓒ To confirm a reservation
- Ⓓ To explain the general manager's opinion

The purpose of the letter is given in the first paragraph of the communication. The writer states that she was asked by the general manager to respond to a previous request for information, and that she is doing so in this letter.

Which of the following is NOT enclosed?
- ● A schedule of events
- Ⓑ A publicity brochure
- Ⓒ A map of downtown Chicago
- Ⓓ A list of room rates

Three enclosures are mentioned: the brochure, the map, and the list of rates for rooms. There is no mention of a schedule of events.

Exercise 7.2

Focus: Understanding and answering questions about business correspondence.

Directions: Read the passages, and then mark the best answers to the questions about them based on the information in the passages.

Questions 1 to 5 are based on the following letter:

Valleyview Labs
740 Potero Avenue
Sunnyvale, California 94086

May 17, 199-

Carlos Reyes
3205 Craycroft Road
Tucson, AZ 85729

Dear Mr. Reyes:

I read with interest your curriculum vitae and letter dated April 30. Your education and prior experience in both research and management were impressive. However, I'm afraid I cannot offer you the position of researcher that you applied for. This is an entry-level position and would not offer the challenge or, frankly, the salary someone with your qualifications should have. I'm afraid you may have been misled by the advertisement, which was not clearly worded, and for that I apologize.

However, due to expansion here at Valleyview, there is a possibility that the position of deputy coordinator of the research and development team may be created. Given your background, you would be a strong candidate for the position.

I plan to be in Tucson on business from May 27 to June 1. If you are still interested in a position with Valleyview Labs, please contact my assistant within the next few weeks to arrange an appointment.

I look forward to meeting you.

Sincerely,

Philip H. Kappler, Executive Director
Valleyview Labs, Inc.

PHK/rs

1. What kind of position did Mr. Reyes apply for?
   (A) Assistant to Mr. Kappler
   (B) Deputy coordinator of a team
   (C) Executive director
   (D) Researcher

2. When did Mr. Reyes apply for a position?
   (A) On April 30   (C) On May 28
   (B) On May 17   (D) On June 1

3. Mr. Reyes was NOT offered the position he applied for because
   (A) he lacked the proper experience for it
   (B) he was overqualified for it
   (C) it had already been filled
   (D) the company decided not to fill it

4. Why does the letter writer apologize?
   (A) Because the advertisement was unclear
   (B) Because the salary is so low
   (C) Because he took so long to respond
   (D) Because the letter is so short

5. What should Mr. Reyes do if he still wants to work at Valleyview Labs?
   (A) Come to the labs for an interview
   (B) Call Mr. Kappler's assistant for an appointment
   (C) Leave for Tucson immediately
   (D) Write Mr. Kappler a letter

Questions 6 and 7 are based on the following note:

To	James		AM
Date	2/17	Time 11:40	PM

WHILE YOU WERE OUT

M s. Bingham
of Product Promotions Team

Phone (   )   6972
Area code   Number   Extension

TELEPHONED   PLEASE CALL   X
CALLED TO SEE YOU   WILL CALL AGAIN
WANTS TO SEE YOU   URGENT
              RETURNED YOUR CALL

Message Came by to discuss your meeting in Rio with Dr. Garofalo on Monday. Call her after lunch.

Sally

6. Who took the message?
   (A) James
   (B) Dr. Garofalo
   (C) Ms. Bingham
   (D) Sally

7. What is James asked to do?
   (A) Join the Product Promotions Team
   (B) Call Dr. Garofalo
   (C) Go out to lunch
   (D) Contact Ms. Bingham

Questions 8 to 10 are based on the following communication:

Northfield Pharmaceuticals International
Interoffice Memo

To **All department heads**

From **Peter Manning, Director**

Subject **United Charity Fund**

Date **Sept. 26**

Next week marks the opening of United Charity Fund's fall campaign drive. As you probably know, UCF is the umbrella organization for about 35 local and regional charity organizations. It solicits funds from businesses and individuals, then divides them up among the member charities.

This is a chance for all of us here at Northfield to repay the community where we work and live. I'd like to have another record year.

Therefore, I'm asking all of you at your departmental meetings this week to remind everyone of Northfield's policy of contributing $.50 for every dollar contributed by employees. And ask everyone in your department to dig deeply into their pockets and purses.

Thanks for your cooperation.

---

8. What are the department heads asked to do?
   - (A) Encourage employees to work harder
   - (B) Inform employees of a company policy
   - (C) Volunteer their time for charitable work
   - (D) Meet with Peter Manning

9. Which of the following is NOT one of United Charity Fund's roles?
   - (A) Asking businesses for contributions
   - (B) Distributing funds to charitable groups
   - (C) Helping individuals who have problems
   - (D) Asking individuals for contributions

10. If an employee of Northfield contributes $20, how much will United Charity Fund receive?
    - (A) $20
    - (B) $30
    - (C) $40
    - (D) $50

Questions 11 and 12 are based on the following letter:

Talon Peripherals, Inc.
800-1444 W. Hastings Street
Vancouver, B.C. V6E 2K3

Dec. 1, 199-

Endang Sujono, Managing Director
Jalan Citarum 82
Jakarta Pusat, Indonesia

Dear Mr. Sujono:

An old friend, Tony Drummond, just returned from Jakarta, and he mentioned to me that you and your firm might find our new line of products, particularly our new Talon Portable Color Laser Printer, of interest. With your marketing expertise, you could turn this into one of the best-selling portable printers in Indonesia, I believe.

One of our marketing representatives will be in Indonesia next month. If it is at all possible, I would like him to meet with you to demonstrate our products' capabilities. If you are interested, I would like you to become sole marketing agent for Talon Peripherals in Indonesia.

I'll ask our representative to contact you in order to arrange a meeting. Please call or fax if you have any questions regarding our company or our product.

Best wishes,

Mary Lymon, Marketing Director
Talon Peripherals, Inc.

---

11. What is the purpose of this letter?
  (A) To persuade Mr. Sujono to buy a printer
  (B) To request some advice from Mr. Sujono
  (C) To ask Mr. Sujono to market a product
  (D) To arrange a meeting in Vancouver

12. Who is Tony Drummond?
  (A) A friend of Mr. Sujono
  (B) A marketing representative
  (C) A friend of Ms. Lymon
  (D) An employee of Talon Peripherals

Questions 13 to 16 are based on the following communication:

Aug. 5	FRI	4:05PM	Redfern Realtors

Fax No. 6038462-884

Dear Mr. Yamaguchi,

Ms. Foster of Ventura Enterprises has asked us here at Redfern Realty to look for a temporary housing situation for you in order to make your process of relocation as smooth as possible. I have located a 3-bedroom condominium close to Ventura Enterprises. It is in a lovely condominium complex called Foxwood Gardens. It has a deck, a fireplace, and a garage. The rent is $925 per month plus heat (oil) and electricity. Rubbish removal, snow removal, and water/sewer are paid by the condominium association.

If you want this unit, send me a check by express mail for the first month's rent, and I will fax you a lease to sign. Make the check out to Atwater Properties, which is leasing the condominium for the owners. We cannot guarantee the lease until your check arrives. Call tomorrow if you have questions.

Best,

Charles Fincastle, Jr.

13. What is Mr. Yamaguchi doing?
    A Moving to a new community
    B Renting out his house
    C Selling his condominium
    D Looking for a new job

14. Where does the writer of this communication work?
    A At Atwater Properties
    B At Redfern Realtors
    C At Ventura Enterprises
    D At Foxwood Gardens

15. All of the following are included in the rent EXCEPT
    A the bill for snow removal
    B the water/sewer bill
    C the heat bill
    D the bill for rubbish removal

16. What must Mr. Yamaguchi do to guarantee the lease?
    A Bring in a signed copy of the lease
    B Call Mr. Fincastle immediately
    C Send a check for $925 by express mail
    D Fax a copy of an agreement to Redfern Realtors

C. Advertisements

These readings are similar to the commercial advertisements you see in newspapers and magazines. They may also include classified ads, especially from "Help Wanted," "Positions Wanted," and "Businesses Available" sections.

Overview questions about advertisements generally ask what the purpose of the ad is or what good or service is being offered. They may also ask what type of reader would be interested in this ad or where this ad probably appeared.

Detail questions often ask about the price of a good that is offered or about the time or place the goods or services are available.

Owning a franchise can be magical!

The expanding children's service market offers an excellent return on your investment — and puts a little magic into your summer. Summer Magic Day Camps franchises provide door-to-door pick-up services for children (ages 6–13) and a wide variety of activities in parks and other locations. No need to invest in expensive camp facilities, as all activities are held off-premises. You can operate the business part-time and from home. We provide all the know-how and direction needed for start-up and day-to-day operations. Very reasonable franchise fees.

For whom is this advertisement intended?
- ● People who want to operate their own business
- Ⓑ Parents of young children
- Ⓒ People who own summer camps
- Ⓓ People who want to work as camp counselors

This is an advertisement meant to attract people interested in owning a summer camp franchise as a business.

The company placing this advertisement would probably NOT provide information on which of the following?
- Ⓐ Where to hold activities
- Ⓑ What kind of activities to provide
- Ⓒ How to attract campers
- ● How to choose a site for the camp

The summer camps described in this advertisement do not have permanent camp facilities— "all activities are held off-premises." There would be no need for franchise owners to choose a site.

Exercise 7.3

Focus: Understanding and answering questions about advertisements.

Directions: Read the passages, and then mark the best answers to the questions about them based on the information in the passages.

Questions 1 to 4 are based on the following advertisement:

• • ACCESS YOUR FUTURE! • •

Today's software is wonderful, but the average software package takes about 100 hours to learn properly by yourself. Professional instruction can cut this to 20 hours — 12 hours in the computer lab and 8 hours of personal effort.

CompuClass offers instruction from top teachers in leading-edge, hands-on computer labs. Courses in all areas available, from basics to advanced applications. Mention this ad and get 25% off on any course priced less than $200.
Day sessions — Tues. and Thurs. 9-12, 1-4 (one-hour lunch break)
Evening sessions — Mon., Wed., and Fri. 5:30-9:30

Introduction to computers		$129	Database $189
Word processing	$169	Desktop publishing	$229
Spreadsheeting	$189	Internet seminar	$149
Graphics programs	$209		

Call for a complete information bulletin.

1. What is being offered?
   - (A) Training
   - (B) Computers
   - (C) Software
   - (D) Jobs

2. At what time do Tuesday and Thursday sessions end?
   - (A) At noon
   - (B) At 1 PM
   - (C) At 4 PM
   - (D) At 9:30 PM

3. According to the advertisement, how many hours of lab work are recommended to learn a typical software package?
   - (A) 8 hours
   - (B) 12 hours
   - (C) 20 hours
   - (D) 100 hours

4. Which of the following is NOT available at a 20% discount?
   - (A) Introduction to computers
   - (B) Word processing
   - (C) Internet seminar
   - (D) Desktop publishing

Questions 5 and 6 refer to the following advertisement:

This is the Sonic Brush — a remarkable new toothbrush that uses imperceptible ultrasonic vibrations to massage the tissues of your gums and interrupt the growth of bacteria. Tests show the Sonic Brush significantly reduces bacterial plaque and gum bleeding. Use as you would a regular toothbrush. No harsh vibrations, no messy water sprays. Dentist recommended. Regularly $149, now only $119 — a discount of almost 20%!

5. What claim is NOT made for this toothbrush?
   - (A) It is easier to use than ordinary toothbrushes.
   - (B) It reduces gum infections and plaque.
   - (C) It is recommended by dentists.
   - (D) It does not cause pain.

6. What is the current price of this toothbrush?
   - (A) $20
   - (B) $30
   - (C) $119
   - (D) $149

Questions 7 to 9 refer to this classified advertisement:

TWO AMBITIOUS PEOPLE NEEDED FOR INTERNATIONAL SALES TEAM

International publishing company requires diligent, articulate personnel to sell advertising for our worldwide family of magazines.

Successful candidates will receive comprehensive training in London. Posting to Singapore, Dubai, or Toronto follows. Generous base salary plus one of highest commissions in the industry. Some top agents have earned up to £45,000 in their first year.

Experience in international sales very desirable. Initially do not send CV but call the Personnel Office mornings only.

7. In which of the following cities is a successful candidate NOT likely to work on a permanent basis?
   - (A) Toronto
   - (B) London
   - (C) Dubai
   - (D) Singapore

8. How should the figure of £45,000 mentioned in the advertisement be regarded?
   - (A) As a base salary
   - (B) As an average first-year commission
   - (C) As a maximum salary
   - (D) As an excellent first-year income

9. What should someone who is interested in one of these positions do first?
   - (A) Mail a CV to the company
   - (B) Call the Personnel Office in the morning
   - (C) Come to the office for an interview
   - (D) Attend the training session

Questions 10 and 11 refer to the following advertisement:

World Fares Travel
Great Business Rates to Europe

(no Saturday overnight stay required)

	One way	Round trip
London	$320	
Paris	$340	
Frankfurt		$600
Rome		$640
Athens	$390	

Offer good only on flights before May 31.
All fares require a 2-week advance purchase.
Non-refundable, no changes.

Call for other cities.

10. A trip to and from which of the following cities would be LEAST expensive?
    - Ⓐ London
    - Ⓑ Paris
    - Ⓒ Frankfurt
    - Ⓓ Rome

11. Which of the following is NOT a requirement for purchasers of these tickets?
    - Ⓐ Buying tickets before May 31
    - Ⓑ Staying at least two days in these cities
    - Ⓒ Buying tickets at least two weeks before flying
    - Ⓓ Spending the weekend in the destination city

D. Announcements

Announcements (and notices) are brief readings meant to inform the public. Typically they concern the hours of a new business, the introduction of a new product or service, the availability of a business opportunity, the statement of a government or business policy, the opening of a cultural attraction, and other similar situations.

Overview questions about announcements often ask about the purpose of the announcement or the audience for it. Detail questions often ask about time, place, and price.

Sample Items: Announcements

"American Impressionism and Realism: The Paintings of Modern Life, 1885–1915." This display features more than 80 paintings that contrast two important turn-of-the-century schools of art. Featured artists include impressionists John Singer Sargent and Mary Cassatt and realists Robert Henri, John Sloan, and William Blackins. At the Los Angeles Museum of Art through May 24.

What is the main theme of this display?
- Ⓐ The range of contemporary painting in Los Angeles
- Ⓑ The contrast between today's art and turn-of-the-century art
- Ⓒ Paintings produced by students from two universities
- ⬤ Differences between two important styles of art

The announcement states that the paintings in the display "contrast two important turn-of-the-century schools of art." (In this context, "school of art" means "style of art"— it does not refer to a university.)

Which of the following artists is NOT considered a realist?
- Ⓐ John Sloan
- ⬤ Mary Cassatt
- Ⓒ William Blackins
- Ⓓ Robert Henri

The passage identifies Mary Cassatt as an impressionist and the other three choices as realists.

Exercise 7.4

Focus: Understanding and answering questions about announcements.

Directions: Read the passages, and then mark the best answers to the questions about them based on the information in the passages.

Questions 1 to 5 refer to the following notice:

All passengers who are nationals of countries other than the United States or Canada must complete an Immigration Form before arrival in the U.S. Fill out one for each family member. Do not write on the back. Write in English in all capital letters. Keep the form until your departure from the United States. Use the white I-94 form if you have a valid U.S. visa. Use the green I-94W form if you hold a passport from one of the 22 countries participating in the visa-waiver program and do not have a valid U.S. visa. Use the blue I-94T form if you are only making an in-transit stop en route to another country.

All passengers (or one passenger per family) are required to complete a Customs Declaration Form prior to arrival. Complete it in English and in capital letters. Be sure to sign your name on the back of the form.

1. How many Immigration Forms must be filled out by a family of two adults and one child who are not U.S. or Canadian nationals?
   Ⓐ None   Ⓒ Two
   Ⓑ One   Ⓓ Three

2. What should a traveler do with the Immigration Form?
   Ⓐ Give it to an immigrations agent
   Ⓑ Keep it until leaving the U.S.
   Ⓒ Fill it out after arrival
   Ⓓ Give it to a U.S. Customs agent

3. If you are changing planes in Miami on a flight from Madrid to Mexico City, which form should you fill out?
   Ⓐ A white one   Ⓒ A blue one
   Ⓑ A green one   Ⓓ No form is required

4. Who must fill out a Customs Declaration Form?
   Ⓐ Each passenger, or one passenger per family
   Ⓑ Everyone except U.S. and Canadian nationals
   Ⓒ Only U.S. residents
   Ⓓ Only passengers from 22 designated countries

5. What should passengers write on the back of the Customs Declaration Forms?
   Ⓐ Nothing
   Ⓑ Their signatures
   Ⓒ Their flight number
   Ⓓ The date

Questions 6 to 8 refer to the following notice:

By signing this airbill, sender agrees that Nova Express is not responsible for any claim due to loss, damage, non-delivery, or misdelivery in excess of $100 unless the sender declares a higher value and pays additional charges based on that higher value. Declared value of the package cannot exceed $500. In the event of untimely delivery, Nova Express will at sender's request refund delivery charges. See back of airbill for further information.

6. What is the purpose of this notice?
   - (A) To discuss how Nova Express can improve its service
   - (B) To inform customers of Nova Express's limits of liabilities
   - (C) To convince potential customers to choose Nova Express
   - (D) To explain how government regulations affect Nova Express

7. If a package is delivered late, how much money will Nova Express give to the sender?
   - (A) None
   - (B) $100
   - (C) $500
   - (D) The amount paid for delivery

8. To obtain more information, what should the sender do?
   - (A) Read the back of the airbill
   - (B) Ask for a special form
   - (C) Sign the airbill
   - (D) Call a Nova Express office

Questions 9 to 13 are based on the following announcement:

Have you always wanted to know the secrets of professional quality black-and-white nature photography? In our first class, held on Thursday evening, we will discuss exposure, composition, lighting, and equipment. Saturday involves an all-day outdoor shooting session. Sunday, participants practice simple darkroom techniques and develop the photos shot on Saturday. (Instructor provides darkroom equipment and supplies.) The workshop ends Monday evening with a review and critique of photographs taken. Bring camera, four rolls of black-and-white film, and enthusiasm.

Location:	Middleton Recreation Center	
Dates:	Oct. 12, 14, 15, and 16	
Fees:	City residents	— advance registration $75
		on-site registration $80
	Non-city residents	— advance registration $95
		on-site registration $100

9. On what type of photographs will the participants focus?
   - (A) Color photographs
   - (B) Photographs taken by professionals
   - (C) Portraits taken in a studio
   - (D) Nature photographs

10. According to the announcement, what does the instructor provide?
   - (A) Film
   - (B) Darkroom chemicals
   - (C) Cameras
   - (D) An enthusiastic attitude

11. What will participants do during the Sunday session?
   - (A) Take photographs
   - (B) Develop photographs taken the day before
   - (C) Plan photographs to take the next day
   - (D) Pose for photographs

12. On what date will participants have their photographs evaluated?
   - (A) October 12   (C) October 15
   - (B) October 14   (D) October 16

13. For whom is this class LEAST expensive?
   - (A) Residents who register in advance
   - (B) Nonresidents who register in advance
   - (C) Residents who register on-site
   - (D) Nonresidents who register on-site

E. Non-prose Readings

These readings are not written in standard paragraph style and may not employ complete sentences. This category of readings includes forms (especially those used by businesses), lists, charts, graphs, schedules, and maps. There are usually one or two non-prose readings per test.

Unlike other types of readings, you should *not* read non-prose readings word for word. Glance at the reading to see what the reading is and what it concerns; then start working on the questions. Refer back to the reading to find specific information.

Sample Items: Non-Prose Reading

METRO LODGING REPORT: JULY

Location	Room Nights		Occupancy Percentage	Average Room Cost
	Occupied	Available		
Airport	89,649	104,847	85.5%	$68.28
North suburban	29,686	35,065	84.7%	$53.75
West suburban	46,279	50,950	90.8%	$57.78
Midtown	29,681	37,851	78.0%	$49.70
Downtown	62,620	77,271	81.0%	$79.61

What does this report concern?
- Ⓐ Apartment buildings
- ● Hotels
- Ⓒ Parking lots
- Ⓓ Office buildings

The term "lodging" indicates that the report deals with hotel rooms.

Which area had the highest rate of occupancy in July?
- Ⓐ North Suburban
- Ⓑ Midtown
- ● West suburban
- Ⓓ Downtown

At 90.8%, the West Suburban area had the highest occupancy rate. (North Suburban had 84.7%, Midtown had 78%, and Downtown had 81%.)

What information does the chart provide about Downtown?
- ● On the average, it had the most expensive rooms.
- Ⓑ It had fewer empty rooms in July than Midtown did.
- Ⓒ It had more rooms than any other area.
- Ⓓ There were more rooms per building than in other areas.

At an average price of $79.61, Downtown hotel rooms were the most expensive.

Exercise 7.5

Focus: Understanding and answering questions about non-prose readings.

Directions: Read the passages, and then mark the best answers to the questions about them based on the information in the passages.

Questions 1 to 4 refer to the following itinerary:

NORTHERN ODYSSEY TOUR
DEPARTING SEPT. 9

For your convenience, we recommend that you check your luggage through to Helsinki, Finland. Please wear your NORTHERN ODYSSEY TOUR badge during transfers to facilitate identification by our representatives.

SAT. SEPT. 9	DEPART USA via air (Please refer to your personal air itineraries for departure/arrival times.)
SUN. SEPT. 10	ARRIVE HELSINKI, FINLAND Accommodations Presidenti Hotel
TUE. SEPT. 12	DEPART HELSINKI motorcoach to dock Accommodations SS Northern Lights
FRI. SEPT. 15	ARRIVE STOCKHOLM, SWEDEN via ship Accommodations Royal Viking Hotel
MON.	SEPT. 18 DEPART STOCKHOLM via Air Scandinavia ARRIVE COPENHAGEN, DENMARK Accommodations Air Scandinavia Hotel
SAT. SEPT. 23	DEPART COPENHAGEN via Air Scandinavia Arrive OSLO, NORWAY Accommodations Princess Christiana Hotel
WED.	SEPT. 27 DEPART OSLO via railroad ARRIVE BERGEN, NORWAY Accommodations Hotel Bryggen
SUN. OCT. 1	DEPART BERGEN by air ARRIVE USA (Please refer to your personal air itineraries. All passengers are required to clear U.S. Customs.)

---

1. Why are the members of the tour asked to wear badges?
   - (A) To get seats on the plane
   - (B) To be recognized by tour representatives
   - (C) To get through customs quickly
   - (D) To recognize each other easily

2. How will members of the tour go from Helsinki to Stockholm?
   - (A) By motorcoach
   - (B) By air
   - (C) By train
   - (D) By ship

3. In which of these cities will members of the tour spend the most time?
   - (A) Copenhagen
   - (B) Stockholm
   - (C) Bergen
   - (D) Helsinki

4. How long will the complete tour take?
   - (A) 1 week
   - (B) 2 weeks
   - (C) 3 weeks
   - (D) 4 weeks

Questions 5 to 8 refer to the following form:

PURCHASE ORDER

Requested by _____

Date _____

Date needed _____

The following form is to be filled in for any purchase other than office supplies.

(A) Budgeted item ☐

(B) Non-budgeted item ☐

1. Item description (Be specific) _____
   _____
2. Quantity _____
3. Intended use _____
4. Recommended place of purchase _____
5. Actual cost (if available)/Estimated cost _____
6. Justification (non-budgeted items only) _____
   _____

- Approval _____
  Supervisor

- Non-budgeted approval _____
  Director

If unapproved, return Copy 1 to originator with comments.

Copy 1: Purchase coordinator

Copy 2: Finance office

Copy 3: Originator

5. This form is needed to purchase all of the following EXCEPT
   (A) a new computer
   (B) a box of envelopes
   (C) a desk
   (D) a file cabinet

6. What is asked for in the line marked "1" on the form?
   (A) Details about the item requested
   (B) The reasons for the purchase
   (C) The date the purchase should be made
   (D) The cost of the item purchased

7. The director does NOT have to sign this form if
   (A) the supervisor has already signed it
   (B) box B has been marked on the form
   (C) the item has been previously budgeted
   (D) line 6 has been left blank

8. Who receives Copy 1 of this form if it is not approved?
   (A) The purchase coordinator
   (B) The finance officer
   (C) The supervisor
   (D) The person requesting the item

Questions 9 to 13 refer to the following instructions:

DIALING INSTRUCTIONS

Room to room	Floors 1 through 9 (6) + room number Floors 10 through 17 (7) + room number
Local calls	8 + phone number ($.75 access charge)
Long distance direct dial	8 + 1 + area code + phone number ($1.00 access charge)
International direct dial	8 + 1 + 011 + country code + city code + phone number ($1.00 access charge)
Credit card calls	8 + 0 + area code + phone number, then follow instructions on card ($1.00 access charge)
Local information	8 + 411 ($.75 access fee)
Long distance information	8 + 1 + area code + 555-1212

Bell captain	57	Housekeeping/laundry	56	Messages	2
Business center	50	Concierge	3	Sports club	59
Front desk	0	Room service	59	Coffee shop	51

---

9. Where would these instructions probably be found?
    - (A) In an office building
    - (B) In a phone booth
    - (C) In a hotel room
    - (D) In a hotel lobby

10. What number would one call to speak to someone in Room 921?
    - (A) 921
    - (B) 6 + 921
    - (C) 7 + 921
    - (D) 8 + 921

11. According to the instructions, how is a person informed of messages?
    - (A) By a phone call from the front desk
    - (B) By visiting the Message Center
    - (C) By a written note
    - (D) By a blinking light

12. How much is the access fee to obtain the phone number of someone who lives in this city?
    - (A) Nothing
    - (B) $.75
    - (C) $1.00
    - (D) $1.25

13. What number would someone dial to have a room cleaned?
    - (A) 2
    - (B) 3
    - (C) 56
    - (D) 59

Question 14 and 15 refer to the following chart:
Figure A: "Short and wide"

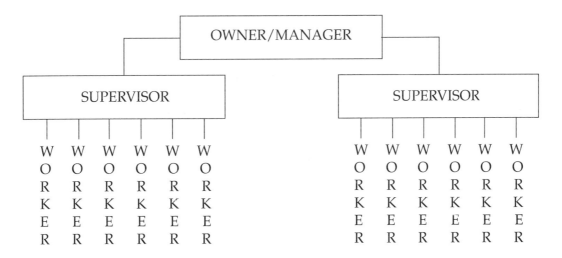

Figure B: "Tall and skinny"

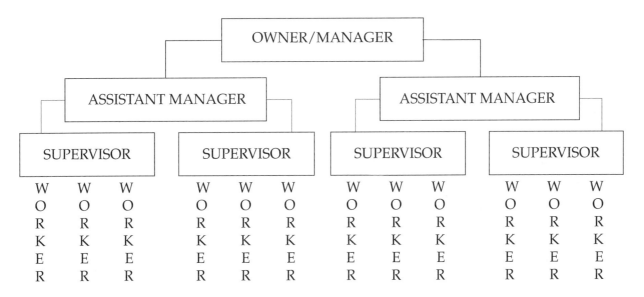

14. What would be the best title for this chart?
    Ⓐ "Two Methods for Organizing Small Businesses"
    Ⓑ "The Changing Structure of Management"
    Ⓒ "The Role of the Owner/Manager"
    Ⓓ "Workers' Responsibility: Before and After"

15. Based on the information in the chart, which of the following statements is true?
    Ⓐ "Short and wide" involves fewer workers.
    Ⓑ "Tall and skinny" involves another level of management.
    Ⓒ "Short and wide" provides more jobs for more people.
    Ⓓ "Tall and skinny" puts the owner/manager in closer contact with the workers.

More Practice

Directions: Read the passages, and then mark the best answers to the questions about them based on the information in the passages.

Questions 1 to 3 are based on the following notice:

City Golf Course encourages reservations. Only one reservation per call. For weekdays, call one full day in advance. Call Wednesday between 5 and 8 PM for Saturday and Thursday between 5 and 8 PM for Sunday. **Anyone making reservations is expected to check in with the pro shop a quarter hour prior to tee time.**

---

1. Which of these is the best heading for this notice?
   - Ⓐ "Tips for Improving Your Golf Game"
   - Ⓑ "Procedures for Making Golf Reservations"
   - Ⓒ "City Golf Course: Hours of Operation"
   - Ⓓ "Special Activities This Week at the Golf Course"

2. If you want to play golf on Tuesday, when should you call?
   - Ⓐ Monday
   - Ⓑ Tuesday
   - Ⓒ Wednesday between 5 and 8 PM
   - Ⓓ Thursday between 5 and 8 PM

3. What should you do on the day of your golf game?
   - Ⓐ Confirm your reservation by phone
   - Ⓑ Practice your golf strokes
   - Ⓒ Stop by the pro shop 15 minutes before playing
   - Ⓓ Purchase necessary equipment in the pro shop

Questions 4 to 7 are based on the following article:

Getting the right octane level in gasoline — a key to engine performance — is costly because of current evaluation methods. To ensure compliance with government regulations, refineries add more octane than necessary. Now an oil company based in Ashland, Kentucky, has developed a more accurate testing technique.

Currently, octane levels are measured by determining how much a special engine "knocks" during combustion. A new procedure called InfraTane uses infrared light to evaluate octane levels and adjust them on-line.

InfraTane has been installed in the company's St. Paul, Minnesota, refinery and will save more than $1 million a year. InfraTane has been licensed to a firm in Merrick, New York, that is expected to offer it to other refineries around the world for around $300,000.

---

4. Why do refineries add more octane than is necessary?
   - Ⓐ To save money on insurance
   - Ⓑ To follow government rules
   - Ⓒ To simplify the refining process
   - Ⓓ To satisfy customer demand

5. Which of the following is NOT true about the InfraTane procedure?
   - Ⓐ It is used during the refining process.
   - Ⓑ It involves a special testing engine.
   - Ⓒ It is more accurate than the current method.
   - Ⓓ It utilizes infrared light.

6. Where is the InfraTane procedure currently being used?
   - Ⓐ All over the world
   - Ⓑ In Ashland, Kentucky
   - Ⓒ In Merrick, New York
   - Ⓓ In St. Paul, Minnesota

7. Approximately how much will it cost for a refinery to license Infratane?
   - Ⓐ $100,000
   - Ⓑ $300,000
   - Ⓒ $1 million
   - Ⓓ $3 million

Questions 8 to 12 are based on the following introduction:

WRITE THAT CONTRACT YOURSELF workbooks contain examples of the contracts most commonly used today. The purpose of this series of workbooks is *not* to replace attorneys. Rather, it is to take the mystery and expense from contractual work by making these simple contract forms accessible to everyone.

Each workbook has a wide range of contract forms related to the area designated by the workbook title. The contracts are simplified in language to make them easier to understand. Each workbook has a glossary at the back, defining terms found in the book.

Many forms are so uncomplicated that they can be taken from the books and used right away. There will be times when readers will decide to get legal advice. In those cases, readers who have already familiarized themselves with terminology and typical contractual agreements will realize a savings in time and expense.

8. Who are the workbooks meant for?
   - (A) The general public
   - (B) Contract attorneys
   - (C) Business executives
   - (D) Authors

9. The material in the series is organized according to
   - (A) subject matter
   - (B) alphabetical order
   - (C) level of difficulty
   - (D) chronological order

10. How do actual contracts differ from the ones in these workbooks?
   - (A) They are shorter.
   - (B) They are less expensive.
   - (C) They are more complicated.
   - (D) They are less specific.

11. What is found at the end of each workbook?
   - (A) Some actual contracts
   - (B) A list of attorneys
   - (C) An index of contracts
   - (D) Definitions of terms

12. What would the author probably suggest to someone who wanted legal assistance with writing a contract?
   - (A) To use these books instead
   - (B) To consult with more than one attorney
   - (C) To refer to these workbooks first
   - (D) To give the lawyer copies of these

Drake Industries
900 McCollough Ave., Charlotte, North Carolina 28262

Lucy Rickenbach, Director
Office of Financial Planning
SouthBank
3520 Rawlins Drive
Dallas, Texas 75219

Dear Ms. Rickenbach:

Bonnie Whitmer has requested that I write to recommend her for a position in your office. Ms. Whitmer worked in my department for two years. She is well-organized and has excellent workplace communication skills. She is honest and energetic. With her degree in economics and her experience in accounting, I am sure she will contribute positively to your organization. Her only fault, as far as I know, is that, because she is such a perfectionist, she sometimes spends too much time on details.

We at Drake Industries are anxious to find positions for our employees whose jobs will be eliminated in the reorganization that will follow our upcoming merger with the Hammond Group. I'd appreciate your considering her for this position.

Please feel free to contact me for further particulars.

Sincerely,

Quinten Howe, Chief Financial Officer/Comptroller
Drake Industries

---

13. Who asked that this letter be sent?
- (A) Ann Rickenbach
- (B) Bonnie Whitmer
- (C) A representative of the Hammond Group
- (D) Ms. Whitmer's supervisor

14. The writer praises Ms. Whitmer for all of the following EXCEPT
- (A) her communication skills
- (B) her honesty
- (C) her energy
- (D) her attention to detail

15. Why is Ms. Whitmer looking for another job?
- (A) Because her position will soon be eliminated
- (B) Because she disagreed with her supervisor
- (C) Because the company where she works has gone bankrupt
- (D) Because she wants to earn a higher salary

Questions 16 to 19 are based on the following review:

THE BARONG GRILL

Service ∗∗		**Value** ∗∗∗	
Atmosphere ∗∗∗∗		**Food** ∗∗∗	

Weekday evenings $$$
Weekend evenings $$$$

120 Stanhope Street
Open 6-10 Tues-Thurs
9-11 Fri-Sun

This new Indonesian restaurant, located in a building that has housed a Mexican and an Indian restaurant in recent times, seems headed for success. The restaurant has been completely remodeled and decorated with fascinating Javanese and Balinese artifacts. Indonesian gamelin music plays in the background. Indonesian favorites, such as *satay* (grilled meat on a skewer), *gado gado* (spinach salad with peanut dressing), and *nasi goreng* (fried rice) are specialties here. On Friday, Saturday, and Sunday nights, a *rijstafel* (a Dutch word meaning "rice table") is served. This is a magnificent feast involving dozens of exotic Indonesian dishes. My only complaint was the service, which was a bit slow the night I dined there.

Ratings guide:		Price per person	
Poor	∗	Less than $10	$
Fair	∗∗	$10 to $20	$$
Good	∗∗∗	$20 to $35	$$$
Excellent	∗∗∗∗	$35 to $50	$$$$
Best in town	∗∗∗∗∗	Over $50	$$$$$

16. What did the reviewer like best about this restaurant?
Ⓐ The service
Ⓑ The food
Ⓒ The value
Ⓓ The atmosphere

17. When is this restaurant closed?
Ⓐ Monday
Ⓑ Tuesday
Ⓒ Thursday
Ⓓ Sunday

18. What kind of food is served in the restaurant reviewed here?
Ⓐ Indian
Ⓑ Dutch
Ⓒ Indonesian
Ⓓ Mexican

19. How much does an average dinner cost per person on Saturday evening?
Ⓐ Less than $10
Ⓑ Between $20 and $35
Ⓒ Between $35 and $50
Ⓓ Over $50

Questions 20 to 22 are based on the following chart:

	Verbal interpretation (per hour)	Text translation (per page)	Phrase book
Bangkok	$10	$8	$3–$7
Hong Kong	$20	$21	$4+
Jakarta	$9	$5	$2–$16
Kuala Lumpur	$16	$12	$4–$7
Manila	$10	$6	$1–$9
Seoul	$67	$7	$3
Singapore	$28	$9	$10–$23
Taipei	$12	$5	$2–$4
Tokyo	$43	$38	$12–$26

20. What is the best heading for this chart?
- Ⓐ "The Cost of Communicating in Asia"
- Ⓑ "The Growing Cost of Translation"
- Ⓒ "The World's Best Phrase Books"
- Ⓓ "How to Communicate in Asia"

21. In which city do all phrase books cost more than a page of text translation?
- Ⓐ Bangkok
- Ⓒ Singapore
- Ⓑ Manila
- Ⓓ Taipei

22. In which city is the price discrepancy between verbal interpretation and text translation greatest?
- Ⓐ Hong Kong
- Ⓒ Seoul
- Ⓑ Jakarta
- Ⓓ Tokyo

Questions 23 to 25 are based on the following article:

Australian archaeologists have found a huge Stone Age "factory" where, 2,000 years ago, aboriginal people crafted stone blades and cutting tools for barter. The site at Tiboobura is so large that archaeologists believe it formed the basis for an export business. The ancient toolmakers probably traded for *pituri*, a drug used to counteract hunger pangs during long treks between hunting grounds. The find follows the recent discovery of a 60,000-year-old human bone in central Australia. That discovery pushed back the date of human habitation in Australia by 20,000 years.

23. Why did the aboriginal people make tools at Tiboobura?
- Ⓐ For hunting
- Ⓑ To trade them
- Ⓒ For self-defense
- Ⓓ To make other tools

24. How did the aboriginal people use the drug *pituri*?
- Ⓐ To relieve feelings of hunger
- Ⓑ To make themselves more alert
- Ⓒ To treat injuries
- Ⓓ To relax

25. Before the discovery of the bone in central Australia, when were humans believed to have first come to Australia?
- Ⓐ 2,000 years ago
- Ⓒ 40,000 years ago
- Ⓑ 20,000 years ago
- Ⓓ 60,000 years ago

Questions 26 to 28 refer to the following reading:

26. What does the reading probably represent?
    (A) The index of a business textbook
    (B) The outline of a business plan
    (C) The table of contents for a company's policy manual
    (D) The schedule for a corporate training program

27. A person who wanted information about taking a business trip would look on what page?
    (A) Page 2   (C) Page 22
    (B) Page 19   (D) Page 36

28. The most information is probably available regarding
    (A) insurance
    (B) overtime
    (C) profit sharing plan
    (D) educational assistance

Questions 29 to 31 are based on the following article:

Hong Kong toy manufacturers have been shifting some of their operations from Hong Kong and China to Macao, Indonesia, and Malaysia. Indonesia and Malaysia are attractive because of their GSP (Generalized System of Preferences) export benefits from the United States. Macao is also a GSP beneficiary and is permitted to export Chinese labor. China, however, remains the most important center of Hong Kong toy-making, which is the territory's fifth largest export industry. The U.S. is the most important customer, buying 50% of the toys exported by Hong Kong last year.

29. Which of the following countries did NOT benefit from the recent shift in Hong Kong's toy-making operations?
    (A) Macao   (C) Indonesia
    (B) China   (D) Malaysia

30. What is the GSP?
    (A) A system of improving the quality of toys
    (B) A contract between Hong Kong toy-makers and those in other Asian countries
    (C) An agreement giving preferential treatment to Hong Kong
    (D) Trade benefits provided by the United States to certain countries

31. According to the article, which of the following is a truthful statement about Hong Kong's toy-making industry?
    (A) It has been moved entirely out of Hong Kong.
    (B) Only four other export industries are of more importance to Hong Kong.
    (C) It provides more than 50% of the toys bought by the United States.
    (D) Competition from other countries has

Questions 32 and 33 deal with the following article:

If you are driving in the snow and need to stop, "pump the brakes." This technique allows you to stop your car on the slickest street. Depress the brake pedal firmly with a single stroke, then release the pressure immediately. Repeat until you come to a stop. When turning on icy streets, if your car starts to spin, steer into the turn. In other words, if your car's rear end slides to the right, gently steer to the right. If it slides to the left, gently steer to the left. Once the car has begun to straighten, steer straight ahead. When at a dead stop, use gentle acceleration to move forward in order to avoid spinning the tires so rapidly that they fail to grip the snow.

32. Which of these techniques is NOT discussed in the reading?
- (A) Turning the car on icy streets
- (B) Getting the engine started on cold days
- (C) Stopping the car on slick streets
- (D) Getting the car into motion on snowy streets

33. Which of the following should you do if your car's rear end starts to slide to the right?
- (A) Gently steer to the right
- (B) Hit the brakes hard, then release
- (C) Quickly turn the steering wheel to the left
- (D) Accelerate, then steer straight ahead

Questions 34 and 35 are based on the following advertisement:

> **Rooms available at 1890s bed-and-breakfast lodge, near Jackson Hole, Wyoming. Views of the Grand Teton range from our four decks and ten-person outdoor hot tub. Horseback riding, tennis, fishing on our property. Call Tom or Norma Blake at the Bighorn Lodge.**

34. Who is this advertisement intended for?
- (A) People who want lodging at a vacation resort
- (B) People who want to work at a hotel
- (C) People who are traveling on business
- (D) People who want to own property in Wyoming

35. Which of the following is probably NOT located on the property of the Bighorn Lodge?
- (A) A tennis court
- (B) A stable for horses
- (C) A swimming pool
- (D) A place to fish

Questions 36 and 37 refer to the following passage:

> **free trade association:** An organization involving two or more countries which have mutually agreed to eliminate tariffs, quotas, and other restrictions on trade. Unlike customs unions, which also eliminate trade barriers, free trade associations do not have a common external trade policy or common external tariff. Member nations are free to set their own tariffs with the rest of the world. (See also *common market, customs union, federation,* and *free trade policy.*)

36. Where did this passage probably appear?
- (A) In a dictionary of terms used in international trade
- (B) In a newspaper article concerning a recent trade agreement
- (C) In a textbook dealing with international diplomacy
- (D) In a footnote to an article in an economics journal

37. In what way is a free trade association similar to a customs union?
- (A) In both, members share the same external trade policy.
- (B) Both make it easier for members to trade with other members.
- (C) In both, members eliminate tariffs and quotas with the rest of the world.
- (D) Both make it possible for members to collect more tariffs from other members.

Questions 38 to 40 refer to the following chart:

SOCORRO COUNTY'S WORKFORCE

	1985	1990	1995
Average age	34.2	33.5	31.6
Bachelor's degree or higher	56.4 %	57.0 %	59.2 %
Executive, managerial, or administrative	14.0 %	13.8 %	15.6 %
Professional	18.1 %	20.8 %	22.6 %
Retail trade	16.4 %	16.5 %	16.5 %
Manufacturing	25.4 %	23.8 %	21.0 %
Government	18.1 %	20.8 %	17.0 %
Construction	5.4 %	5.2 %	4.0 %
Finance, insurance, and real estate	2.5 %	2.9 %	3.3 %

38. Which of the following could account for the changes in the "average age" data from 1985 to 1995?
  Ⓐ County families had more children.
  Ⓑ Some retired workers returned to the workforce.
  Ⓒ A number of workers in their twenties moved to the county.
  Ⓓ Many young workers returned to the university to get better jobs later.

39. Based on the information in the chart, which of the following trends reversed itself between 1985 and 1995?
  Ⓐ The growth in the percentage of people with at least bachelor degrees
  Ⓑ The decline in the percentage of people working in manufacturing
  Ⓒ The drop in the percentage of people working in the construction field
  Ⓓ The increase in the number of people working for the government

40. The percentage of people working in which of these fields remained most stable during the ten-year period?
  Ⓐ Executive, managerial, and administrative
  Ⓑ Retail trade
  Ⓒ Professional
  Ⓓ Finance, insurance, and real estate

Practice TOEIC Test

How to Take the Practice Test

This practice test is designed to be as close as possible to those given by ETS in terms of length, format, and level of difficulty.

If you are taking this test at home, be sure to follow these procedures:

- Take the entire test at one time. This will help you work on your overall timing and give you a feel for what it is like to take an actual test.

- Work at a desk or table, not in an easy chair or sofa. Work away from distractors such as televisions and stereos.

- Mark your answers on the answer sheet provided rather than on the test.

- Check your answers in the Answer Key and read the explanations provided for parts IV, VI, and VII.

- Go back and look at items that you answered incorrectly. Make sure you understand *why* you answered that item incorrectly.

- If possible, take the entire test a second time, using another answer sheet. (You may want to copy the answer sheet before you take the test the first time.)

Scoring the Practice Test

No practice test can provide you with a completely accurate prediction of what your score will be on an actual test. However, this chart will help you make a reasonable estimate of what your score on TOEIC may be.

To use the chart, calculate your raw score from both Listening and Reading by counting the number of correct answers. Then use the chart to calculate your converted score for each section. Add these two scores for your overall test score.

For example, if your raw score for Listening is 63, your converted score is 315. If your raw score for Reading is 74, your converted score is 320.

$$315 + 320 = 635$$

Your overall score is 635.

Score Conversion Chart

Raw Scores	Converted Scores: Listening	Converted Scores: Reading	Raw Scores	Converted Scores: Listening	Converted Scores: Reading
98 – 100	495	470	56	260	215
97	495	465	55	255	210
96	495	460	54	250	205
95	495	455	53	245	200
94	490	450	52	235	190
93	490	445	51	230	185
92	485	435	50	225	180
91	480	430	49	220	175
90	475	425	48	215	165
89	470	415	47	205	160
88	465	410	46	200	155
87	460	400	45	195	150
86	455	395	44	185	140
85	450	390	43	180	135
84	445	385	42	175	130
83	435	380	41	165	125
82	430	370	40	160	120
81	425	365	39	155	115
80	420	360	38	145	105
79	410	350	37	140	100
78	400	345	36	135	95
77	390	340	35	130	90
76	385	335	34	120	85
75	380	330	33	115	80
74	375	320	32	110	75
73	365	315	31	105	65
72	360	310	30	100	60
71	350	305	29	90	55
70	345	300	28	85	50
69	340	295	27	80	40
68	335	285	26	70	35
67	330	280	25	65	30
66	325	275	24	60	25
65	320	270	23	50	20
64	310	265	22	45	15
63	305	255	21	40	10
62	300	250	20	35	10
61	290	245	19	30	10
60	285	240	18	25	5
59	275	230	17	20	5
58	270	225	16	15	5
57	265	220	0 – 15	5	5

Practice Test: Answer Sheet

Listening Comprehension

1. Ⓐ Ⓑ Ⓒ Ⓓ	35. Ⓐ Ⓑ Ⓒ Ⓓ	69. Ⓐ Ⓑ Ⓒ Ⓓ
2. Ⓐ Ⓑ Ⓒ Ⓓ	36. Ⓐ Ⓑ Ⓒ Ⓓ	70. Ⓐ Ⓑ Ⓒ Ⓓ
3. Ⓐ Ⓑ Ⓒ Ⓓ	37. Ⓐ Ⓑ Ⓒ Ⓓ	71. Ⓐ Ⓑ Ⓒ Ⓓ
4. Ⓐ Ⓑ Ⓒ Ⓓ	38. Ⓐ Ⓑ Ⓒ Ⓓ	72. Ⓐ Ⓑ Ⓒ Ⓓ
5. Ⓐ Ⓑ Ⓒ Ⓓ	39. Ⓐ Ⓑ Ⓒ Ⓓ	73. Ⓐ Ⓑ Ⓒ Ⓓ
6. Ⓐ Ⓑ Ⓒ Ⓓ	40. Ⓐ Ⓑ Ⓒ Ⓓ	74. Ⓐ Ⓑ Ⓒ Ⓓ
7. Ⓐ Ⓑ Ⓒ Ⓓ	41. Ⓐ Ⓑ Ⓒ Ⓓ	75. Ⓐ Ⓑ Ⓒ Ⓓ
8. Ⓐ Ⓑ Ⓒ Ⓓ	42. Ⓐ Ⓑ Ⓒ Ⓓ	76. Ⓐ Ⓑ Ⓒ Ⓓ
9. Ⓐ Ⓑ Ⓒ Ⓓ	43. Ⓐ Ⓑ Ⓒ Ⓓ	77. Ⓐ Ⓑ Ⓒ Ⓓ
10. Ⓐ Ⓑ Ⓒ Ⓓ	44. Ⓐ Ⓑ Ⓒ Ⓓ	78. Ⓐ Ⓑ Ⓒ Ⓓ
11. Ⓐ Ⓑ Ⓒ Ⓓ	45. Ⓐ Ⓑ Ⓒ Ⓓ	79. Ⓐ Ⓑ Ⓒ Ⓓ
12. Ⓐ Ⓑ Ⓒ Ⓓ	46. Ⓐ Ⓑ Ⓒ Ⓓ	80. Ⓐ Ⓑ Ⓒ Ⓓ
13. Ⓐ Ⓑ Ⓒ Ⓓ	47. Ⓐ Ⓑ Ⓒ Ⓓ	81. Ⓐ Ⓑ Ⓒ Ⓓ
14. Ⓐ Ⓑ Ⓒ Ⓓ	48. Ⓐ Ⓑ Ⓒ Ⓓ	82. Ⓐ Ⓑ Ⓒ Ⓓ
15. Ⓐ Ⓑ Ⓒ Ⓓ	49. Ⓐ Ⓑ Ⓒ Ⓓ	83. Ⓐ Ⓑ Ⓒ Ⓓ
16. Ⓐ Ⓑ Ⓒ Ⓓ	50. Ⓐ Ⓑ Ⓒ Ⓓ	84. Ⓐ Ⓑ Ⓒ Ⓓ
17. Ⓐ Ⓑ Ⓒ Ⓓ	51. Ⓐ Ⓑ Ⓒ Ⓓ	85. Ⓐ Ⓑ Ⓒ Ⓓ
18. Ⓐ Ⓑ Ⓒ Ⓓ	52. Ⓐ Ⓑ Ⓒ Ⓓ	86. Ⓐ Ⓑ Ⓒ Ⓓ
19. Ⓐ Ⓑ Ⓒ Ⓓ	53. Ⓐ Ⓑ Ⓒ Ⓓ	87. Ⓐ Ⓑ Ⓒ Ⓓ
20. Ⓐ Ⓑ Ⓒ Ⓓ	54. Ⓐ Ⓑ Ⓒ Ⓓ	88. Ⓐ Ⓑ Ⓒ Ⓓ
21. Ⓐ Ⓑ Ⓒ Ⓓ	55. Ⓐ Ⓑ Ⓒ Ⓓ	89. Ⓐ Ⓑ Ⓒ Ⓓ
22. Ⓐ Ⓑ Ⓒ Ⓓ	56. Ⓐ Ⓑ Ⓒ Ⓓ	90. Ⓐ Ⓑ Ⓒ Ⓓ
23. Ⓐ Ⓑ Ⓒ Ⓓ	57. Ⓐ Ⓑ Ⓒ Ⓓ	91. Ⓐ Ⓑ Ⓒ Ⓓ
24. Ⓐ Ⓑ Ⓒ Ⓓ	58. Ⓐ Ⓑ Ⓒ Ⓓ	92. Ⓐ Ⓑ Ⓒ Ⓓ
25. Ⓐ Ⓑ Ⓒ Ⓓ	59. Ⓐ Ⓑ Ⓒ Ⓓ	93. Ⓐ Ⓑ Ⓒ Ⓓ
26. Ⓐ Ⓑ Ⓒ Ⓓ	60. Ⓐ Ⓑ Ⓒ Ⓓ	94. Ⓐ Ⓑ Ⓒ Ⓓ
27. Ⓐ Ⓑ Ⓒ Ⓓ	61. Ⓐ Ⓑ Ⓒ Ⓓ	95. Ⓐ Ⓑ Ⓒ Ⓓ
28. Ⓐ Ⓑ Ⓒ Ⓓ	62. Ⓐ Ⓑ Ⓒ Ⓓ	96. Ⓐ Ⓑ Ⓒ Ⓓ
29. Ⓐ Ⓑ Ⓒ Ⓓ	63. Ⓐ Ⓑ Ⓒ Ⓓ	97. Ⓐ Ⓑ Ⓒ Ⓓ
30. Ⓐ Ⓑ Ⓒ Ⓓ	64. Ⓐ Ⓑ Ⓒ Ⓓ	98. Ⓐ Ⓑ Ⓒ Ⓓ
31. Ⓐ Ⓑ Ⓒ Ⓓ	65. Ⓐ Ⓑ Ⓒ Ⓓ	99. Ⓐ Ⓑ Ⓒ Ⓓ
32. Ⓐ Ⓑ Ⓒ Ⓓ	66. Ⓐ Ⓑ Ⓒ Ⓓ	100. Ⓐ Ⓑ Ⓒ Ⓓ
33. Ⓐ Ⓑ Ⓒ Ⓓ	67. Ⓐ Ⓑ Ⓒ Ⓓ	
34. Ⓐ Ⓑ Ⓒ Ⓓ	68. Ⓐ Ⓑ Ⓒ Ⓓ	

Reading Comprehension

101. Ⓐ Ⓑ Ⓒ Ⓓ	135. Ⓐ Ⓑ Ⓒ Ⓓ	169. Ⓐ Ⓑ Ⓒ Ⓓ
102. Ⓐ Ⓑ Ⓒ Ⓓ	136. Ⓐ Ⓑ Ⓒ Ⓓ	170. Ⓐ Ⓑ Ⓒ Ⓓ
103. Ⓐ Ⓑ Ⓒ Ⓓ	137. Ⓐ Ⓑ Ⓒ Ⓓ	171. Ⓐ Ⓑ Ⓒ Ⓓ
104. Ⓐ Ⓑ Ⓒ Ⓓ	138. Ⓐ Ⓑ Ⓒ Ⓓ	172. Ⓐ Ⓑ Ⓒ Ⓓ
105. Ⓐ Ⓑ Ⓒ Ⓓ	139. Ⓐ Ⓑ Ⓒ Ⓓ	173. Ⓐ Ⓑ Ⓒ Ⓓ
106. Ⓐ Ⓑ Ⓒ Ⓓ	140. Ⓐ Ⓑ Ⓒ Ⓓ	174. Ⓐ Ⓑ Ⓒ Ⓓ
107. Ⓐ Ⓑ Ⓒ Ⓓ	141. Ⓐ Ⓑ Ⓒ Ⓓ	175. Ⓐ Ⓑ Ⓒ Ⓓ
108. Ⓐ Ⓑ Ⓒ Ⓓ	142. Ⓐ Ⓑ Ⓒ Ⓓ	176. Ⓐ Ⓑ Ⓒ Ⓓ
109. Ⓐ Ⓑ Ⓒ Ⓓ	143. Ⓐ Ⓑ Ⓒ Ⓓ	177. Ⓐ Ⓑ Ⓒ Ⓓ
110. Ⓐ Ⓑ Ⓒ Ⓓ	144. Ⓐ Ⓑ Ⓒ Ⓓ	178. Ⓐ Ⓑ Ⓒ Ⓓ
111. Ⓐ Ⓑ Ⓒ Ⓓ	145. Ⓐ Ⓑ Ⓒ Ⓓ	179. Ⓐ Ⓑ Ⓒ Ⓓ
112. Ⓐ Ⓑ Ⓒ Ⓓ	146. Ⓐ Ⓑ Ⓒ Ⓓ	180. Ⓐ Ⓑ Ⓒ Ⓓ
113. Ⓐ Ⓑ Ⓒ Ⓓ	147. Ⓐ Ⓑ Ⓒ Ⓓ	181. Ⓐ Ⓑ Ⓒ Ⓓ
114. Ⓐ Ⓑ Ⓒ Ⓓ	148. Ⓐ Ⓑ Ⓒ Ⓓ	182. Ⓐ Ⓑ Ⓒ Ⓓ
115. Ⓐ Ⓑ Ⓒ Ⓓ	149. Ⓐ Ⓑ Ⓒ Ⓓ	183. Ⓐ Ⓑ Ⓒ Ⓓ
116. Ⓐ Ⓑ Ⓒ Ⓓ	150. Ⓐ Ⓑ Ⓒ Ⓓ	184. Ⓐ Ⓑ Ⓒ Ⓓ
117. Ⓐ Ⓑ Ⓒ Ⓓ	151. Ⓐ Ⓑ Ⓒ Ⓓ	185. Ⓐ Ⓑ Ⓒ Ⓓ
118. Ⓐ Ⓑ Ⓒ Ⓓ	152. Ⓐ Ⓑ Ⓒ Ⓓ	186. Ⓐ Ⓑ Ⓒ Ⓓ
119. Ⓐ Ⓑ Ⓒ Ⓓ	153. Ⓐ Ⓑ Ⓒ Ⓓ	187. Ⓐ Ⓑ Ⓒ Ⓓ
120. Ⓐ Ⓑ Ⓒ Ⓓ	154. Ⓐ Ⓑ Ⓒ Ⓓ	188. Ⓐ Ⓑ Ⓒ Ⓓ
121. Ⓐ Ⓑ Ⓒ Ⓓ	155. Ⓐ Ⓑ Ⓒ Ⓓ	189. Ⓐ Ⓑ Ⓒ Ⓓ
122. Ⓐ Ⓑ Ⓒ Ⓓ	156. Ⓐ Ⓑ Ⓒ Ⓓ	190. Ⓐ Ⓑ Ⓒ Ⓓ
123. Ⓐ Ⓑ Ⓒ Ⓓ	157. Ⓐ Ⓑ Ⓒ Ⓓ	191. Ⓐ Ⓑ Ⓒ Ⓓ
124. Ⓐ Ⓑ Ⓒ Ⓓ	158. Ⓐ Ⓑ Ⓒ Ⓓ	192. Ⓐ Ⓑ Ⓒ Ⓓ
125. Ⓐ Ⓑ Ⓒ Ⓓ	159. Ⓐ Ⓑ Ⓒ Ⓓ	193. Ⓐ Ⓑ Ⓒ Ⓓ
126. Ⓐ Ⓑ Ⓒ Ⓓ	160. Ⓐ Ⓑ Ⓒ Ⓓ	194. Ⓐ Ⓑ Ⓒ Ⓓ
127. Ⓐ Ⓑ Ⓒ Ⓓ	161. Ⓐ Ⓑ Ⓒ Ⓓ	195. Ⓐ Ⓑ Ⓒ Ⓓ
128. Ⓐ Ⓑ Ⓒ Ⓓ	162. Ⓐ Ⓑ Ⓒ Ⓓ	196. Ⓐ Ⓑ Ⓒ Ⓓ
129. Ⓐ Ⓑ Ⓒ Ⓓ	163. Ⓐ Ⓑ Ⓒ Ⓓ	197. Ⓐ Ⓑ Ⓒ Ⓓ
130. Ⓐ Ⓑ Ⓒ Ⓓ	164. Ⓐ Ⓑ Ⓒ Ⓓ	198. Ⓐ Ⓑ Ⓒ Ⓓ
131. Ⓐ Ⓑ Ⓒ Ⓓ	165. Ⓐ Ⓑ Ⓒ Ⓓ	199. Ⓐ Ⓑ Ⓒ Ⓓ
132. Ⓐ Ⓑ Ⓒ Ⓓ	166. Ⓐ Ⓑ Ⓒ Ⓓ	200. Ⓐ Ⓑ Ⓒ Ⓓ
133. Ⓐ Ⓑ Ⓒ Ⓓ	167. Ⓐ Ⓑ Ⓒ Ⓓ	
134. Ⓐ Ⓑ Ⓒ Ⓓ	168. Ⓐ Ⓑ Ⓒ Ⓓ	

General Directions

This exam is designed to test how well you can understand and use the English language. The test takes approximately two and a half hours to complete. It consists of seven separate parts, each with its own directions. Before you begin to work on a part, be certain that you understand the directions.

Some items will seem harder than other items. However, you should answer every one if possible. Remember, you are not penalized for guessing. If you are not able to answer every question, don't worry.

All your answers should be marked on the answer sheet found on pages 199-200. Remove this sheet before the test begins. When you are marking an answer, fill in the circle corresponding to the letter that you have chosen. The space in the circle should be completely filled in so that the letter inside is not visible, as shown in the example below:

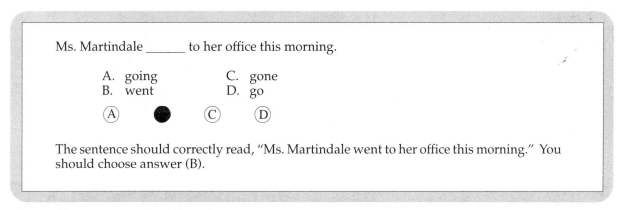

Ms. Martindale _____ to her office this morning.

    A. going   C. gone
    B. went   D. go

    Ⓐ   ●   Ⓒ   Ⓓ

The sentence should correctly read, "Ms. Martindale went to her office this morning." You should choose answer (B).

For each question, you may mark only one answer. If you decide to change your answer, you should erase your original answer completely.

Listening Comprehension

In this first section of the exam, your ability to understand spoken English will be tested. This section consists of four separate parts, each having its own directions.

Part I

Directions: For each item, there is a photograph in the book and four short sentences about it on the tape. The sentences are NOT written out, so you must listen carefully.

You must choose the one sentence — (A), (B), (C), or (D) — that is the best description of what can be seen in the photograph. Then mark the correct answer.

Look at the example

Ⓐ   Ⓑ   ●   Ⓓ

Listen to the four sentences:
Choice (C) — "He's waving to someone" — is the best description of what can be seen in the photograph.

5

9

6

10

7

11

8

12

13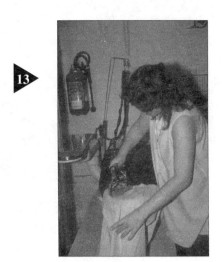

17

14

18

15

19

16

20

Part II

Directions: In this part of the test, you hear a question asked on the tape. After that, you hear three possible responses to the question. Each question and response is given only once and is not written out in your book, so listen carefully. Mark the answer that corresponds to the best response to the question.

Listen to a sample

You hear: Where have you been, Steve?

You then hear: A. At the gymnasium.
　　　　　　　　B. Very well, thanks.
　　　　　　　　C. Yes, I have.　　　　●　　Ⓑ　　Ⓒ

Choice (A), "At the gymnasium," is the best response to the question "Where have you been, Steve?" You should mark (A) on your answer sheet.

21. Mark your answer on the answer sheet.	**31.** Mark your answer on the answer sheet.	**41.** Mark your answer on the answer sheet.
22. Mark your answer on the answer sheet.	**32.** Mark your answer on the answer sheet.	**42.** Mark your answer on the answer sheet.
23. Mark your answer on the answer sheet.	**33.** Mark your answer on the answer sheet.	**43.** Mark your answer on the answer sheet.
24. Mark your answer on the answer sheet.	**34.** Mark your answer on the answer sheet.	**44.** Mark your answer on the answer sheet.
25. Mark your answer on the answer sheet.	**35.** Mark your answer on the answer sheet.	**45.** Mark your answer on the answer sheet.
26. Mark your answer on the answer sheet.	**36.** Mark your answer on the answer sheet.	**46.** Mark your answer on the answer sheet.
27. Mark your answer on the answer sheet.	**37.** Mark your answer on the answer sheet.	**47.** Mark your answer on the answer sheet.
28. Mark your answer on the answer sheet.	**38.** Mark your answer on the answer sheet.	**48.** Mark your answer on the answer sheet.
29. Mark your answer on the answer sheet.	**39.** Mark your answer on the answer sheet.	**49.** Mark your answer on the answer sheet.
30. Mark your answer on the answer sheet.	**40.** Mark your answer on the answer sheet.	**50.** Mark your answer on the answer sheet.

Part III

Directions: In this part of the test, you hear short dialogs involving two speakers. Each dialog is spoken only once and is not written out in the book, so listen carefully.

In your book, you read a question about each dialog. Following each question are four answer choices. Choose the best answer — (A), (B), (C), or (D).

Listen to a sample

You hear: Man: My wife and I plan to visit the Grand Canyon when we're in the United States.

Woman: You'll love it — it's a beautiful sight! Are you going on a bus tour?

Man: No, we're going to rent a car at the Los Angeles airport and drive there ourselves.

You read: How will the man and his wife travel to the Grand Canyon?

  A. By plane.
  B. In a rental car.
  C. By bus.
  D. In a taxi.   (A)   ●   (C)   (D)

Choice (B), "In a rental car," is the best answer to the question, "How will the man and his wife travel to the Grand Canyon?" You should choose (B).

51. At about what time is this conversation taking place?
  A. 10 AM   C. 12 noon
  B. 11 AM   D. 1 PM

52. What does Ann suggest Yoshi rent?
  A. An office
  B. Another apartment
  C. A car
  D. Some furniture

53. Where does this conversation take place?
  A. At a fruit market
  B. On a farm
  C. At customs
  D. In a restaurant

54. When must the brochures be mailed?
  A. Wednesday
  B. Thursday
  C. Next Monday
  D. Next month

55. Where should he call Linda?
  A. At home   C. At her hotel
  B. At her office   D. At the airport

56. How many big sales has the man made?
  A. None   C. Two
  B. One   D. Three

57. What has Marina found?
  A. A budget
  B. Some notes
  C. Some books
  D. A pen

58. What is Mr. Heath's plan?
  A. To increase the number of workers
  B. To obtain new orders
  C. To ask employees to work overtime
  D. To take an inventory

59. What are they discussing?
  A. A car   C. A sale
  B. A movie   D. A book

60. Why did Marcia call Mr. Stevens?
  A. To make an appointment with him
  B. To reschedule his appointment
  C. To cancel his appointment
  D. To remind him of an appointment

61. Where does David work?
   A. At a radio station
   B. At an advertising agency
   C. At a recording studio
   D. At a newspaper office

62. What is the problem?
   A. The shipping company could not find the package.
   B. The unit was not packaged.
   C. The package was not addressed properly.
   D. The invoice was not enclosed.

63. What will Rosa be doing Saturday?
   A. Skiing   C. Working
   B. Packing   D. Moving

64. What does Amy say about the watch?
   A. It is very fashionable.
   B. It belongs to her father.
   C. It is part of a collection.
   D. It is quite valuable.

65. How many evenings a week does Paul want to work?
   A. Two   C. Five
   B. Four   D. Six

66. What are they discussing?
   A. A hotel room
   B. An apartment house
   C. A hospital room
   D. A furniture store

67. What does Mr. Perkins tell her?
   A. The repairs will probably not be finished today.
   B. The copy machine must be replaced.
   C. The commercial copy center makes better copies.
   D. The meeting should probably be postponed.

68. Why is Phil concerned?
   A. He might not be reimbursed.
   B. His company is having financial problems.
   C. He might not be able to take a trip.
   D. He has lost his tickets.

69. How do they feel about the book?
   A. The man likes it, but the woman doesn't.
   B. They both think it is an impressive book.
   C. Neither of them wants to read it.
   D. They both find it too long.

70. What are they doing?
   A. Attending a play
   B. Going to a sporting event
   C. Reading newspapers
   D. Watching television

71. What does Loraine want?
   A. A glass of lemonade
   B. A hot drink
   C. Just some ice
   D. Some cold water

72. When will he call the box office?
   A. At three this afternoon
   B. At nine tonight
   C. At three on Friday afternoon
   D. At nine on Friday night

73. What is Frank upset about?
   A. The waiter's rudeness
   B. The high prices
   C. The cold soup
   D. The slow service

74. Who is the man?
   A. George Nielsen
   B. George Nielsen's cousin
   C. Eric Nielsen
   D. The host of the party

75. What kind of books does the man look for?
   A. Cheap books
   B. New books
   C. Children's books
   D. Rare books

76. Where is this conversation taking place?
   A. At a bank
   B. At a grocery store
   C. At a bus stop
   D. At a cafeteria

77. What is Ms. Anspach's occupation?
    A. Photographer
    B. Painter
    C. Nurse
    D. Salesperson

78. Why does Mr. Devon want to speak to Lee?
    A. To ask him to work on another project
    B. To criticize his work on a previous project
    C. To invite him out for a meal
    D. To offer him another office

79. What does he say about the consultants?
    A. They are not in agreement.
    B. They have not finished their work yet.
    C. They have not formed their opinions yet.
    D. They do not think there is a problem.

80. What is John's primary concern?
    A. Motivating the sales staff
    B. Bringing in new business
    C. Creating a long-term policy
    D. Saving the company money

Part IV

Directions: During this part of the exam, there are a number of brief talks. These talks are not written out and are spoken only once, so you must listen carefully.

There are two or more questions about each of the talks. Following the questions are four possible answers — (A), (B), (C), and (D). You must decide which of these best answer the questions and then mark the correct answers.

81. What is the best title for this talk?
    A. "Types of Bicycles and Their Uses"
    B. "Bicycle Safety Regulations"
    C. "How to Maintain Your Bicycle"
    D. "Recent Developments in Bicycle Design"

82. What does the speaker say about mountain bicycles?
    A. They are the least expensive.
    B. They are designed for difficult terrain.
    C. They are very lightweight.
    D. They are the most recently developed type.

83. What type of bicycle would the speaker recommend for someone who rides on both paved and unpaved surfaces?
    A. A three-speed bicycle
    B. A ten-speed bicycle
    C. A mountain bicycle
    D. A hybrid bicycle

84. When is this announcement being made?
    A. In early winter
    B. Just after a holiday weekend
    C. In late spring
    D. Just before a holiday weekend

85. Why is the blood supply low?
    A. Because of a typical seasonal drop
    B. Because donations have been lower than usual
    C. Because of numerous accidents
    D. Because the blood center has been closed

86. Which of these will a donor NOT receive?
    A. Free blood for a year
    B. A decorative pin
    C. Special mention on the radio
    D. A small snack

87. What type of blood is especially needed?
    A. AB positive
    B. AB negative
    C. A negative
    D. B positive

88. How did airline industry analysts react to the announcement?
    A. They were disappointed.
    B. They were angry.
    C. They were pleased.
    D. They were surprised.

89. Where is North American Airline's training facility presently located?
    A. In Minneapolis
    B. In Salt Lake City
    C. In Saint Louis
    D. In Atlanta

90. What benefit will the city of Minneapolis receive?
    A. Cash payments
    B. The prospect of jobs
    C. Tax revenues
    D. The status of hub city

91. When will a roll of film be available if it is brought in on Monday morning?
    A. By noon on Monday
    B. By three PM on Monday
    C. After three PM on Tuesday
    D. On Thursday or Friday

92. Which of the following is available at a special discount price?
    A. Cameras
    B. Black-and-white film
    C. Enlargements
    D. Color film

93. In what field are Clio Awards given?
    A. Film   C. Advertising
    B. Music   D. Television

94. According to the speaker, what happened in 1991?
    A. The first Clio Award ceremony was held.
    B. The Clio Award organization was reorganized.
    C. The Clio Award organization collapsed.
    D. The Clio Award ceremony was first televised.

95. How did the ceremony change after reorganization?
    A. Fewer prizes were awarded
    B. The international judges were dismissed
    C. More money was given
    D. New categories were created

96. Who is Diana Hartwick?
    A. An office worker
    B. A physical therapist
    C. A university professor
    D. A medical doctor

97. Which of these is Diana Hartwick LEAST likely to tell her seminar audience?
    A. How to sit properly in a desk chair
    B. How to arrange office equipment
    C. How to exercise to recover from injury
    D. How to position one's hands while working at a computer

98. What is the main purpose of this talk?
    A. To forecast a change in the weather
    B. To advertise a new brand of juice
    C. To explain the coming citrus-fruit shortage
    D. To describe a flood in California

99. When is the change in prices expected to occur?
    A. Tonight or tomorrow
    B. In a month
    C. In two or three months
    D. In five years

100. What does the speaker suggest?
    A. Instituting flood control
    B. Eating more fruit
    C. Stabilizing fruit prices
    D. Buying low-cost juice

THIS IS THE END OF THE LISTENING COMPREHENSION SECTION OF THE TEST.
GO ON TO THE READING COMPREHENSION SECTION.

YOU HAVE ONE HOUR AND FIFTEEN MINUTES IN WHICH TO COMPLETE
THE LAST THREE PARTS OF THE TEST.

Reading Comprehension

In this second section of the exam, your ability to understand written English will be tested. This section consists of three separate parts, each with its own directions.

Part V

Directions: This part of the test consists of incomplete sentences. Beneath each sentence, four words or phrases appear. Mark the answer choice — (A), (B), (C), or (D) — that best completes the sentence.

Example

Mr. Morales read over the contract with great _____.

    A. interesting
    B. interest
    C. interested
    D. interestingly   Ⓐ ● Ⓒ Ⓓ

This sentence should correctly read, "Mr. Morales read over the contract with great interest." Therefore the best answer is (B).

101. Ms. Nicholson was hired because of her experience, skill, and _____.
    A. creation   C. creativity
    B. creative   D. create

102. The new arrangement of machines on the factory floor _____ a number of advantages over the old arrangement.
    A. is   C. makes
    B. takes   D. has

103. There is a radio antenna _____ top of the Empire State Building in New York City.
    A. at   C. of
    B. on   D. in

104. The incidence of computer crime has _____ in recent years.
    A. been grown   C. growing
    B. grow   D. been growing

105. Welders use special masks to protect _____ faces.
    A. their   C. themselves
    B. them   D. theirs

106. This paint is meant to be used on the _____ of houses.
    A. external   C. exteriors
    B. outsiders   D. outer

107. Mr. Stavo took his car to the mechanic to have it _____.
    A. referred   C. repaired
    B. renewed   D. reformed

108. London's Heathrow Airport is _____ airports in the world.
    A. the one busiest of
    B. one of the busiest
    C. the busiest one of
    D. of the busiest one

109. William has been busy ever _____ he got to work this week.
    A. since   C. from
    B. until   D. to

110. Unemployment has dipped to its lowest _____ in several years.
    A. stage   C. step
    B. measure   D. level

111. Shinji enjoys _____ crossword puzzles while commuting to work on the train.
    A. work   C. works
    B. to work   D. working

112. The Ruhr Valley in Germany is _____ area.
    A. a heavy industrial
    B. a heavily industrialized
    C. an industrially heavy
    D. a heavily industry

113. The new bridge is not as picturesque _____ the old one, but it is much safer.
    A. as   C. like
    B. so   D. than

114. The scientific method is the _____ of all scientific research.
    A. basic   C. basing
    B. basis   D. base

115. Temporary and part-time workers make _____ a higher proportion of the work force today than they did in the past.
    A. out   C. away
    B. up   D. on

116. I invited Beverly to join us _____ work.
    A. afterwards   C. subsequent
    B. later   D. after

117. Information about employees' salaries is considered _____.
    A. confidence   C. confidential
    B. confiding   D. confident

118. This new policy must be _____ gradually to avoid confusion.
    A. implemented   C. exercised
    B. affected   D. resulted

119. Please _____ these contracts at the lawyer's office.
    A. take in   C. drop off
    B. put off   D. take over

120. The architects _____ up some preliminary plans for the new office building.
    A. draw   C. drawn
    B. drawing   D. drew

121. There are some very interesting _____ to see in New Zealand.
    A. sights   C. viewings
    B. looks   D. sightings

122. In her speech, she offered several _____ examples to support her ideas.
    A. expelling   C. repelling
    B. compelling   D. impelling

123. Mr. Chen cautioned _____ adopting the plan.
    A. along   C. at
    B. to   D. against

124. It was such an excellent report that Mrs. Tyler _____ the fact that it had been turned in late.
    A. oversaw   C. overruled
    B. overwhelmed   D. overlooked

125. She uses a time-management chart _____ how much time she should spend on each project.
    A. in determination
    B. determines
    C. to determine
    D. determination of

126. Throwing litter from cars is _____ by law.
    A. forbidding   C. inadmissible
    B. prohibited   D. permissive

127. The _____ from the sale are being donated to charity.
    A. processes   C. proceeds
    B. procedures   D. proceedings

128. Nonprofit corporations are established for purposes of public service and _____ special privileges by the government.
    A. are given   C. gave
    B. give   D. are giving

129. Lucia has finally _____ the position she always wanted.
    A. attained   C. attired
    B. attended   D. attuned

130. These beautiful rugs are all woven _____.
    A. with hands   C. by the hand
    B. by hand   D. at hand

131. Mr. and Mrs. Wills have been planning to attend the home show, but they _____ have not had the opportunity.
    A. already   C. anymore
    B. still   D. yet

132. Let's _____ at the Harbor House for dinner tonight.
    A. meet   C. to meet
    B. meeting   D. met

133. The information in this data bank is constantly being _____.
    A. dated   C. updated
    B. outdated   D. undated

134. The departmental meeting _____ next Tuesday.
    A. to be held   C. holds
    B. has held   D. will be held

135. We should get _____ to that new journal.
    A. a subscription
    B. a prescription
    C. an inscription
    D. a conscription

136. _____ Mr. Addison was not feeling well, he went to work anyway.
    A. Despite   C. Although
    B. However   D. Even so

137. I asked Habib to _____ me of the meeting.
    A. remember   C. review
    B. remark   D. remind

138. We were certain _____ we could reach an agreement by the next day.
    A. of   C. that
    B. about   D. to

139. During periods of "stagflation," inflation is high, and _____.
    A. so unemployment is
    B. unemployment too is
    C. is unemployment too
    D. so is unemployment

140. Mr. Morrison was _____ as the firm's accountant after it was learned that he had not been involved in the scheme to embezzle funds.
    A. reinstated
    B. overstated
    C. countermanded
    D. reprimanded

GO ON TO THE NEXT PART. ☞

Part VI

Directions: In each sentence in this section, four words or phrases are underlined and marked (A), (B), (C), and (D). You must choose the *one* underlined expression that must be rewritten in order to form a correct sentence. Then mark the correct answer.

Example

Every <u>workers</u> in <u>this</u> department <u>will receive</u> a bonus <u>in</u> September.
     A   B   C   D

●   Ⓑ   Ⓒ   Ⓓ

Choice (A), "workers" is incorrectly used in this sentence. The correct sentence should read, "Every worker in this department will receive a bonus in September." You should mark letter (A).

As soon as you are ready, you can begin working on this section.

141. My brother is not a <u>professionally</u>
                              A
musician, <u>but</u> he enjoys <u>playing</u> in a band
          B   C
<u>on weekends</u>.
  D

142. Mr. Shim <u>bought</u> <u>a lots</u> of <u>gifts</u> <u>at the</u>
               A   B   C   D
duty-free shops.

143. The museum <u>owns</u> several <u>works</u> <u>that</u>
                 A   B   C
were <u>painting</u> by Picasso.
     D

144. I am <u>in favor</u> of <u>adjourn</u> the <u>meeting</u> now
        A   B   C
and continuing it <u>tomorrow</u> morning.
              D

145. Before it <u>was edited</u>, the <u>training</u> video
           A   B
was <u>double</u> as long <u>as it is</u> now.
     C   D

146. I am <u>looking for</u> a roommate <u>who</u> is
           A   B
<u>easy-going</u> and has a good sense of
    C
<u>humorous</u>.
  D

147. The memo was <u>sent</u> <u>to</u> all <u>of clerical</u>
               A B   C
workers in <u>the office</u>.
       D

148. A vehicle <u>pulling</u> a trailer is four <u>times</u>
          A   B
more <u>likeable</u> to <u>be involved</u> in an acci-
      C   D
dent than a vehicle without a trailer.

149. This is <u>so</u> a difficult decision <u>that</u> I need
        A   B
more <u>time</u> to think <u>about it</u>.
    C   D

150. The <u>translation</u> was generally <u>done</u> quite
        A   B
<u>well</u>, but there were a <u>little</u> minor errors.
 C   D

151. <u>Every</u> day <u>around</u> 2.5 <u>millions</u> passengers
     A   B   C
<u>travel</u> on London's Underground.
 D

152. There is <u>no</u> question <u>in my mind</u> that, of
         A   B
the two <u>applicants</u>, Ms. Coalway has the
         C
<u>strongest</u> credentials.
    D

153. A region's hotel industry is considered

<u>health</u> when 80% <u>or more</u> of all its
 A   B
<u>hotel rooms</u> are <u>occupied</u>.
    C   D

154. One <u>of</u> my favorite <u>city</u> <u>to visit</u> in Italy <u>is</u>
     A   B   C   D
Florence.

155. Our profits were down <u>slightly</u> in the last
                  A
quarter, but we expect <u>it</u> will <u>go up</u> again
              B   C
<u>in this</u> quarter.
 D

156. Due to increased <u>competitions</u> from <u>other</u>
               A   B
airlines, Worldwide Airlines has again

<u>lowered</u> its <u>ticket</u> prices.
 C   D

157. There is <u>always</u> some <u>risk</u> <u>involved</u> in
         A   B   C
launching a new line of <u>produces</u>.
                D

158. <u>In</u> North America, January is <u>typically</u> the
 A   B
month when the greatest <u>amount</u> of
                 C
workers <u>change</u> jobs.
       D

159. Diamonds that are not of <u>enough high</u>
                     A
quality <u>to be</u> gemstones <u>may be used</u> as
       B   C
<u>industrial</u> diamonds.
 D

160. A nation's highways <u>make up</u> a
               A
<u>major, important</u> component <u>of its</u>
    B   C
<u>economic</u> infrastructure.
 D

GO ON TO THE NEXT PART. ☞

Part VII

Directions: Questions in this part of the test are based on a wide range of reading materials, including articles, letters, advertisements, and notices. After reading the passage, decide which of the four choices — (A), (B), (C), or (D) — best answers the question, and mark your answer. All answers should be based on what is stated in or on what can be inferred from the readings.

Now read the following example

La Plata Dinner Theater announces the opening of *Life on the River*, a musical play based on a book by Mark Twain. Dinner is served from 6:30 to 8:00, and the performance begins at 8:30 every evening.

What is opening?
- A. A bookstore
- B. An art exhibit
- C. A musical play
- D. A new restaurant   Ⓐ   Ⓑ   ●   Ⓓ

The reading states that *Life on the River* is a musical play that is opening at La Plata Dinner Theater. You should choose (C).

Questions 161 to 163 refer to the following notice:

If you are not fully satisfied with your Consolidated Sales purchase, please return it within 90 days to any Consolidated Sales store.

If you have your original sales receipt, we will exchange the item for a similar item, return your cash, remove the charge from your credit card account, or mail a cash refund within 10 days. Checks will be mailed for all refunds of $100 or greater.

If you do not have a receipt and the store still carries the item, we will mail you a refund within two weeks.

---

161. For whom is this notice intended?
- A. Customers
- B. Executives
- C. Manufacturers
- D. Advertisers

162. How long does this policy remain in effect?
- A. 10 days
- B. 14 days
- C. 90 days
- D. 100 days

163. Under which of these circumstances will a check be mailed to a customer?
- A. The purchase is made by credit card.
- B. The customer returns the purchase to a Consolidated Sales store other than the one where it was bought.
- C. The store no longer carries the item.
- D. The purchase costs more than $100.

Questions 164 and 165 are based on the following article:

While unusual restaurant decor is not a new concept, its popularity is growing for one good reason: increased competition. Three hundred billion dollars was spent in restaurants in the United States last year, an increase of about 5% from the previous year, and the number of restaurants increased by 3%. Restaurateurs can no longer focus entirely on food and service. Ambience — the synthesis of architecture, furniture, fixtures, lighting, and even staff attire — is now an important criterion when consumers choose a restaurant.

---

164. By how much did the amount of money spent in United States restaurants increase since last year?

    A. 3%   C. 50%

    B. 5%   D. 100%

165. Which of these is NOT given as a component of restaurant ambience?

    A. The architecture of a restaurant

    B. The quality of the food and service

    C. The tables and chairs

    D. The clothing worn by waiters and waitresses

Questions 166 and 167 are based on the following advertisement:

THE FAIRCHILD HOTEL, SAN FRANCISCO
PRESENTS THE EXECUTIVE CLUB
FOR THE FREQUENT BUSINESS TRAVELER

For immediate enrollment, dial the number listed below and receive:

- Suite upgrades when available at check-in
- Guaranteed room reservations when booked 48 hours in advance
- Twice-daily maid service
- Free valet parking
- Free use of facilities at the Nob Hill Health Spa
- In-room welcome gift
- Complimentary morning newspaper and continental breakfast
- Many additional benefits

---

166. When must a member of the Executive Club book a room to guarantee a reservation?

    A. Eight hours in advance

    B. A day in advance

    C. Two days in advance

    D. A week in advance

167. Which is NOT mentioned as being free of charge for members?

    A. Valet parking

    B. Continental breakfasts

    C. Use of health-spa facilities

    D. Suite upgrades

Questions 168 and 169 are based on the following article:

Singapore is a pioneer in "agro-tech" farming in Asia. Since growing urbanization is reducing Singapore's farmland, soon only a few thousand hectares will be available for cultivation. Hence, agro-technology — the application of technology to achieve higher crop yields than traditional farming methods — is being urgently developed.

As of 1990, there were 49 high-tech farms in Singapore. From 1985 to 1990, these farms produced 450 million Singapore dollars' worth of vegetables, shrimp, flowers, poultry, and aquarium fish. During this same 5-year period, Singapore was able to export over S$60 million worth of aquarium fish, S$8.5 million worth of aquatic plants, S$12.4 million worth of cut orchids, and S$6.0 million worth of ornamental plants.

---

168. What does this article mainly concern?
- A. Traditional Asian farming methods
- B. Agro-technology in Singapore
- C. Singapore's export policy
- D. Methods of high-tech farming

169. Which of these was the most valuable export commodity for Singapore from 1985 to 1990?
- A. Aquarium fish
- B. Cut orchids
- C. Aquatic plants
- D. Ornamental plants

Questions 170 to 172 refer to the following communication:

MEMO

TO: ALL PERMANENT EMPLOYEES
FROM: SOHEILA DARVISHALA, BENEFITS OFFICER
SUBJECT: NEW BENEFITS PLAN
DATE: AUG. 7, 199-

SYNCO MEDICAL TECHNOLOGIES IS INITIATING A NEW BENEFITS PLAN FOR ALL ELIGIBLE EMPLOYEES* BEGINNING SEPT. 1. IT IS IMPORTANT THAT THEY UNDERSTAND HOW THIS PLAN WORKS IN ORDER TO MAKE INFORMED DECISIONS. IT IS ALSO REQUIRED BY LAW THAT ALL ELIGIBLE EMPLOYEES ACCEPT OR DECLINE THIS NEW BENEFIT PLAN IN WRITING. (A FORM WILL BE PROVIDED AT THE MEETING.)

THERE WILL BE A MANDATORY MEETING ON FRIDAY, AUGUST 11 AT NOON IN ROOM 202 OF THE CENTER BUILDING. PLEASE MAKE A POINT OF ATTENDING. (THE MEETING OF AUGUST 4 WAS CANCELED BECAUSE OF POOR ATTENDANCE.)

A BROCHURE IS ATTACHED WHICH PROVIDES GENERAL INFORMATION ABOUT THE PLAN. EMPLOYEES SHOULD FAMILIARIZE THEMSELVES WITH THIS INFORMATION BEFORE THE MEETING AND BRING QUESTIONS.

*ELIGIBILITY FOR PARTICIPATION IS THE SAME AS ELIGIBILITY FOR HEALTH INSURANCE COVERAGE. IT IS LIMITED TO PERMANENT EMPLOYEES WHO WORK AT LEAST 30 HOURS A WEEK.

---

170. What is true about the August 11 meeting?
- A. It has to be canceled.
- B. Eligible employees must attend.
- C. Health insurance issues will be discussed.
- D. It will be held early in the morning.

171. Who is eligible for the benefits package?
- A. All Synco employees
- B. Permanent employees who work over 30 hours weekly
- C. Employees who do not currently have health insurance
- D. Part-time employees only

172. What is attached to this memo?
- A. A form
- B. An agenda
- C. A brochure
- D. A check

Questions 173 to 175 are based on the following reading:

The Moroccan government encourages foreign investment, especially when it creates jobs and transfers technology. Foreign-owned holdings are subject to the same regulations as locally owned businesses. Any regulations that do exist are principally related to financial service companies. There are also certain restrictions on businesses concerned with rail and air transport, water and energy supply, mining, and industries potentially harmful to public health or safety.

The Industrial Investment Code provides tax relief and other incentives to non-service companies with investment programs exceeding DH100,000, certain service industries (including engineering and consulting), and small- and medium-sized businesses with investment programs not exceeding DH5 million.

173. What is the purpose of this reading?
    A. To acquaint readers with Morocco's foreign investment policy
    B. To explain the best way to start a business in Morocco
    C. To discuss the current financial situation in Morocco
    D. To encourage Moroccans to invest in certain industries

174. Which of the following types of foreign companies are NOT mentioned as being regulated?
    A. Banks   C. Hotels
    B. Mining companies D. Airlines

175. All of the following might receive incentives under the Industrial Investment Code EXCEPT
    A. a non-service company investing more than DH100,000
    B. an engineering firm
    C. a medium-sided corporation investing less than DH5 million
    D. a large service company investing more than DH5 million

Questions 176 to 180 are based on the following schedule:

21ST ANNUAL INTERNATIONAL SALES CONFERENCE

Thursday
9 AM-4 PM	Registration and badge pick-up
7-8 PM	Informal reception at West Ballroom, New Plaza Hotel
8-9 PM	Opening address by Ted Singer, Vice President for Sales

Friday
7:30 AM	Attendees bused to Carleton Ranch
8:30-9 AM	Coffee and rolls
9 AM-12	Plenary Session
12-1 PM	Lunch
1-3:30 PM	Meetings with regional sales managers
4-7 PM	Horseback ride and old-fashioned barbecue
7 PM	Attendees bused back to their hotels

Saturday
9 AM-12	Sales seminars, New Plaza Hotel
12-1:30 PM	Lunch, closing ceremony, and "Sales Reps of the Year" awards

Your badge is your "ticket" to all events.

Dress: Business dress for Thursday and Saturday events. Casual western wear (blue jeans, boots, and cowboy hats!) for events at the Carleton Ranch.

All meals not listed on this schedule must be paid for by attendees. Room service bills are the responsibility of attendees. Attendees who stay over Saturday night must pay for accommodations for that night. Taxis, rental cars, and other ground transportation other than shuttle van to and from the airport will not be reimbursed. Keep receipts for hotel bills and airline tickets in order to be reimbursed.

176. On what day should attendees wear casual Western clothing?
   A. Wednesday   C. Friday
   B. Thursday   D. Saturday

177. How will attendees get to the Carleton Ranch?
   A. By bus   C. By rental car
   B. By air   D. By taxi

178. When will awards be presented?
   A. During the opening address
   B. At the plenary session
   C. At the barbecue dinner
   D. During the final event

179. What must attendees bring to all events?
   A. Boots   C. A badge
   B. A ticket   D. Receipts

180. For which of the following will attendees be reimbursed?
   A. Airfares
   B. Room service charges
   C. Taxi fares
   D. Saturday night's hotel bill

Questions 181 to 184 refer to the following article:

NEWSPAPER sales fell in most countries last year, especially in the developed world, according to an annual survey released by the International Federation of Newspaper Publishers.

Daily circulation fell in 23 of the 40 countries surveyed, slipping 1.2% in the United States, 1.87% in the European Union countries, and 0.17% in Japan.

But among less developed nations, Peru had a dramatic rise of 90% and India showed an increase of 28.5%.

The survey showed that Japan continued to lead the world in daily sales with 71.9 million, followed by the United States with 5.9 million and Germany with 25.7 million.

181. What is the author's main purpose in writing?
   A. To announce an increase in the number of newspapers worldwide
   B. To discuss the changing nature of journalism
   C. To contrast the way newspapers are operated in different nations
   D. To report on a survey regarding newspaper sales

182. In how many of the countries surveyed did sales NOT decline?
   A. 13   C. 23
   B. 17   D. 40

183. In which of these was there the greatest increase in sales?
   A. Peru
   B. The United States
   C. India
   D. The European Union countries

184. Which of these conclusions can be made about the sale of newspapers in Japan?
   A. Although there was a modest rise in sales, Japan still trails the United States and Germany.
   B. This year, sales continued their dramatic decline.
   C. Sales dropped slightly, but Japan continues to lead the world in daily sales.
   D. The sharp rise in sales was higher than that of any other country.

Questions 185 to 187 are based on the following notice:

Wildlife Protection League

Membership Renewal Reminder

March, 1996

Dear Member,
Your membership in the Wildlife Protection League is going to expire in a month.
Please continue helping us in our work to conserve the Siberian tiger, the African
elephant, the mountain gorilla, and all the other at-risk species around the globe.
Your early renewal will continue your membership until April 1997.
And please, while you're at it, subscribe to *Wild!,* the WPL newsletter which
details our wildlife-saving efforts and contains superb wildlife photography. For
just $15, you'll receive six copies of this attractive bi-monthly journal.
Thank you for your continuing support.

Karen McCauley, President

Enclosed please find:
Basic membership contribution   ☐ $25
Subscription to *Wild!*   ☐ $15
Additional contribution:
  ☐ $50   ☐ $100   ☐ Other $ _____

Total enclosed $ _____

---

185. How long will the recipient's member-
ship continue if he or she renews now?
   A. Until March 1996
   B. Until April 1996
   C. Until March 1997
   D. Until April 1997

186. How often is the journal *Wild!* published?
   A. Every month
   B. Every two months
   C. Every six months
   D. Every year

187. How much is the basic membership fee?
   A. $15   C. $50
   B. $25   D. $100

Questions 188 and 189 are based on the following article:

Basically, there are two types of patents: mechanical and design. A mechanical patent is employed when the concept involves a new product that works mechanically and has never been developed before. A design patent involves a previously patented product. The new design must somehow improve the original. Mechanical designs last for seventeen years and can be renewed, while design patents last for only three years.

188. What is the main purpose of this article?
   A. To distinguish between two types of patents
   B. To define and give examples of mechanical patents
   C. To discuss the steps needed to obtain patents
   D. To describe a typical design improvement

189. How long does a design patent remain in effect?
   A. For the lifetime of the product
   B. For three years
   C. Until the design is fundamentally changed
   D. For seventeen years

Questions 190 to 192 are based on the following form:

SANDIA TECHNOLOGY SYSTEMS
Worksheet: Telephone Reference Check

Name of applicant: Carolina Sanchez

Previous/Current Employer   BFA Graphics
Dates of employment: May 1 1995   to   Present
Position: Data entry clerk
Salary: Approx $24,000
Reason for leaving: See "Additl comments"

Does applicant get along well with others?   Yes __X__   No ____   Not sure ____

Does applicant have leadership qualities?   Yes ____   No ____   Not sure __X__

Is employee reliable?   Yes ____   No ____   Not sure ____
Would you rehire?   Yes __X__   No ____

Additional comments   Mgr of Accts Recvble Dept stated that he hated to lose Ms. Sanchez but that, because BFA is a relatively small co, there was not much room for her to advance in near future. Asst mgr of dept. told me that Ms. Sanchez was very conscientious and that she was certain Ms. Sanchez would make an excellent data coordr for us.

Information received from   Dennis Longhurst, Mgr, and Kay Barret, Asst Mgr Accts Recvble Dept at BFA

Information taken by   M. Nakayoshi, Pers'l Dir

190. What is the purpose of this form?
  A. To record information obtained by checking with an employment reference
  B. To determine if an employee should be given a promotion
  C. To record notes taken during a telephone interview with a job applicant
  D. To explain why an applicant is unsuitable for a position

191. Who filled out this form?
  A. Carolina Sanchez
  B. Dennis Longhurst
  C. Kay Barrett
  D. M. Nakayoshi

192. What position is the applicant seeking?
  A. Manager, Accounts Receivable
  B. Data coordinator
  C. Personnel director
  D. Data entry clerk

Questions 193 to 195 refer to the following article:

It is difficult to explain the Pareto Principle (or Pareto Law) in completely abstract terms. However, it is easy to explain it by reference to practical examples. Suppose that a firm sells 100 products. One would not expect that each customer would contribute equally to the total sales value. In fact, the Pareto Principle (Law) states that there will probably be such an imbalance, and that a very large proportion of variables (in this, case customers) contributes in only a small degree to the result (in this case, total sales) and that a small proportion of variables contributes in a very great degree to the result. Because it is so often found that some 80% of a firm's sales are made to only 20% of the customers, the Pareto Principle is sometimes called the 80/20 Technique or the 80/20 Rule.

193. Which of the following does the author say about the Pareto Principle?
  A. It is simple to explain through examples.
  B. It is an interesting theory, but it has little practical value.
  C. It was once an important tool but is no longer used.
  D. It is too complex for the average businessperson to employ.

194. Which of these is NOT another term for the Pareto Principle?
  A. The 80/20 Technique
  B. The Proportional Effect
  C. The Pareto Law
  D. The 80/20 Rule

195. If the Pareto Principle is perfectly accurate, and if a company sells $100,000 worth of goods to 100 customers, then
  A. 20 of the customers will account for sales of $80,000
  B. each of the 100 customers will spend $1,000
  C. 80% of the sales will be to one customer
  D. the company will make $20,000 in profit

Questions 196 and 197 are based on the following advertisement:

Relocating Your Business?

For a smooth move across town or around the world, call C & J Relocation Specialists and take the worry and inconvenience out of your move.

Sure, you could
- research moving companies
- deal with phone and utility companies
- order new stationery
- prepare checklists
- take care of 1,001 other details

Our business is to manage the details of the move so that you can STAY in business.

But don't you have a business to run?

Call for a free consultation!

196. For whom is this advertisement intended?
- A. Businesses that want to expand their operations
- B. Executives being transferred to another city
- C. Employees who want to change careers
- D. Companies moving to another location

197. What does the advertiser offer potential clients?
- A. Lower prices
- B. Less inconvenience
- C. Greater speed
- D. More prestige

Questions 198 to 200 are based on the following notice:

TRADE TIPS

1. **United Arab Emirates** is seeking direct sales to end users of insulated fiber optic cables, multimeters, pipes and fittings, paint, varnishes, lumber, and pumps.
2. **Qatar** is seeking other investors for a frozen orange juice and dried milk plant.
3. **Hungary** is seeking a distributorship for telephone modems.
4. **Egypt** is seeking an agency for second-grade paper.
5. **Australia** is seeking a distributorship for a picture-hanging system.
6. **Brazil** is seeking a joint-venture opportunity with an environmental-technology firm.

For further information and more tips, contact the International Trade Center Tip Program. Trade Tips is a service offered to our members, who may request as many tips as they desire. For nonmembers, there is a three-tip request limit. Call for membership information.

198. What is Qatar looking for?
    A. A distributorship
    B. A source of orange juice and milk
    C. Additional investment
    D. Further information

199. Which of these countries is seeking a joint-venture partner?
    A. Egypt
    B. Australia
    C. Hungary
    D. Brazil

200. How many tips can a non-member request?
    A. None
    B. One
    C. Three
    D. An unlimited number

THIS IS THE END OF THE READING COMPREHENSION SECTION. IF YOU FINISH BEFORE TIME IS UP, YOU MUST WORK ONLY ON PROBLEMS IN THIS SECTION.

Tapescript and Answer Key

Sample Test

Example

A. He's waiting in a line.
B. He's reading a newspaper.
C. He's waving to someone.
D. He's writing on a paper.

1. _D_
A. The boy is holding the fruit.
B. He's playing a game by himself.
C. The boy is preparing some food.
D. He's playing music on the flute.

2. _A_
A. She's painting the wall.
B. She's pushing the stroller.
C. She's climbing the ladder.
D. She's planting flowers by the wall.

3. _C_
A. The cards are on the rock.
B. The lock is on the machine.
C. The time clock is below the bulletin board.
D. The cars are in a line.

4. _B_
A. The barges appear to be empty.
B. Trees grow on both sides of the river.
C. The boat is passing under a bridge.
D. The river is too narrow for the boat.

5. _C_
A. He's pushing a steel barrel.
B. He's going the wrong way.
C. He has just stepped out of the shadow.
D. He's waiting at a stop sign.

6. _A_
A. The man is holding the book open.
B. They're standing by themselves.
C. The books are all of different sizes.
D. The woman is pointing at the page.

Exercise 1.1

1. _C_
  _M+S_
  _M_
  _M+S_
A. She's painting the wall.
B. She's pushing the stroller.
C. She's climbing the ladder.
D. She's planting flowers by the wall.

Explanation
A. Correct.
B. She is using a roller, not pushing a stroller. (A stroller is a chair with wheels used to take small children for walks.)
C. The ladder is in the background — she's not climbing it.
D. She's not planting; she is painting. (*Planting* sounds a little like *painting*.)

2. _S_
  _M+S_
  _C_
  _S_
A. The cards are on the rock.
B. The lock is on the machine.
C. The time clock is below the bulletin board.
D. The cars are in a line.

Explanation
A. The cards are on a rack, not a rock.
B. There's no lock in the picture. (*Lock* sounds like *clock*.)
C. Correct.
D. There are no cars in the photograph. (*Cars* sounds like *cards*.)

3. _M_
  _C_
  _M_
  _M_
A. The barges appear to be empty.
B. Trees grow on both sides of the river.
C. The boat is passing under a bridge.
D. The river is too narrow for the boat.

Explanation
A. The barges appear to be full.
B. Correct.
C. The bridge is far behind the boat.
D. The river is wide enough for the boat.

4. _S_
  _M_
  _C_
  _M_
A. He's pushing a steel barrel.
B. He's going the wrong way.
C. He has just stepped out of the shadow.
D. He's waiting at a stop sign.

Explanation
  A. He's pushing a wheelbarrow.
     (*Steel barrel* sounds like *wheelbarrow*.)
  B. He would be going the wrong way only if
     he were in a car.
  C. Correct.
  D. He's not waiting, and he's not at the stop
     sign.

5. __C__   A. The man is holding the book open.
   _S+M_   B. They're standing by themselves.
   __M__   C. The books are all of different sizes.
   __M__   D. The woman is pointing at the page.

Explanation
  A. Correct.
  B. Only one of them is standing. (*The shelves*
     sounds like *themselves*.)
  C. Most of the books are exactly the same
     height.
  D. She's not pointing at anything.

Exercise 1.2

1. __F__   (a) The airport appears to be closed.
   __T__   (b) There's a crowd of customers at the
              counter.
   __T__   (c) There are some brochures on the
              counter.
   __F__   (d) No one is behind the counter.
   __F__   (e) The lights have been turned off.
   __T__   (f) The man is wearing a tie.

2. __F.__ (a) They're standing behind a curtain.
   __T__   (b) They seem to be enjoying
              themselves.
   __F__   (c) They're at a fancy nightclub.
   __F__   (d) They're up on a stage.

3. __T__   (a) The round building is between two
              other buildings.
   __F__   (b) The trees block the view of the
              buildings.
   __F__   (c) One of the buildings is being
              demolished.
   __T__   (d) The round building is the tallest of
              the three.
   __T__   (e) Palm trees grow around the round
              building.
   __F__   (f) It's late at night.

4. __F__   (a) The elevator is too crowded to
              get on.
   __F__   (b) The elevator is going up.
   __F__   (c) The railing in the elevator seems
              to be made of metal.
   __F__   (d) The floor of the elevator is covered
              with carpeting.
   __T__   (e) The doors are wide open.
   __F__   (f) The elevator is probably in the
              basement.

5. __F__   (a) The man is starting the motorcycle.
   __F__   (b) The crowd is watching the
              motorcycle races.
   __T__   (c) The man in the jacket is carrying a
              walking stick.
   __T__   (d) Some people are crossing the
              street.
   __T__   (e) The motorcycle is parked by the
              curb.

6. __T__   (a) They appear to be at an art exhibit.
   __F__   (b) Both of the men are wearing ties.
   __F__   (c) They are studying the pictures.
   __F__   (d) The woman has a flower in her
              hand.
   __T__   (e) The man with the glasses has his
              coat on his arm.

7. __F__   (a) Here is a blank sheet of paper.
   __F__   (b) The ticket has been torn in two.
   __F__   (c) The card is made of plastic.
   __F__   (d) Someone is holding the ticket.

8. __F__   (a) They're going for a ride in the boat.
   __T__   (b) One of them is fishing.
   __F__   (c) They're walking in the water.
   __T__   (d) A child is on a bicycle.
   __F__   (e) All of them are dressed in white.

9. __T__   (a) Books are piled on the table.
   __F__   (b) They're skating down the aisle.
   __F__   (c) They're both wearing glasses.
   __T__   (d) One man is looking at a book.
   __T__   (e) One man has skates over his
              shoulder.
   __F__   (f) They seem to be in a bookstore.

10. __T__ (a) People are sitting on the steps.
    __F__ (b) They're working in an office.
    __F__ (c) Everyone is talking together.
    __F__ (d) They're meeting at an outdoor
              cafe.
    __T__ (e) Some people are eating lunch.
    __F__ (f) Everyone is wearing a helmet.

Exercise 1.3

Part A

1. **B** A. The woman has a pain in her hand.
      B. The woman is writing at her desk.

2. **A** A. The boots are standing in a row.
      B. The boats are all lined up.

3. **B** A. There are many resources here.
      B. The racehorses are running down the track.

4. **A** A. She's packing up her clothes.
      B. She's picking up her suitcase.

5. **A** A. He's diving off the board.
      B. He's ready to start driving.

6. **B** A. A woman is having her hair dyed.
      B. The stylist is drying the woman's hair.

7. **B** A. He's started singing.
      B. He's about to hit the ball.

8. **A** A. She's making a copy.
      B. She's making coffee.

9. **A** A. She's tasting the water.
      B. She's taking a test.

10. **B** A. The child is playing on the sled.
      B. The child is coming down the slide.

Part B

Sound-Alike Word	"Correct" Word
1. pain	(pen)
2. boats	boots
3. resources	racehorses
4. picking	packing
5. driving	diving
6. dyed	(dried)
7. singing	(swinging)
8. coffee	copy
9. test	(taste)
10. sled	slide

Exercise 1.4

1. **B** A. All of the men are drinking from cups.
      B. One of the men is wearing a jacket.

2. **B** A. The skirts are hanging in the closet.
      B. The shirts are stacked on the shelves.

3. **A** A. He's up on a ladder.
      B. He's writing a letter.

4. **B** A. The truck is in the right lane.
      B. The truck is right in front of the plane.

5. **A** A. The man is standing in front of the desk.
      B. The woman is sitting on the deck.

6. **B** A. Fish are swimming in the tank.
      B. Dishes are stacked in the sink.

7. **A** A. The arrow points the way.
      B. The sign is long and narrow.

8. **A** A. She's sitting near the flowers.
      B. She's putting out the fires.

9. **A** A. He's pointing at the board.
      B. He's looking at the bird.

10. **B** A. Grain is stored in these towers.
      B. The cranes tower over the trees.

Part B

Sound-Alike Word	"Correct" Word
1. cups	(caps)
2. skirts	shirts
3. letter	ladder
4. lane	plane
5. deck	desk
6. fish*	dishes*
7. narrow	arrow
8. fires**	flowers**
9. bird	board
10. grain	cranes

* *Tank* also sounds a little like *sink*.
** *Sitting* also sounds a little like *putting*.

More Practice

1. __A__ A. They're signaling the bus driver.
    B. The weather is warm and sunny.
    C. They're waving good-bye to each other.
    D. The driver has been waiting for them.

2. __C__ A. They're feeding the baby.
    B. The baby appears to be crying.
    C. The baby is on the table between them.
    D. They're both looking down at the baby.

3. __B__ A. Someone is looking at the newspaper.
    B. Newspapers and magazines are on display.
    C. The new neighbors are very interesting.
    D. The papers are all blowing away.

4. __D__ A. The driver is waiting to use the phone.
    B. The man is standing by the taxi.
    C. The telephone is inside the car.
    D. The driver has one hand on the wheel.

5. __C__ A. The barber is cutting the man's hair.
    B. They're entering the gymnasium.
    C. One of the men is lifting weights.
    D. They're waiting for a ride.

6. __B__ A. Someone is watching the show.
    B. He's suspended from above.
    C. The building is made of glass and steel.
    D. Someone is climbing a mountain.

7. __D__ A. The letter is in his hands.
    B. He's sawing a board.
    C. He's making an announcement.
    D. Some notices are on the board.

8. __A__ A. The attendant is pointing to the rear of the plane.
    B. The pots are full of beans.
    C. Some of the apartments are still open.
    D. There's someone sitting in every seat on the plane.

9. __A__ A. The globe is surrounded by maps.
    B. The charts are hanging on the wall.
    C. Some mops are on the floor.
    D. People are taking naps.

10. __B__ A. He's making the bed.
    B. The oven is open.
    C. He's shoveling some snow.
    D. The leaves have been raked.

11. __D__ A. Both of them have paper cups.
    B. They're talking on the phone to each other.
    C. Wearing a coat is a requirement in this office.
    D. There's a computer in front of both of them.

12. __A__ A. The sign lists some prices.
    B. She's showing the clothes to a customer.
    C. The lamp is shining right in her face.
    D. She's marking the calendar.

13. __C__ A. He's paying the cashier.
    B. He's performing in a play.
    C. He's playing a song.
    D. He's arranging the flowers.

14. __D__ A. The table is round.
    B. There's a cable stretched across the floor.
    C. Someone needs to set the table.
    D. There's a view of the street from this table.

15. __D__ A. She's rearranging the furniture.
    B. She's leaning against the chair.
    C. She's sleeping on the sofa.
    D. She's cleaning up the area.

16. __B__ A. The two men are facing each other.
    B. The doctor is giving the patient a check-up.
    C. The dentist is checking the man's teeth.
    D. One man is handing the other a check.

17. __B__ A. The guitarists are up on the stage.
    B. There's a tag on each of the guitars.
    C. Stars can be seen overhead.
    D. There are many instruments on the control panel.

18. __A__ A. There's a row of trees along the street.
         B. The buildings are hidden by the trees.
         C. There are three buses in a row.
         D. Traffic is heavy at this time of day.

19. __C__ A. They're speaking to each other through the fence.
         B. The police officer is giving her directions.
         C. He's taking notes on what she is saying.
         D. She seems to be under arrest.

20. __B__ A. Children are not allowed in this restaurant.
         B. Some cups and dishes are on the table.
         C. The family is sitting in front of a mirror.
         D. The restaurant is empty except for these three.

LESSON 2

Sample Test

1. __B__ Did you finish that project yet?
   A. It was a difficult one.
   B. Yes, finally, a week ago.
   C. No, there's only one.

2. __C__ What color is your new car?
   A. I bought a sports car.
   B. New cars are expensive.
   C. It's bright blue.

3. __B__ Can you tell me when the next planning meeting will be?
   A. Every month
   B. This Monday at ten
   C. Yes, that's the plan

4. __C__ Are you taking the 3 PM flight to Paris?
   A. From New York
   B. It leaves in an hour
   C. No, the 7 PM flight

5. __A__ How was the party Friday night?
   A. Very enjoyable
   B. By car
   C. Until around midnight

6. __B__ Do you prefer playing tennis or golf?
   A. All right, let's play.
   B. I like both.
   C. I didn't play tennis.

7. __A__ What do you think of the plan to open an office in Yokohama?
   A. I think it's a great idea.
   B. I'll leave the office open.
   C. I'm going next month.

8. __A__ May I talk to you for a few minutes?
   A. Sure. What about?
   B. Yes, thanks to you.
   C. If you're not too busy.

9. __C__ Wasn't that a fascinating article?
   A. Yes, he was fascinating.
   B. It will be finished soon.
   C. Yes, it was very interesting.

10. __C__ How many suitcases are you bringing?
    A. Quite expensive
    B. They're very full
    C. Two or three

11. __B__ That presentation wasn't very long, was it?
    A. No, it wasn't very difficult.
    B. You're right — it was quite short.
    C. Thanks, I enjoyed it.

12. __B__ Did you catch the plane?
    A. No, I didn't change my plan.
    B. Yes, but I almost missed it.
    C. No, I didn't catch a cold.

Exercise 2.1

1. How long have you known Mr. Park?
   Information question
2. What kind of company do you work for?
   Information question
3. Does Martha still work here?
   Yes/no question
4. Do you want to stay in tonight or go out?
   Other
5. Why did you ask me that?
   Information question
6. Could you come back for another interview tomorrow?
   Yes/no question
7. Should I press this button?
   Yes/no question
8. Don't you like this food?
   Other
9. When did the movie start?
   Information question
10. Harry is a good friend of yours, isn't he?
    Other
11. Were you involved in an accident?
    Yes/no question
12. Can you tell me where the sales meeting will be held?
    Other

230

Exercise 2.2

1. __A__ What has Roger been doing?
   A. He's been busy with his job.
   B. He's fine, I'm sure.
   C. He's been in New York City.

2. __C__ What's the name of that restaurant?
   A. They mainly serve seafood.
   B. On Harborside Boulevard.
   C. It's called the Dolphin Cafe.

3. __A__ What's the matter with the tape player?
   A. I think the batteries are dead.
   B. I bought it at an electronics store.
   C. Yes, it's a good brand.

4. __C__ What kind of music does that band play?
   A. At a nightclub
   B. Around 8 o'clock
   C. Rock and roll, mostly

5. __B__ What time is Mr. Abe's flight due?
   A. In June
   B. Three in the afternoon
   C. He'll be leaving soon

6. __A__ What does Lily do for a living?
   A. She's an architect.
   B. She lives in Montreal.
   C. She has a nice apartment.

7. __A__ What's it like out today?
   A. It's sunny and warm.
   B. I'd like to go to the beach today.
   C. I was out all day.

8. __B__ What do you think of the new software?
   A. I've been thinking about it all day.
   B. It certainly seems easy to use.
   C. It's available now.

9. __A__ What flight are you taking to Rio?
   A. Flight 649, leaving at 9 PM
   B. It was quite pleasant, thanks
   C. Nearly eight hours

10. __C__ What does Mr. Weis look like?
    A. He enjoys sports a lot.
    B. He's looking for another position.
    C. He's tall and has dark hair and a beard.

Exercise 2.3

1. __A__ How well can Pamela ski?
   A. She's an expert.
   B. Every few weeks.
   C. In Switzerland.

2. __A__ How about another cup of coffee?
   A. No thanks, I've already had two.
   B. It's quite strong.
   C. One dollar.

3. __C__ How much is that sweater?
   A. It's made of wool.
   B. At the shopping mall
   C. It's on sale for half price.

4. __B__ How many eggs do you need for the cake?
   A. Sure, I'd enjoy some
   B. Half a dozen
   C. They're large eggs

5. __C__ How old is your car?
   A. It's a bright red sports car.
   B. It handles very well, don't you think?
   C. It's over five years old, but it looks newer.

6. __A__ How often do you play golf?
   A. At least once a week
   B. Hundreds of times
   C. I need more practice.

7. __B__ How far do you jog every day?
   A. Early in the morning
   B. A couple of kilometers
   C. Before breakfast

8. __C__ How did you find the mistake?
   A. It was excellent, thanks.
   B. Just a little one
   C. By going over the problem again and again

9. __C__ How will I recognize you at the airport?
   A. There are signs that direct you to it.
   B. I'll get there by bus.
   C. I'll be holding a sign with your name on it.

10. __C__ How about coming over for dinner this evening?
    A. Salad, soup, and pasta
    B. It was delicious, thanks.
    B. Sorry, but I can't this evening.

11. __A__ How many times have you been to
Sydney before?
A. This is my second trip here.
B. It took fifteen hours to get here.
C. For around a month

12. __B__ How long have you worked in
marketing?
A. It's on the twenty-third floor.
B. For around five years
C. It's an interesting field.

13. __A__ How early will we have to leave?
A. By six AM, at least
B. Let's take a taxi.
C. About ten miles from here

14. __C__ How did you like Prague?
A. Yes, very much.
B. Only a week
C. It's a charming city.

Exercise 2.4

1. __C__ When did the flight to Los Angeles
leave?
A. In about an hour
B. From Tokyo
C. Twenty minutes ago

2. __A__ When do you usually listen to the radio?
A. When I'm in my car
B. Since about noon
C. Not for a long time

3. __A__ Where is Mr. Arikan from?
A. He's from Turkey.
B. He's in his room.
C. He went to his office.

4. __C__ Where did I put those stamps?
A. No, not at this time
B. At the post office
C. In your desk drawer, I think

5. __C__ When will the company picnic be held?
A. Until about four o'clock
B. In Buckingham Park
C. On Saturday at noon

6. __B__ When was this company founded?
A. By Mr. DeClerque
B. In 1952
C. In Paris

7. __A__ Where will you stay when you're in
Seoul?
A. At a hotel downtown
B. In around three days
C. I'm going there on business.

8. __C__ Where are you moving?
A. Next Saturday
B. Because I have a better job there
C. To San Francisco

Exercise 2.5

1. __A__ Why did Mr. Maas go to Singapore this
week?
A. To attend a trade fair
B. He flew on Far Eastern Airlines.
C. I believe he will.

2. __A__ Why don't you take a public speaking
class?
A. That's a good idea.
B. Because I enjoy public speaking
C. I was speaking with my boss.

3. __C__ Who's that woman you spoke to in the
lobby?
A. I told her I'd meet her in the lobby.
B. To get some important information
from her
C. She's an old friend of mine from
college.

4. __B__ Whose apartment did you sublet?
A. On the second floor
B. Mr. Krause's
C. For the next six months

5. __C__ Which jacket is yours?
A. Yes, it's mine.
B. I have one just like that.
C. The brown leather one

6. __B__ Which way did Mr. Nishida go?
A. He left over an hour ago.
B. He turned right when he went out
the door.
C. He's traveling by train.

7. __C__ Whose car is this parked behind mine?
A. It's been there all afternoon.
B. This parking lot is owned by the
city.
C. I think it belongs to Mark.

8. __A__ Which page is missing from the report?
   A. The last page
   B. It's five pages long.
   C. The report is on your desk.

Exercise 2.6

1. __A__ Who lives upstairs?
   A. My cousin Brigid
   B. On the second floor
   C. No, I'm going downstairs.

2. __C__ Where is Udo from?
   A. Back to Hamburg
   B. A few years ago
   C. He comes from Hamburg.

3. __A__ When did the merger take place?
   A. Last January
   B. In Miami
   C. Early next year

4. __C__ Why don't we get something to eat before the game?
   A. A sandwich and some coffee, please.
   B. The game starts in an hour.
   C. That sounds like a good idea.

5. __B__ How long has Fred been working on this project?
   A. He's worked very hard on it.
   B. For at least six months
   C. The project should be finished soon.

6. __C__ What are you going to order for dinner?
   A. Because I'm very hungry
   B. To the restaurant around the corner
   C. Salad, steak, and baked potato

7. __A__ What's the matter with the copier?
   A. I don't know — it just stopped working.
   B. I made several copies.
   C. No, it's not hard to use.

8. __B__ When's the last time you went scuba diving?
   A. This is the last time
   B. Last summer, I guess
   C. In the Virgin Islands

9. __B__ What business is Mr. Tang in?
   A. He's very busy these days.
   B. He owns a small trading company.
   C. Right down the street

10. __C__ What time should we leave for the airport?
   A. A few hours ago
   B. We should take the shuttle bus.
   C. About seven-thirty

11. __B__ How late did they work last night?
   A. They were quite late for work.
   B. Until 10 PM
   C. By this morning

12. __A__ Whose computer disk is this?
   A. It's mine — I've been looking all over for it.
   B. Joan is using that computer right now.
   C. It's on the desk.

13. __C__ What did you think of Barcelona?
   A. Yes, quite often.
   B. I was there last year.
   C. What an exciting city!

14. __A__ How do you like the new office furniture?
   A. To tell you the truth, I preferred the old.
   B. It's brand-new furniture.
   C. My new office is across the hall.

15. __A__ Where are these goods going to be stored?
   A. In our warehouse
   B. The store is on Nelson Road.
   C. Maybe, if they're good enough.

16. __C__ Which channel is the early news on?
   A. It's on at ten o'clock.
   B. No, it's not too late.
   C. It's on Channel eight.

Exercise 2.7

1. __A__ Are you a friend of Shio's?
   A. Oh, sure, I've known Shio for years.
   B. No, I've never met Shio's friend.
   C. I met him at a trade conference.

2. __C__ Did you enjoy the game?
   A. The game started at four.
   B. Thanks, I will.
   C. It was great.

3. __A__ Have you had a chance to look around the city yet?
A. I haven't even been out of my hotel.
B. I've been to that city several times.
C. I can't find it on the map.

4. __B__ Is the highway still closed?
A. No, it's a long way from here.
B. It is, but it should be open again soon.
C. For weeks now

5. __B__ Did you know many people at the party?
A. There were about twenty people there.
B. A few, but not many
C. A lot of fun

6. __B__ Are you still planning to attend that conference in Rotterdam?
A. It's been planned for over a year.
B. Unfortunately, I had to change my plans.
C. It's going to last all week.

7. __C__ Will you be back to work on Monday?
A. In the human resources department
B. I work every Monday.
C. If I feel better by then

8. __B__ Were there any calls while I was out?
A. Yes, you can use my telephone.
B. One from your travel agent
C. No, I didn't call you.

9. __B__ Have you ever been mountain climbing?
A. It's thousands of feet high.
B. Never, but I'd love to go sometime.
C. That's a good idea.

10. __C__ Do you have to spend the night in Atlanta?
A. Yes, there's a lot to do there at night.
B. Several hundred dollars
C. No, I'll probably return here later this evening.

Exercise 2.8

1. __C__ May I take your picture, please?
A. Here's one
B. It's a picture of my brother.
C. Of course, go ahead

2. __C__ Would you mind if I skipped this meeting?
A. For about an hour
B. Yes, you can attend if you like.
C. No, you don't really have to be here.

3. __B__ Could you take this file to Ms. Del Rio?
A. The file is in Ms. Del Rio's office.
B. I'll see that she gets it right away.
C. Because she asked me to.

4. __B__ Do you want to go out and hear some music tonight?
A. Yes, I can hear it clearly.
B. That would be fun
C. At a concert hall.

5. __A__ Can I get you a couple of aspirin?
A. Thanks — I have a terrible headache.
B. Yes, there are a few.
C. In the cabinet

6. __B__ Would you and your partner be able to join us for a game of golf this weekend?
A. We've already joined.
B. We'd be delighted.
C. We won that game.

7. __C__ Should I open the window?
A. No, it shouldn't be.
B. Yes, it is.
C. Please don't.

8. __A__ May I take your order now, sir?
A. In a moment — I'm still looking at the menu.
B. I'd be happy to take your order.
C. Yes, I believe I will.

9. __A__ Is there anything I can do to help with the mailing?
A. You could stuff these envelopes.
B. That isn't very helpful.
C. I'm sure the mailing will help.

10. __B__ Would you like to use the phone?
A. The line was busy.
B. It's in the kitchen.
C. Just to make a quick call

11. __C__ Do you have a match?
  A. It doesn't match your shirt.
  B. I haven't seen it.
  C. I never carry matches.

12. __C__ Have you bought your airline tickets yet?
  A. It hasn't arrived yet.
  B. I still have them.
  C. I've already got them.

Exercise 2.9

1. __A__ Can you tell me where I can change my money?
  A. At most banks and large hotels
  B. I don't know where your money is.
  C. No, I don't have any change.

2. __C__ Do you know when the museum opens?
  A. Yes, I think it is
  B. On Seventh Street
  C. At 10, I believe

3. __B__ Do you want a small drink or a large one?
  A. Yes, please.
  B. I'll have a small one, please.
  C. No, it isn't.

4. __B__ Would you rather spend your vacation in Bermuda or the Bahamas?
  A. I sure would
  B. Either would be wonderful
  C. Yes, it's an expensive trip.

5. __B__ Does anyone know whose address book this is?
  A. I don't know him well.
  B. It looks like Allen's.
  C. I'm not sure where he lives.

6. __C__ Do people in your country drive on the left side of the road or the right?
  A. Yes, we do.
  B. You're right about that.
  C. On the left

7. __A__ Will you let me know if Mr. Constas calls?
  A. I'll transfer the call to you if he does.
  B. If he calls, tell him I'm out.
  C. He can use my phone if he wants.

8. __C__ Do you know whether the contract was signed?
  A. In the president's office
  B. Late yesterday, I think
  C. I believe it was.

9. __C__ Should I put your groceries in paper or plastic bags?
  A. Put them in bags, please.
  B. Yes, you should.
  C. Paper, please.

10. __B__ Do you know that your plane is already boarding?
  A. Yes, it's ready to be boarded.
  B. Already? Then I'd better get on board.
  C. In about an hour

11. __A__ Will you be paying by cash, check, or credit card?
  A. I'll write you a check.
  B. Whenever you want
  C. You have an excellent credit rating.

12. __A__ Do you want the chicken or the fish?
  A. I don't know — they both sound good.
  B. I'd like chicken or fish.
  C. No, not at all.

13. __C__ Do you know why Stefano is late?
  A. He's late again.
  B. Almost an hour
  C. Maybe he had car trouble

14. __C__ Can you tell me where the keys are?
  A. They're for my car.
  B. No, they're not the right keys.
  C. I have them in my pocket.

15. __B__ Did you know that Bill's sister is a pop singer?
  A. No, I've never heard that song.
  B. Really? I never knew that.
  C. Yes, I've heard that Bill is a good singer.

16. __B__ Will that be economy class, business class, or first class?
  A. I think so
  B. Business class, please
  C. It was first class.

Exercise 2.10

1. __B__ There was another malfunction, wasn't there?
   A. That's its function.
   B. I'm afraid there was.
   C. No, it wasn't there.

2. __A__ Cathy speaks Japanese very well, doesn't she?
   A. She's quite fluent.
   B. She'd like to learn Japanese.
   C. She enjoyed her trip to Japan.

3. __B__ Haven't you heard that joke before?
   A. No, I never have.
   B. Yes, I've told it before.
   C. It wasn't very funny.

4. __C__ Aren't you hungry?
   A. I'm not angry.
   B. I can't do it.
   C. I'm starving!

5. __B__ He didn't have to get an X-ray, did he?
   A. He doesn't know where it is.
   B. Fortunately, he didn't
   C. The X-ray machine is on the second floor.

6. __C__ You don't need any more copier paper, do you?
   A. Yes, I'm sure it is.
   B. We've copied everything.
   C. No, we have enough.

7. __A__ Shouldn't we get some gasoline?
   A. Why? We still have half a tank.
   B. We shouldn't have bought it.
   C. They should be more careful.

8. __A__ Won't you have a seat?
   A. Thanks, but I don't mind standing.
   B. Yes, it's quite comfortable.
   C. I don't think it is.

9. __A__ Doesn't that display look great?
   A. It looks wonderful.
   B. It's not on display.
   C. This play is very interesting.

10. __C__ That's your briefcase, isn't it?
    A. Yes, quite brief.
    B. It's very important.
    C. It's mine all right.

11. __B__ You won first prize, right?
    A. The prize was perfect.
    B. No, second prize
    C. That's the right answer.

12. __C__ This is a sharp knife, wouldn't you say?
    A. Yes, if we can.
    B. I'd like a sharp knife.
    C. Very sharp

Exercise 2.11

1. __B__ How long have you been at your present address?
   A. I didn't buy a present.
   B. I've lived here two years.
   C. She's wearing a new dress.

2. __A__ Where should we meet for dinner?
   A. Let's meet at Felicia's Restaurant.
   B. No, I prefer fish.
   C. I don't know what to wear for dinner.

3. __C__ Where did you park the car?
   A. The park is across the street.
   B. I sent the postcard.
   C. I parked around the corner.

4. __A__ Does anyone know where a blank computer disk is?
   A. There are some in that cabinet.
   B. The computer desk should be against the wall.
   C. Yes, the desk is black.

5. __A__ Did you write the report yet?
   A. Yes, I finished it last night.
   B. That's the wrong report.
   C. No, jets can't land at this airport.

6. __C__ How long did you have to wait?
   A. About thirty miles
   B. About thirty pounds
   C. About thirty minutes

7. __B__ Did you buy a new set of golf clubs?
   A. No, I didn't join the club.
   B. No, this is my old set.
   C. Yes, I was slightly upset.

8. __B__ What shape was the table?
   A. It was in an antique shop.
   B. It was round.
   C. It was in excellent condition.

9. __B__ Do you have a cold?
   A. Yes, I haven't felt well all day.
   B. Yes, it's freezing out there.
   C. No, not here.

10. __A__ Did you see the tables in the back of the book?
   A. Yes, they contained a lot of useful information.
   B. Yes, they were made of dark wood.
   C. No, I haven't brought the book back yet.

Exercise 2.12

1. Did John already talk to you?
   Yes, I did. *Wrong person*
2. When will the work on the Hughes' account be done?
   Catherine is doing the work on it.
   Wrong type of question
3. Do you want an aisle seat or a window seat?
   No, thank you. *Wrong type of question*
4. How long did you spend in Lisbon?
   I'll be there for four days. *Wrong tense*
5. Is your sister a teacher?
   No, he isn't. *Wrong person*
6. Where did you buy that book?
   Last week. *Wrong type of question*
7. Did the police investigate the incident?
   Yes, they will. *Wrong tense*
8. Can you repair the machine?
   Yes, you can. *Wrong person*
9. Were you in the hospital?
   It's on Regent Street.
   Wrong type of question
10. Where was the training manual?
   Yes, it was. *Wrong type of question*

More Practice

1. __A__ How long has Claire worked in this department?
   A. Since last summer
   B. Sure, it's easy for her.
   C. In the shipping department

2. __B__ Why don't we take a break now?
   A. I couldn't help it.
   B. All right, but just for ten minutes.
   C. No, we don't know what it is.

3. __C__ Would you rather eat with chopsticks or with a fork?
   A. Yes, thank you.
   B. I'm not very hungry.
   C. With chopsticks, please

4. __B__ Where was the ticket found?
   A. I've got it in my briefcase.
   B. On the floor in the concourse
   C. From a travel agent

5. __A__ Would you like to leave a message for Mr. Campbell?
   A. Yes, please ask him to call his travel agent.
   B. I'm going to leave soon.
   C. No, I didn't like the message.

6. __C__ Can you tell me where to catch the bus?
   A. At 4:30
   B. To the museum
   C. Right around the corner

7. __B__ What's the matter with Ms. Braun?
   A. I'm not mad at her.
   B. She has a bad headache.
   C. There she is.

8. __C__ Are you sure this is the right road?
   A. Yes, I'm sure it will be tonight.
   B. It's on the left side of the road, I think.
   C. No — we'd better stop and get directions.

9. __A__ How did you get to work today?
   A. I rode my motorcycle.
   B. I saw an ad in the newspaper.
   C. I worked hard all day.

10. __C__ The weather sure is nice, isn't it?
   A. I don't know what the weather will be like.
   B. Don't worry, it's not icy.
   C. It couldn't be any nicer.

11. __B__ May I have another helping of dessert?
   A. Yes, you can help make it.
   B. Sure, help yourself.
   C. No, I've had enough, thanks.

12. __C__ Don't you just love these paintings?
   A. No, I hate to paint.
   B. They should be finished soon.
   C. Yes, they're very impressive.

13. __A__ How serious was the accident?
   A. Fortunately, it was fairly minor.
   B. One car ran a red light.
   C. No, I was only joking.

14. C   Would you mind turning on the air conditioner?
   A. This room is air conditioned.
   B. Thanks a lot.
   C. I'm sorry, but it's out of order.

15. B   Do you take checks?
   A. Yes, thanks.
   B. No, just cash.
   C. I have them.

16. B   Do you think Akiko is free this weekend?
   A. I don't think about it very often.
   B. No, she probably has to work.
   C. It didn't cost her anything.

17. C   I wonder why the traffic is moving so slowly?
   A. I'm going as fast as I can.
   B. About twenty miles an hour
   C. Maybe there is an accident up ahead.

18. A   How about going swimming?
   A. Fine, I'd like that.
   B. I swim fairly well.
   C. It's too far to swim.

19. A   You haven't been abroad for a long time, have you?
   A. No, I haven't been overseas for years.
   B. I lived abroad for several years.
   C. It won't be possible for me to leave the country.

20. C   What's Benjamin like?
   A. He enjoyed playing golf.
   B. I like him a lot.
   C. He seems very nice.

21. C   Do you want her to call you back?
   A. Yes, I'll return her call.
   B. She should be back soon.
   C. Yes, if it's convenient for her.

22. A   Do you speak any Indonesian?
   A. Just a few phrases
   B. I've been to Indonesia.
   C. I spoke to all of them.

23. A   Won't you two join us for dinner?
   A. We'll be glad to.
   B. We don't want to join.
   C. There will be two of us.

24. C   What time do you usually eat breakfast?
   A. I already did.
   B. Just coffee and toast, usually.
   C. About seven

25. B   Do you know if Ms. da Silva is planning to go to Lisbon?
   A. If you want to.
   B. I think that's her plan.
   C. It will be in Lisbon.

26. C   When did this package arrive?
   A. I sent it yesterday afternoon.
   B. From Toronto, I think
   C. Earlier this morning

27. C   In what room will the presentation be?
   A. I'll be there in a few minutes.
   B. It was on the first floor.
   C. In the meeting room on the first floor

28. B   Whose pen is this?
   A. Tom has my pen.
   B. It's mine.
   C. It's a black one.

29. A   Shouldn't we have a going-away party for André?
   A. Great idea — how about this Friday?
   B. It was a lot of fun.
   C. André should be leaving soon.

30. C   What kind of books do you like best?
   A. I read a biography.
   B. This book is the best.
   C. Mystery novels are my favorites.

Sample Test

1. __B__ F: <u>There</u> you are. I needed that contract half an hour ago.

M1: Sorry — I got lost on the way over here.

F: You should have gotten better directions.

2. __C__ M2: So you're still leaving on Tuesday, Rita?

F: No, I'm going to delay my trip for a day.

M2: That's probably a good idea.

3. __D__ M1: We don't have any reservations. Is it possible for us to get a table?

F: You're in luck — a party of two just canceled their reservations. We can seat you in a few minutes.

M1: Great.

4. __B__ F: Is there a dress code at your company?

M2: No, but most of the men wear coats and ties, and the women wear dresses or suits.

F: Oh, it's pretty formal then.

5. __A__ F: Good morning, National Office Supplies.

M1: Yes, this is Mr. Tupton. I'm calling about an order I just received. There were twenty packages of blue paper, and we ordered white paper.

F: I'll connect you with the customer service department, Mr. Tupton.

6. __A__ F: George, have you seen that video about new management techniques?

M1: No, but I intend to. I've heard it's interesting.

F: It's more than interesting — it could change your whole style of management.

7. __A__ F: So, do you like working here?

M1: Not nearly as much as I thought I would.

F: Give it a chance — you've only been here for a month.

8. __A__ M2: Front desk.

M1: Yes, I'd like to have my suit cleaned and pressed.

M2: Certainly. I'll have someone come by your room in a few minutes to pick it up.

9. __D__ F: Have you read this new book by Donald Hobart?

M1: I tried to, but I found it hard to follow.

F: So did I, but the critics sure seemed to like it.

10. __C__ M1: I haven't seen Brian lately. Isn't he working in the design department anymore?

F: Actually, he's in the management training program now.

M1: I didn't know that Brian wanted to be a manager.

Exercise 3.1 (no tapescript)

1. c	**4.** p	**7.** a	**10.** k
2. u	**5.** f	**8.** e	**11.** o
3. g	**6.** q	**9.** t	**12.** h

Exercise 3.2 (no tapescript)

1. l	**3.** a	**5.** b	**7.** m	**9.** g
2. f	**4.** o	**6.** h	**8.** i	**10.** c

Exercise 3.3

1. __A__   M1: There's something wrong with this switch. Can you fix it?
     M2: It's not just the switch, I'm afraid. This whole building needs rewiring.
     M1: But that will cost a fortune!

2. __C__   F: Don't you love shopping here?
     M2: I sure do. The farmers' fruits and vegetables are always so fresh.
     F: And it's nice to be outside when the weather is so warm.

3. __A__   M2: I think that suit looks very nice on you. It's a beautiful color, and the material is very high quality.
     M1: I don't know. The jacket seems too big.
     M2: You can have that taken in a little.

4. __B__   M2: Stacey, do you have those blueprints ready yet?
     F: No, I'm changing the design of the foyer slightly.
     M2: Well, I need to go over them with the builder tomorrow.

5. __D__   F: I want to put a new deck on the back of my house. Do you know anyone who does that kind of work?
     M1: Why don't you ask Thomas? He did a great job repairing the wooden stairway in my house.
     F: I asked him, but he's working on a new construction job.

6. __B__   M2: Could I get another cup of coffee?
     F: Sorry, sir, we're on our final approach now.
     M2: Oh, in that case I'd better buckle my seat belt.

7. __C__   M2: Sorry, ma'am, but no one is allowed in that wing of the plant without an identification badge.
     F: But I have an appointment with Mr. Salazar.
     M2: I'll call him. He can arrange a visitor's badge for you.

8. __A__   M1: Isn't this your usual stop?
     F: Yes, but today I'm going to the library.
     M1: Oh, then you should get off at the next stop and walk up to Clifton Avenue.

9. __D__   M2: I can't decide what to rent — I like funny movies, but my wife prefers European films.
     F: There's a wonderful new French comedy that just came in.
     M2: Sounds great. What shelf is it on?

10. __A__   M1: What color is the director's office going to be painted?
     M2: Lisa decided not to have it painted — she going to have it wallpapered instead.
     M1: Well, I guess that's the kind of decision we hired her to make.

11. __A__   M1: Can you show me your saws?
     M2: Power, or hand saws?
     M1: Power. And I'd like to see your electric drills too.

12. __C__   M2: Mr. Winston, we're going to do a few more tests.
     M1: Why, is there something the matter?
     M2: Your blood pressure is higher than we'd like it to be. I'm going to be prescribing some medicine for you as well.

Exercise 3.4

1. __B__   F: Did you go out in your boat?
     M1: No, we just stood on the dock.
     F: Did you catch anything?

2. __D__   M1: Excuse me, ma'am, that's not your bag.
     F: Oh — it sure looks like mine.
     M1: I know this is mine — see, this is my ID tag on the handle.

3. __C__   M1: Aren't her portraits beautiful?
     F: I like her still lifes even more. The fruit looks so real, you could take a bite out of it.
     M1: She certainly is a talented artist.

4. <u>B</u> M2: Have you signed a lease on a place yet?

F: Not yet, but I'm interested in a location in a shopping mall over in Glenwood.

M2: That would be a convenient location for a lot of your customers.

5. <u>A</u> M1: Have you seen this model yet?

M2: No, but I understand it's very fast.

M1: Not just that — it has a huge memory.

6. <u>D</u> F: You just want a trim, Mr. Krueger?

M1: Yes, just a little off the top.

F: Fine. Step back here, and I'll give you a shampoo.

7. <u>A</u> M1: There was another serious accident at the corner of Lamont Road and Highway 67.

F: Oh, no! That's the third one already this year.

M1: The city needs to put a traffic light there.

8. <u>B</u> F: Do you need to rent equipment?

M1: Just boots and poles.

F: All right. I'll stand in line to get lift tickets.

9. <u>A</u> M2: Did you use computers in your previous jobs?

F: No, but I worked with them in college.

M2: I'm afraid we're looking for someone with on-the-job computer experience.

10. <u>C</u> F: Do you want to see that documentary about deep-sea creatures?

M1: Sure. What time is it on?

F: It's on at eight on Channel 5.

Exercise 3.5

1. <u>D</u> M2: I'm going to pick up my wife at the airport.

F: All right, Mr. Maras. If one of your clients calls, when should I tell him you'll be back in the office?

M2: Oh, I won't be back until tomorrow morning.

2. <u>C</u> M1: I'm sorry, but the office is closed for the weekend.

F: What time will it open Monday?

M1: It isn't open at all then — Monday is a holiday.

3. <u>C</u> M1: Has the 7:30 showing of the movie started yet?

F: Yes, sir, about ten minutes ago.

M1: Guess I'll come back for the nine o'clock showing — I hate to miss the beginning of a film.

4. <u>D</u> M2: Eva, I understand you've been assigned to another sales region.

F: That's right, Carlos. I'm going to be working in the Pacific Northwest region now.

M2: Congratulations. I know you like that part of the country.

5. <u>B</u> F: Frank, I know your brother Joe started working here in 1994. Did you start the year after that?

M1: No, the year before.

F: Oh, I thought Joe started here before you did.

6. <u>B</u> M1: Hello, this is Patrick — I'm not feeling very well, and I don't think I'll be in this morning.

M2: Sorry to hear that, Patrick. Do you think you'll be able to come in tomorrow morning?

M1: Actually, if I feel better, I'm going to come in sometime after lunch.

7. <u>D</u> M2: I had to take a limousine to the airport.

M1: That must have been pretty expensive.

M2: Yes, but there just wasn't time to take the shuttle bus.

8. <u>A</u> F: Dan is sure in a bad mood this morning.

M1: He can't find his new coffee mug.

F: Is that all? Well, I saw it in the conference room.

9. <u>D</u> F: It sure is great to be home.

M1: Welcome back, Ms. Shearson. I forget — how long were you living abroad?

F: It was a year last month.

10. __B__   F: Are you going to the trade fair in Brussels this year, Jim?

   M1: I wish I could — I just have too many things to do here.

   F: Well, at least the distribution manager will be there.

Exercise 3.6

1. __D__   M1: I'm going to take my bicycle to the bike shop.

   F: Why? It just has a flat tire. Can't you fix that yourself?

   M2: I suppose I could, but while I'm there, I want to buy a new bike lock.

2. __C__   M2: I don't want to be disturbed while I'm talking to Mr. Utsumi.

   F: But Mr. Neufield, you have a meeting scheduled with the chief engineer.

   M2: Call him, please, and postpone our meeting. And hold all my calls.

3. __D__   F: I've decided to go back to school this fall.

   M1: What made you decide that, Mary?

   F: There just aren't enough opportunities in this field if you don't have a graduate degree.

4. __A__   F: What happened to the music? Is there something wrong with the tape player?

   M2: Let me look. Umm, no, for some reason, the tape broke.

   F: Too bad — I was really enjoying that song.

5. __D__   M1: Mrs. Powers, did you interview Katie?

   F: Yes, and I think she's well-qualified. If her references give her good recommendations, I'll offer her the position.

   M1: Oh, I'm sure they will.

6. __B__   M1: So, are you still going to Manila next week?

   M2: No, I think we should invite Mr. Quizon to come here instead.

   M1: Good idea. He should get familiar with our side of the operation anyway.

7. __C__   F: Don't get those documents out of order, whatever you do.

   M1: Uh, oh. You should have told me that sooner.

   F: You'd better put them back the way they were, then!

8. __A__   M1: The rent on this apartment is reasonable enough, but I live alone. I don't need this much room.

   F: I have a one-bedroom unit you may like better, and it's even cheaper.

   M1: Let's take a look at that one.

9. __D__   M1: How did your glass tabletop get cracked?

   M2: I dropped that flowerpot on it.

   M1: Well, you can always have the glass replaced.

10. __B__ M2: Did you know that Mr. Dufour is going to start investing in art?

   F: He'd better get some good advice first. Art is a risky field of investment.

   M2: He doesn't need to — he's an expert himself.

Exercise 3.7

1. __B__   M2: Aren't you and your husband going to the party Saturday night?

   F: I'm afraid not, Mr. Lo — we just moved here, and we don't have a babysitter for our children.

   M2: Let me give you my wife's number — she knows lots of good babysitters.

2. __D__   M2: Costs are still too high. They have to be cut.

   M1: Yes, but how?

   M2: For one thing, let's start making more use of our own employees and stop hiring so many outside consultants.

3. __B__   M1: Did you see that new play at the Odeon Theater?

   F: I saw about half of it. It was so trite and boring, I got up and left.

   M1: If I didn't know better, I'd say we saw different plays.

4. __B__   M1: Arlene, do you have to work this weekend again?
       F: I don't mind. They pay me time-and-a-half when I work overtime.
       M1: Yes, but everyone needs some time to relax.

5. __C__   M2: I'm going down to the coffee shop to get something to eat. Do you want to come?
       F: You know, Hans, after all the work we did today, I'm just going to stay in my room and get a good night's sleep.
       M2: If you don't feel like going out, you could order from room service and eat in your room.

6. __C__   F: We need another copier.
       M1: Why? There's nothing wrong with this one.
       F: Maybe not, but it's practically an antique.

7. __B__   M1: Did you know that NorCorp, Inc. just leased its own corporate jet?
       M2: If their executives want to waste that much money to impress customers, fine.
       M1: Well, I don't know if they're wasting money — I've seen figures to show that their plan is very cost effective.

8. __B__   F: I'm sorry, Ms. Bauer is at a sales meeting.
       M1: I see. Will it last much longer?
       F: Probably not. Why don't you get yourself some coffee or tea and have a seat over there?

9. __C__   F: Can we open a window in here? I need some fresh air.
       M2: Sorry, Donna — this is a climate-controlled building. The windows don't even open.
       F: It doesn't *feel* climate-controlled.

10. __D__   F: Did you know the company is going to install its own exercise equipment? We won't have to drive over to this health club every day after work.
       M1: Oh, great — I just bought a three-year membership at this place.
       F: Maybe you can sell it.

Exercise 3.8

1. __B__   F: Douglas, do you have any batteries for your flashlight?
       M1: No. I never think of buying batteries until the electricity goes out.
       F: I guess we'll just have to use candles then.

2. __A__   F: The sky is never this clear at home.
       M2: You can see for miles out here.
       F: And the air smells so fresh.

3. __B__   F: You're going sailing tomorrow?
       M1: Sure. Want to come?
       F: Perhaps. Do you know what the weather is going to be like?

4. __C__   F: As a clerk here, do I get a discount on the clothes I buy?
       M2: Yes, Natalie, we give our clerks thirty percent off retail prices once they've worked here for a month.
       F: Then I guess I'll wait a couple of weeks before I buy any clothes.

5. __D__   M1: How did you get to be so good on the piano?
       F: I took lessons when I was a child.
       M1: So did I, but I sure can't play like you.

6. __A__   M1: When I got to work this morning, the security system had been turned off.
       M2: Really? That's strange.
       M1: That's what I thought too.

7. __B__   M2: It's going to be another warm day.
       M1: Of course. You know, I miss living somewhere that has four seasons.
       M2: Me, too. I especially miss those cool, brisk autumn mornings.

8. __D__   M1: According to this memo, we have to attend a special meeting after work today.
       F: Look again — that's only for new employees.
       M1: Oh, you're right.

More Practice

1. __C__   F: Will my dry cleaning be ready Thursday?
       M2: Yes, Ms. Rao — you can pick it up after four on Thursday.
       F: Not until after four? I'll just get it the next morning.

2. __A__   M1: Could you meet Mr. Saito at the airport at two?
       M2: I'll be giving a presentation at two.
       M1: I guess I'll have to go then. The boss said he's an important client.

3. __B__   M1: We could do a better job on this project if we had more people working on it.
       F: Sure, Mark, but everyone else is working on the MacDougal job.
       M1: True. But we should at least ask for more time to complete it.

4. __C__   M1: The figures from last quarter are in, and it looks like our market share increased.
       M2: Yes, but profits were slightly down.
       M1: That's because our labor costs went up, and so did taxes.

5. __A__   F: Do you have any brothers or sisters?
       M1: I have an older brother and a younger sister.
       F: I'm an only child myself.

6. __D__   M1: Did you read that article about the unemployment rate in the business section?
       M2: Not yet. I'm still reading the front page.
       M1: I always start with the sports page myself.

7. __C__   M2: We're going to have a safety inspection soon.
       M1: Tomorrow?
       M2: No, in two days.

8. __B__   F: I like these blue ones.
       M1: Good choice. They're lightweight but strong, and easy to handle.
       F: Is there a matching carry-on bag?

9. __A__   M2: I can't hear a thing in here. Let's go to another restaurant for dinner.

       F: But Dennis, we've already ordered. The food will be here any minute.
       M2: So what? We'll just tell the waiter to cancel the order.

10. __C__   M1: The scenery here is beautiful.
       F: Wait until we finish hiking up to the top of the hill. The view is even better there.
       M1: When we get there, I'd like to have lunch. I'm getting hungry.

11. __B__   M2: Are you going to Bangkok on business or for a vacation?
       F: I'm going there for a business conference, but I hope to get out of my hotel to see some sights.
       M2: Be sure to visit the Temple of the Dawn. It's famous all over the world.

12. __A__   M2: Did you see those shots Cynthia took for the Canfield Department Store ads?
       F: Those were Cynthia's? They're fabulous!
       M2: Aren't they! She can make anyone's line of clothes look great.

13. __D__   M2: How much would you like to exchange?
       F: I'd like $500 worth of Deutschemarks, please.
       M2: Very well. I'll need to see your passport. Will you be exchanging traveler's checks or cash?

14. __A__   F: I'd like to put this on my credit card.
       M2: Fine. I should mention, however, that there's a small surcharge for paying by credit card here. It's three percent higher than payment by cash.
       F: In that case, I'll pay by traveler's check.

15. __D__   M1: Do you like that office tower they built on Market Street?
       M2: I like it, but it sure doesn't blend in with those old Victorian buildings on Market.
       M1: Personally, I like the contrast of old and new.

16. B
M1: You're taking your vacation in September?
F: Right. I think it's the perfect time. The weather is still warm, but the resorts aren't crowded.
M1: I'd do the same thing, but my kids are in school then.

17. A
M1: Do you happen to have a spare key to the filing cabinet that's in my office?
F: No, why?
M1: I think I locked mine inside it.

18. B
F: Dr. Lamb can see you first thing tomorrow, Mr. Ranglos.
M1: Tomorrow! But I have a *terrible* toothache!
F: Oh, in that case, I'll call you back in a few minutes. He can fit you in later this afternoon.

19. C
M2: Don't you think it's extravagant to buy fresh flowers for the office every Friday?
M1: Not really. The office workers appreciate it, and it's good for morale.
M2: I think it's just another unnecessary expense.

20. C
M1: Did you hear about Roy? He's been transferred to the public relations department.
F: Well, let's hope he likes his new job more than he liked his job in the sales department.
M1: Oh, sure he will. At least he has some training in public relations.

21. B
M2: Our bid for the Rusnak contract arrived too late to be considered.
M1: Impossible. I sent it by express messenger service Monday afternoon.
M2: But it had to be there by Monday morning.

22. A
F: You mean all you have left are compacts?
M1: I'm afraid so.
F: But I specifically requested a mid-sized model when I called in my reservation.

23. C
M1: It's *still* not fixed?
F: No, and of course it had to break down during the hottest week of the year.
M1: Well, if it's not fixed by tomorrow, I'm not wearing a coat and tie in the office.

24. B
M2: Aren't you Ms. Silverman's administrative assistant?
F: You must be confusing me with someone else. I work in the personnel department.
M2: Oh, sorry — you look a lot like her.

25. B
F: I can't believe how nice and sunny it is today.
M1: I know. Last year at this time, there was ten inches of snow on the ground.
F: Unfortunately, there's a cold front moving in tomorrow, and it's supposed to turn cloudy.

26. D
M2: Can you fix this leaky faucet?
M1: Of course. I'll just have to replace a washer. It should only take a few minutes.
M2: Great. I was afraid there might be some serious problems with the pipes.

27. D
F: Why aren't you using the new laser printer?
M1: Tell you the truth, I don't know exactly how it works.
F: There's an instruction manual in that cabinet with the printer paper.

28. A
M1: So I'll bring the sleeping bags and the tent.
M2: And I'll bring the food and the camp stove.
M1: This is going to be fun!

29. B
M2: Jane, you went skiing at Winter Star last week, didn't you?
F: I was going to, but there just wasn't enough snow.
M2: Well, there's plenty now. Conditions are great!

30. C
M1: Where do you want me to leave these boxes?
F: You'll have to take them to the Purchasing and Receiving Department.
M1: Is that on the other side of the plant?

Sample Test

[Questions 1 and 2 refer to the following recorded announcement:]
[Your attention, please. Stopping momentarily in front of the airport terminal building is permitted only for the unloading of passengers and baggage. Short-term parking is available at the airport parking structure, and long-term parking is available at the facility on Jones Road. Do not leave your vehicle unattended for any reason. Unattended vehicles will be ticketed and towed to the police lot downtown. Your cooperation is appreciated.]

1. A   **2.** D

[Questions 3 and 4 refer to this forecast:]
[It looks as though our warm, sunny, summer-like weather will continue at least through Saturday and Sunday, so this weekend will be the perfect time to go out to the countryside to view the colorful fall foliage. On Monday, though, it appears we're in for a change. It should be much cooler, and there's a good chance of rain or perhaps even snow flurries.]

3. D   **4.** C

[Questions 5 and 6 are based on the following announcement:]
[Attention, shoppers: someone has just turned in a pair of prescription sunglasses in a black leather case. They were found on the floor of the sporting goods section. If these glasses are yours, please come to the customer service booth to claim them.]

5. C   **6.** C

[Questions 7 to 9 are based on the following talk:]
[And now, ladies and gentlemen, I'd like to present the award for employee of the month to Elizabeth Bryce from the shipping department. She not only received top evaluations from her supervisor; she also submitted a suggestion that could save the company thousands of dollars a year in shipping costs. Besides a small bonus in next week's paycheck, Ms. Bryce gets a reserved parking place for a month —the one right next to the CEO's spot. She also becomes eligible for the employee of the year award, and as you know, the employee of the year wins a new car.]

7. A   **8.** C   **9.** D

[Questions 10 to 12 refer to the following advertisement:]
[Are you frustrated because you need to know a language for business reasons but you're just too busy to take classes? Then order a language kit from Translingua. Watch our videocassettes and work on our CD-ROM computer program in the comfort of your home. Learn in a natural way by listening to native speakers in business situations and then responding to them in your own words. No boring grammar rules to memorize. Courses now available in English, Spanish, and Japanese. Courses in French and Russian will be available in the next few months. Each kit contains four workbooks, two video-cassettes, and one CD-ROM computer disk. Call Translingua today.]

10. A   **11.** D   **12.** B

Exercise 4.1

[Questions 1 to 3 are based on this announcement:]
[Paging Glasgow-bound passenger Kim, Mr. Chang Su Kim. Mr. Kim, please come to the ticket counter of British Airways International or pick up one of the white information telephones located through-out the airport to receive an important message.]

1. C   **2.** A   **3.** C

[Questions 4 and 5 refer to this talk:]
[Attention, Food Mart shoppers. Stop by our fresh fish department for our catch of the day. Today's catch is delicious salmon steaks, perfect for grilling over charcoal. Today only, these salmon steaks are two for the price of one. And while you're at it, stop by our bakery for some French bread, still warm from the oven.]

4. B   **5.** D

[Questions 6 to 8 are based on this announcement:]
[Attention, all passengers, this is your captain speaking: There is a four-year-old boy named Nicholas who says he became separated from his mother and

father in the snack shop on Deck A. He's waiting for his parents in the purser's office on Deck C. And to all our other passengers: we should be docking in the next few minutes. I hope you've enjoyed your trip despite the rough seas.]

6. _C_   7. _A_   8. _A_

[Questions 9 to 12 are based on this talk:]
[The next two-hour tour of Monument Cavern will depart in fifteen minutes. You may purchase your tickets in the gift shop. Tickets are six dollars for adults, four dollars for children six to twelve, and children under six are free. As soon as you have purchased your tickets, please come to the elevators at the north side of the building. The elevators will take you down to the top level of the cave.]

9. _C_   10. _B_   11. _D_   12. _B_

[Questions 13 to 15 refer to this announcement:]
[Good morning, ladies and gentlemen: we have reached our cruising altitude of 36,000 feet, and we're about 60 miles northwest of Flagstaff, Arizona. Those of you seated on the right-hand side of the aircraft should be able to see the Grand Canyon off in the distance. We're estimating our time of arrival at Denver International Airport at around nine AM Mountain Standard Time — about an hour from now. We're running about twenty minutes late due to our delayed departure from Los Angeles. In just a few minutes, our cabin attendants will begin food and beverage service, but for now, we'd like to invite you to sit back, relax, and enjoy the flight.]

13. _D_   14. _C_   15. _A_

Exercise 4.2

[Questions 1 to 3 refer to the following news item:]
[And now, this item just in from Cape Canaveral, Florida. This morning, the mighty rocket engines of the booster rocket that was to carry the Space Shuttle *Pathfinder* into earth orbit were automatically shut down minutes before lift-off, due to a problem with the on-board computer system. Engineers will work to correct the problem today and tomorrow. The shuttle will be launched two days from now if the weather remains clear. The *Pathfinder*, as you may remember, is the first of the new generation of space shuttles that can stay in orbit considerably longer than the original shuttles.]

1. _D_   2. _B_   3. _D_

[Questions 4 to 6 refer to the following bulletin:]
[Residents of the Eastern Seaboard, especially those in coastal Maryland, Virginia, and North Carolina, can breathe a little easier. Hurricane Charlotte was scheduled to slam into this area with winds of 120 miles per hour. After passing about 80 miles north of Bermuda, Charlotte has turned to the northeast and is heading toward the open Atlantic. It is expected now to pass no closer than 200 miles from the Eastern Seaboard, and no serious damage is expected.]

4. _B_   5. _A_   6. _C_

[Questions 7 to 9 are based on the following public service message:]
[Most of us do not consider balloons toys that have to be handled with special care. In fact, when we think of balloons, we think of birthday parties and other happy childhood occasions. However, balloons pose a risk that many parents overlook. An uninflated balloon or a piece of a popped balloon may lodge in a child's throat if swallowed and cause choking and suffocation. Parents should inflate balloons for young children and supervise their use.]

7. _C_   8. _D_   9. _A_

[Questions 10 to 12 refer to this bulletin:]
[This is Sherry Dobbins in the KDCX traffic copter, with our rush-hour traffic report. There are going to be some major delays if you're headed west on Interstate Highway 74. A truck has spilled its cargo of lumber all across the four westbound lanes. And if you're planning to take the Valley Expressway north, forget it. From up here, looks like two cars were involved in a collision near Lake Avenue. You'll be better off taking Route 8. Traffic is heavy on 8, but at least it's moving.]

10. _B_   11. _A_   12. _D_

Exercise 4.3

[Questions 1 to 3 are based on the following advertisement:]
[When you think of Viking Mountain, you probably think of world-class skiing, and with good reason. But Viking Mountain is much, much more. It's also a world-class summer resort, offering a challenging eighteen-hole golf course and a lake for swimming, fishing, and boating. In late June, there is the famous Viking Mountain jazz music festival, in July an arts and crafts fair, and in August a classical music

festival. And summer hotel rates are more than reasonable. Rooms at the Norseman Lodge and the other hotels are half the ski-season rate. So come on up now for summer fun on Viking Mountain.]

1. __C__   2. __A__   3. __D__

[Questions 4 and 5 refer to this commercial message:]
[Bruhn Design announces a new line of products for the discriminating traveler — all beautifully designed, long-lasting, and ultra lightweight. These include handsome briefcases, travel alarm clocks, electric travel irons, and powerful, portable short-wave radios for the world traveler. Bruhn Design products are available at fine stores everywhere.]

4. __A__   5. __D__

[Questions 6 and 7 are based on this advertisement:]
[Everyone knows that by the time you read something in a monthly or weekly business magazine, it is already old news. International business situations change from day to day. Now *Business Day*, the only major daily business magazine, helps you stay current with the unfolding world of business every day, Monday through Friday. Why wait? Subscribe to *Business Day* today.]

6. __C__   7. __C__

[Questions 8 to 10 refer to this commercial message:]
[Cakes-by-Carolyn now offers cakes for your office birthday party, retirement party, or other special office function. And remember, Carolyn's can customize your cake with any message or design that you like. Also available are our delicious coffee rolls and donuts for those early morning meetings. So call Carolyn's from 6 AM to 3 PM. And don't forget, we deliver!]

8. __D__   9. __A__   10. __B__

Exercise 4.4

[Questions 1 to 3 are based on the following remarks:]
[Good morning, everyone Before we get down to the first item on our agenda, I'd like to say a few words of congratulations. You must really have been paying attention to me at the meeting last month! Virtually everyone's sales figures are up this month. I'd like to single out a few people for special mention. Jane's sales were up 10%, Tom's sales were up 12%, Nina's were up 15%, and Rob's were up an amazing 24%, all just in one month. Great job,

everyone! Let's all get together after work Friday to celebrate.]

1. __D__   2. __C__   3. __B__

[Questions 4 and 5 are based on the following introductory comments:]
[Ladies and gentlemen, I'd like to thank you for inviting me and my colleagues from Hyperdata, Inc. to discuss some innovative systems for storing, retrieving, and then transmitting information via satellites, and to demonstrate some of our products that will allow you to put these systems to work for you here at North American Dynamics. We've prepared a multimedia presentation to acquaint you with our new equipment, but I know some of you have a few questions, so let's begin with those.]

4. __B__   5. __D__

[Questions 6 to 8 are based on the following announcement:]
[Attention, all personnel. Flu season begins soon, so the company is offering flu shots for all employees Friday. The shots will be given in the company nurse's office, just off the lunchroom. They will be administered by health professionals from the county health department. These shots would cost ten dollars if you got them at the Health Department, twenty-five dollars at a clinic, and forty dollars or more if given by a private doctor, but we are offering them at no cost in order to reduce absenteeism. So come get your flu shots on Friday and stay healthy this winter.]

6. __A__   7. __A__   8. __C__

[Questions 9 and 10 are based on this talk:]
[We'd like to extend a warm hello this evening to you, our colleagues from the Singapore branch of the corporation. Tomorrow, you are going to have a busy day. You'll have a chance to tour our plant, meet with the executive board, and discuss technical matters with members of our engineering team. Tonight, though, we just want you to relax, have something to eat and drink, and get to know us.]

9. __B__   10. __D__

Exercise 4.5

[Questions 1 and 2 are based on the following recorded message:]
[Thank you for calling Alpha Airlines. All our customer representatives are busy with other callers

at this moment. Your call will be answered in the order in which it was received. Please hang on, as your call is important to us. And thank you for calling Alpha, the first word in air travel.]

1. _B_   **2.** _A_

[*Questions 3 to 5 are based on the following recording:*]
[Attention, riders. Do not pull down the safety bar. The safety bar will engage automatically before the ride begins. To avoid injuries, do not attempt to stand up or put your arms outside of the roller coaster car. In case of an emergency, do not leave the car. Stay seated, and park personnel will assist you. At the end of the ride, do not attempt to leave your seat until the roller coaster car has come to a complete stop and the safety bar has been automatically disengaged.]

3. _B_   **4.** _A_   **5.** _D_

[*Questions 6 and 7 refer to the following recorded announcement:*]
[Thank you for calling Woodland Gear, where only the finest in camping equipment and outdoor clothing and footwear are sold. If you wish to place a new order, please press "star one" on your touch-tone phone. If you have a question about a previous order, press "star two." For any other business, press "star three."]

6. _C_   **7.** _B_

[*Questions 8 to 10 refer to the following recorded message:*]
[Thanks for calling Triplex Cinema. Today in Cinema 1, we are screening the suspense thriller *Neon Streets*. In Cinema 2, that heart-warming family comedy *Daisy* is being shown, and in Cinema 3, we have the action-adventure hit *Rico's Revenge*. All films are shown at 3, 5, 7, and 9. On Friday and Saturday, there is a special showing of that science fiction classic, *Star Voyage*, beginning at midnight. Admission for the first showing of all movies is $3. Regular admission is $4 for children and $7 for adults. Admission to the midnight movie is $3.]

8. _D_   **9.** _B_   **10.** _B_

More Practice

[*Questions 1 to 3 are based on the following advertisement:*]
[Some exercise machines, such as rowing machines, work out only your upper body. Others, such as stationary bicycles, work out only your lower body. Does this mean you should buy two machines? Not at all. Exercise experts say that you achieve maximum benefit from working out all your muscle systems at one time. That's why the Polaris Exersystem was developed — to provide you with a full-body workout from one machine. Easy to use, even for a beginner. Easy to assemble. And even easy to afford. Make one payment of $100 and we'll send you the Polaris Exersystem. Then make just four payments of $200 for only four months. Act now, and start getting in shape.]

1. _C_   The speaker says a rowing machine works out only the upper body.
2. _D_   Exercise experts say that a person achieves maximum benefit from working out all muscle systems at one
          _B_   time.
3. ____   The monthly payment for four months is $200. (The initial payment is $100.)

[*Questions 4 and 5 are based on the following commercial message:*]
[Do you need to rent a car but have a limited budget? Why not give Bob's Auto rental a call? We provide clean, dependable, quality used cars at unbelievably low rates. So, if you want to impress someone, go to one of those expensive rental agencies. If you just want to get from Point A to Point B and back again, come to Bob's. We're located on Marshall Boulevard, just north of Oxford Mall. We provide free shuttle service to and from the airport and from the major downtown hotels.]

4. _D_   The cars at Bob's Auto Rental are available at "unbelievably low rates."
5. _B_   Bob's is located on Marshall Boulevard near the Oxford Mall.

[*Questions 6 and 7 are based on the following talk:*]
[Before we go on to the next issue, I'd like to go back to the point Jim just made. I don't think his plan to hire temporary help to finish the Shannon project is a good one at all. Sure, it may cost us some in overtime salaries to have our own people do the job, but not as much as it will cost to go through the temporary agencies. Besides, the temporary workers will have to be trained, and think how much time that will take. And in the future, we need to be certain that we have the resources to complete a project on schedule before we accept it.]

6. _C_   The speaker is disagreeing with Jim; he doesn't believe that Jim's plan is "a good one at all."
7. _D_   Jim's plan is to hire temporary workers; the speaker disagrees with it.

[Questions 8 to 11 are based on the following report:]
[This is Max Hampton of the eyewitness news team with the noon update. As you can see, those fires in the warehouse complex in lower downtown that began at about 5 AM are still burning out of control. At least two warehouses have been burned to the ground, and half a dozen are in flames. So far, only one person, a night watchman, has been reported injured, mainly because at the time the fires broke out, the area was virtually deserted. The cause of the blaze remains a mystery although, according to owners, a previous fire here was caused by faulty electrical wiring in these old buildings. There's no evidence of deliberate arson. Now we're going to try to get some more details from Fire Chief Paul Cummings. Chief, would you step over here for a moment, please?]

8. __D__ The speaker identifies himself as part of a news team, so he is obviously a reporter; the fact that people can see the fires indicates that he is a television reporter.
9. __B__ There has been only one reported injury (to a night watchman).
10. __A__ The fire broke out at 5 AM.
11. __D__ The cause of the fire "remains a mystery."

[Questions 12 and 13 are based on the following advertisement:]
[Businesspersons, we at Mario's Restaurant know just how valuable your time is. If you order from our special Businesspersons' Menu and your lunch takes longer than ten minutes to arrive at your table, then it is absolutely free. We also offer private rooms for groups of eight or more, so have your lunch meetings at Mario's. Also, while you're here, don't forget to drop your business card in the goldfish bowl by the cash register. If we pick your card in our weekly drawing, you win a free dinner for two.]

12. __D__ If lunch does not arrive at the table within 10 minutes, it is served for free.
13. __B__ The prize is "a free dinner for two."

[Questions 14 to 16 are based on the following voice-mail message:]
[This is Don Beeson of Beeson and Sitwell Architectural Associates. It's now 2:30 PM. I will be out of the office for the rest of the afternoon, and I won't be returning until tomorrow at 9 AM. If you need to speak with me this afternoon, please leave a message on my voicemail. I'll be checking my voicemail and returning calls from my home. If you have an urgent problem, you can call my partner, Robin Sitwell, at 320-1631. Have a great day.]

14. __C__ He says he will not return until tomorrow.
15. __C__ He asks callers to leave a message on his voice mail, and says that he will then return calls from his home this afternoon.
16. __A__ He identifies Robin Sitwell as his partner.

[Questions 17 to 20 are based on the following talk:]
[Welcome to Radio Station WKYO's show, Garden Spot. This is your host, Peter Brooks. This time of year, with just a few weeks until the first days of fall, is a good time to talk about harvesting your garden vegetables, and today I have a few hints for you. For example, did you know that you should always pick corn in the morning when it's cool? That's because the afternoon heat turns the sugar in the corn to starch and spoils the taste. And did you know that the longer you leave peppers on the vine, the more vitamin C they contain? We'll be back in a moment with more harvesting hints, and a little later, Professor Gail Mueller, an expert on plant parasites, will be dropping by the studio to chat with us, but first, this commercial message from our sponsor, the Colony Seed Company.]

17. __A__ The speaker identifies himself as the host of the radio show "Garden Spot."
18. __B__ Corn should be picked in the morning because the afternoon heat turns the sugar to starch, so it won't taste as sweet.
19. __A__ The speaker says that first, there will be a message from the program's sponsor, Colony Seed Company.
20. __B__ Fall is a few weeks away, so it must still be summer.

Sample Test

1. C	3. B	5. C	7. D	9. A
2. D	4. C	6. A	8. D	10. C

Exercise 5.1

1. d	5. b	9. d	13. d	17. b	21. d
2. b	6. a	10. c	14. a	18. c
3. c	7. a	11. a	15. b	19. a
4. d	8. b	12. d	16. d	20. b

Exercise 5.2

1. so	11. No
2. some	12. alike almost
3. enough	13. any
4. such never	14. too much
5. Most	15. amounts
6. many	16. Like
7. yet	17. already
8. Fewer	18. such not
9. anymore	19. Among the most
10. Like	20. Little yet

Exercise 5.3

1. b	4. a	7. c	10. d	13. a
2. d	5. c	8. b	11. c	14. c
3. c	6. d	9. a	12. a	15. d

Exercise 5.4

1. said — *Said* is not used with an object before the clause (*said that*); *told* must take an object.
2. Visitors — Only *visitors* is used with the preposition *to*.
3. twice — Only *twice* can be used as an adverb (meaning "two times").
4. advised — Only *advised* is used with an object + an infinitive (*advised him to study*).
5. goods — A plural subject is required because the verb *are* is plural.
6. looking — Only *looking* is used with the words *out of*.
7. pay — Only *pay* can be used with *for*.
8. tell — *Tell* is used with an object (*tell you*); *say* is not.
9. close — Only *close* can be used with the preposition *to*.
10. standards — Only *standards* is used after the verb *set*.
11. regarded — *Regarded* is followed by *as*; *considered* is not.
12. heard — *Heard* is not used with a preposition; *listened* is used with the preposition *to*.

Exercise 5.5

1. A	4. A	7. D	10. A	13. A
2. D	5. B	8. D	11. B	14. C
3. C	6. A	9. A	12. A	15. C

Exercise 5.6

1. b	5. a	9. a	13. c	17. d	21. c
2. a	6. b	10. a	14. d	18. c	22. c
3. d	7. d	11. c	15. a	19. a	23. d
4. c	8. c	12. b	16. b	20. d	24. b

Exercise 5.7

1. A	3. D	5. D	7. A	9. D	11. A
2. B	4. A	6. C	8. A	10. C	12. D

Exercise 5.8

1. C	3. D	5. D	7. C	9. B	11. D
2. A	4. B	6. D	8. A	10. A	12. D

Exercise 5.9

1. rises	10. discuss
2. has been played	11. taken
3. was watching	12. has been published
4. had just returned	13. is giving
5. will finish	14. be promoted
6. spend	15. driven
7. snowed	
8. has owned	
9. was written	

Exercise 5.10

1. d	4. c	7. b	10. b	13. a
2. a	5. b	8. a	11. a	14. d
3. b	6. a	9. c	12. d	15. b

Exercise 5.11

1. D	4. C	7. B	10. B	13. B
2. B	5. D	8. C	11. C	14. D
3. A	6. A	9. A	12. A	15. B

Exercise 5.12

1.	of	for		
2.	of	to		
3.	into	to		
4.	with	in	of	with
5.	of	of		
6.	for	for		
7.	to	for	for	

8.	of	to/for		
9.	of	to		
10.	for	to		
11.	to	in	of	
12.	with	about		
13.	for	for		
14.	to	of	on	
15.	of	of		
16.	with	at		
17.	to	of		
18.	with	to		
19.	with	on	to	in
20.	of	by	of	of

Exercise 5.13

1.	by	in	in	
2.	in	for		
3.	In	with		
4.	at	by	until	
5.	by	between		
6.	in	on	at	in/within
7.	in	with		
8.	in	at		
9.	in	at	since	for
10.	by	in		
11.	on	during/in		
12.	During/In	on	at	
13.	at	in	at	
14.	At	in	in/within	
15.	in	on	in	
16.	by	until	during/in	
17.	on	in		
18.	in	by	in	
19.	in	on		
20.	From	on	in	

Exercise 5.14

1. A	4. D	7. B	10. D
2. B	5. C	8. C	11. C
3. D	6. A	9. A	12. A

Exercise 5.15

1. d	5. b	9. b	13. b
2. a	6. c	10. c	14. d
3. c	7. e	11. a	15. a
4. e	8. a	12. d	16. c

Exercise 5.16

1. a	5. a	9. b	13. d
2. d	6. e	10. a	14. a
3. e	7. c	11. c	15. c
4. c	8. d	12. e	16. e

Exercise 5.17

1. e	5. e	9. a	13. e
2. c	6. b	10. c	14. a
3. b	7. a	11. e	15. c
4. a	8. d	12. b	16. d

Exercise 5.18

1. B	4. D	7. A	10. A	13. A	16. C
2. C	5. A	8. B	11. C	14. A	
3. A	6. C	9. B	12. B	15. D	

Exercise 5.19

1.	singing	to deliver	paying
2.	to implement		
3.	cooking	cleaning up	
4.	hiking		
5.	miss		
6.	to practice	speaking	
7.	to be		
8.	to go shopping		
9.	taking	to drop	
10.	fix	to change	
11.	to stop	drinking	
12.	to pay		
13.	work	to arrange	
14.	going		
15.	go	hiking	stay

Exercise 5.20

1. A	4. D	7. A	10. C
2. C	5. A	8. B	11. D
3. C	6. D	9. A	12. D

More Practice

1. B	11. C	21. D	31. D
2. D	12. C	22. A	32. D
3. D	13. D	23. D	33. A
4. B	14. B	24. B	34. B
5. C	15. A	25. D	35. C
6. B	16. B	26. D	36. B
7. A	17. A	27. C	37. A
8. D	18. B	28. C	38. B
9. B	19. C	29. B	39. D
10. A	20. C	30. A	40. B

Sample Test

1. D	4. C	7. A	10. A
2. D	5. C	8. C	11. C
3. A	6. A	9. C	12. B

Exercise 6.1

1. X were	6. X is	11. X is	16. C
2. C	7. C	12. X was	17. C
3. X have	8. X is	13. X was	18. X has
4. C	9. C	14. C	19. C
5. C	10. C	15. X attend	20. X are

Exercise 6.2

1. X have become
2. C
3. X took
4. C
5. X have
6. X was not
7. C
8. X have visited
9. X had just boarded
10. X pays off
11. X have not had
12. X worked
13. X will have already returned
14. C
15. X like

Exercise 6.3

1. X produced	6. X strengthened	11. X grown
2. X jogging	7. C	12. C
3. X read	8. X worn	13. X sang
4. X seen	9. X flew	14. X driving
5. C	10. C	15. X changed

Exercise 6.4

1. C	6. C	11. C
2. X so much	7. X so	12. X beside
3. X too	8. X so often	13. C
4. C	9. X Like	14. X between
5. X After	10. X no longer	

Exercise 6.5

1. X lend	8. X lie	15. X made
2. X do	9. C	16. X robbed
3. X common	10. X late	17. X customs
4. X made	11. X nearly	18. X made
5. X major	12. X raised	19. C
6. X unanimously	13. X felt	20. X accept
7. X old	14. X owe	

Exercise 6.6

1. X recent	5. X smooth	9. X sudden
2. C	6. X annual	10. X well
3. X particularly	7. X dense	
4. X loyal	8. C	

Exercise 6.7

1. X health	11. X confidence
2. X analyze	12. X warm
3. X drama	13. X walks
4. X speech	14. X Tourism
5. C	15. X French
6. X safety	16. X full
7. X delivers	17. X prove
8. C	18. C
9. X Payment	19. X relief
10. X advice	20. X leader

Exercise 6.8

1. A   The past participle *given* is required after the auxiliary *has*.
2. C   The correct word is *hard*. (*Hardly* means "only a little.")
3. A   *Popular* means well-liked, but no one likes the flu! The proper word is *common*.
4. B   The negative adjective *no* must be used before a noun.
5. C   The future perfect tense is needed: *will have increased*.
6. B   The adverb *carefully* is required.
7. B   The past tense *wore* is needed in place of the past participle (*worn*).
8. C   The noun *list* is needed in place of the gerund.
9. D   In a time clause about the future, the simple present tense is needed.
10. A   The verb *are* must be used to agree with the grammatical subject, *several people*.
11. B   The past participle *held* is required after the auxiliary *are*.
12. B   Before an adjective + noun (*beautiful sight*), the phrase *such a* must be used in place of *so*.
13. A   The correct phrase is *in general*.
14. B   The verb *choose* is needed.
15. A   The noun *importance* is needed.
16. C   The correct expression is *fell asleep*. (*Fell* is the past tense of *fall; felt* is the past tense of *feel*.)
17. B   The past tense is needed because the verb is a passive form, not a progressive form.
18. A   The correct word is *did*.

19. A The verb *told* should be used because the verb *said* cannot be followed by an indirect object such as *you*.
20. D The noun form *seniority* is needed.

Exercise 6.9
1. X at	6. C	11. X in
2. X for	7. X by	12. C
3. X for	8. X on	13. X with/by
4. X on	9. X in	14. X on
5. X from	10. X by	15. X to

Exercise 6.10
1. X overseas	7. X Most of the
2. X next Friday	8. C
3. C	9. X Hundreds of people
4. X spite of the problems	10. X contact one
5. X which	11. X in the rear of the
6. X belongs to Patty	12. X approved by the director

Exercise 6.11
1. X to risk	6. X get	11. X to import
2. X getting	7. C	12. X helping
3. X to follow	8. X to record	13. X to pick
4. C	9. C	14. C
5. C	10. X work	15. C

Exercise 6.12
1. X and me	11. C
2. X it	12. C
3. X Your	13. X we saw
4. X These	14. C
5. X whose	15. X it
6. X yourselves	16. X herself
7. C	17. X her
8. X his	18. X to
9. X their	19. X them
10. X this	20. X offers

Exercise 6.13
1. X pounds of coffee	11. X minutes
2. C	12. C
3. X ten years old	13. X mountain roads
4. X discoveries	14. X participants
5. X two-room suite	15. C
6. C	16. X the women
7. X advice	17. X coin collectors
8. C	18. X eight-month-old
9. X feet	19. X jewelry
10. C	20. C

Exercise 6.14
1. C The correct form of the infinitive is *to enter* (omit *for*).
2. D *Equipment* is a noncount noun and should not be pluralized.
3. C After the verb *allow*, the infinitive (*to enter*) must be used.
4. B No preposition is used before the word *abroad*.
5. A *Thousand* should be pluralized.
6. A The preposition *in* should be used: *in line*.
7. C The preposition *to* is needed after the verb *lead*.
8. B The noun *example* should be pluralized.
9. A After the verb *let*, a simple form is needed.
10. D The first noun of a compound noun (*professional golfers*) should not be pluralized.
11. B The correct possessive form is *their*.
12. D *Tooth* has an irregular plural form, *teeth*.
13. B The plural first person pronoun *we* should be used in place of the singular first person pronoun *I* to agree with the plural noun *foreigners*.
14. A The gerund *seeing* is needed after the verb *missed*.
15. C The plural noun *weeks* should be used.
16. C The feminine possessive form *her* should be used to agree with the feminine noun *actress*.
17. C The correct preposition is *for*: *for rent*.
18. A No preposition is used after the verb *attended*.
19. B The pronoun *it* should be omitted.
20. B The noun *plane* should be pluralized.

Exercise 6.15
1. C	6. X highest
2. X hotter	7. X less
3. X the most reliable	8. X most important
4. X worst	9. C
5. C	10. X faster

Exercise 6.16
1. C	11. X a third
2. X Volume	12. X the near future
3. C	13. X a university
4. X the airport	14. X The first
5. X an idea	15. C
6. C	16. X The water
7. X Water	17. X an hour
8. X the photographs	18. X most
9. X the roof	19. C
10. X a week	20. X business administration

Exercise 6.17
1. X big enough problems	7. X environmental
2. X fully grown	8. X miles long
3. X that means	9. X us to show him
4. C	10. X there were
5. X in which	11. X almost entirely
6. C	12. X much too

Exercise 6.18

1. X Because of
2. X what
3. X which/that
4. X if
5. C
6. X who/that
7. X neither
8. C
9. X which/that
10. X When
11. X that
12. X but also

Exercise 6.19

1. X limited
2. X disappointing
3. X frustrating
4. C
5. X written
6. X amazed
7. C
8. C
9. X disgusting
10. X stolen

Exercise 6.20

1. C   Before a word beginning with a consonant sound, the article *a* must be used.
2. A   The past participle *frozen* is required.
3. C   The article *the* is missing: *near the end.*
4. B   Before a noun phrase (*his strong background*) *because of* must be used.
5. B   The correct word order is *at which* (preposition + relative word).
6. C   The noun-clause marker *what* should be used.
7. C   The correct pattern is *either . . . or.*
8. D   The correct word order is *working too slow.*
9. C   The possessive form *whose* must be replaced with the subject form *who.*
10. B   The correct word order is *warm enough.* (Adjectives precede the word *enough.*)
11. D   The present participle *amusing* is required.
12. D   The comparative form of the adjective (*clearer*) is needed to compare two things.
13. A   The definite article *the* should be used before the superlative form of the adjective.
14. C   The article *a* should be omitted before the noncount noun *life.*
15. A   The indefinite article *the* should be used because the noncount noun *ice cream* is followed by a modifier (*that we bought at the store*).
16. C   The correct word order is *widely spoken.*
17. D   No article is needed before the noncount noun *electricity.*
18. D   The past participle *deserted* must be used.
19. C   The correct form of the comparative is *warmer.* (Omit *more.*)

More Practice

1. C   The plural form *servings* should be used.
2. D   The phrase should correctly read *to do business.*
3. B   The past participle *met* is needed in place of the simple form.
4. B   The infinitive *to open* is required in place of the gerund.
5. A   Before a word beginning with a vowel sound. the article *an* must be used in place of *a.*
6. B   The noun *form* must be pluralized.
7. A   The word *for* must be omitted; the correct form of the infinitive is *to relocate.*
8. B   The preposition *on* must be used before the phrase *the morning.*
9. D   The past participle *confusing* is needed.
10. B   The plural pronoun *these* is needed to refer to the three types of organization.
11. C   The noun *gallons* should not be pluralized.
12. C   The adjective form *ordinary* should be used in place of the adverb.
13. C   The adjective-clause marker *whom* should be used to refer to persons.
14. A   The word *like* would be used in place of *alike.*
15. B   The correct comparative form is *easier.*
16. A   Before a clause, the adverb-clause marker *although* must be used.
17. B   The word *remind* must be used in place of *remember* because *remember* cannot be used with an object (*me*).
18. D   The correct word order is *it is.*
19. C   The adjective *dangerous* is needed in place of the plural noun.
20. C   The present participle *challenging* is needed

Sample Test

1. D	3. C	5. C	7. A	9. B	11. D
2. C	4. B	6. A	8. D	10. A	12. B

Exercise 7.1

1. B	4. B	7. A	10. B	13. C	16. C
2. C	5. C	8. C	11. D	14. B	17. A
3. D	6. C	9. D	12. B	15. D	

Exercise 7.2

1. D	4. A	7. D	10. B	13. A	16. C
2. A	5. B	8. B	11. C	14. B	
3. B	6. D	9. C	12. C	15. C	

Exercise 7.3

1. A	4. D	7. B	10. C
2. C	5. A	8. D	11. D
3. B	6. C	9. B	

Exercise 7.4

1. D	4. A	7. D	10. B	13. A
2. B	5. B	8. A	11. B	
3. C	6. B	9. D	12. D	

Exercise 7.5

1. B	4. C	7. C	10. B	13. C
2. D	5. B	8. D	11. D	14. A
3. A	6. A	9. C	12. B	15. B

More Practice

1. B   This passage provides directions for making reservations to play golf. There are no tips for playing golf in the passage, and the hours of operation are not given. There is no mention of special events.

2. A   To play on weekdays, you must call a full day in advance. Therefore, to play on Tuesday, you must call on Monday.

3. C   The notice says that you must check in with the pro shop a quarter hour (15 minutes) prior to tee time. (*Tee time* is the time a golfer begins playing.)

4. B   The first paragraph of the article says, "To ensure compliance with government regulations, refineries add more octane than necessary."

5. B   The InfraTane process does NOT involve a special testing engine — the current testing

method does. The other statements about InfraTane are true.

6. D   The third paragraph says that "InfraTane has been installed in the company's St. Paul, Minnesota refinery."

7. B   The article says in the third paragraph that the firm in Merrick, New York, will "offer it to other refineries around the world for around $300,000."

8. A   The first paragraph of the passage states that these books make "contract forms accessible to everyone."

9. A   The second paragraph says that "each workbook has a wide range of contract forms related to the area designated by the workbook title." This indicates that contracts on similar subjects will be found in the same workbook.

10. C   The second paragraph says that, "the contracts are simplified in language," indicating that actual contracts must be more complex.

11. D   The second paragraph states that "each workbook has a glossary at the back, defining terms found in the book."

12. C   The third paragraph says that, if people decide to get legal assistance, "they will realize a savings in time and money" if they are already familiar with terminology and typical contracts, so the author would recommend that people refer to the workbooks before speaking to an attorney.

13. B   The writer says "Bonnie Whitmer has requested that I write . . . "

14. D   The one fault that the writer mentions is that Ms. Whitmer "sometimes spends too much time on details."

15. A   The writer suggests that Ms. Whitmer is one of the employees whose jobs will be eliminated.

16. D   At the top of the review, the reviewer gives the restaurant four stars for atmosphere. The Ratings Guide at the bottom of the review explains that this symbol means "Excellent." The other qualities of the restaurant that the reviewer considers have fewer than four stars.

17. A   The restaurant is open from Tuesday to Thursday and Friday through Sunday. It

18. C The reviewer is discussing "a new Indonesian restaurant."

19. C At the top of the review, "Weekend evenings" (which would include Saturday evening) are marked with the symbol $$$$. The Ratings Guide explains that this symbol means that each person pays, on the average, $35 to $50.

20. A This chart shows the relative costs of three methods of communicating — through verbal interpreters, text translators, and phrase books — and the costs of all three in nine Asian capitals. Choice A best summarizes this concept. Choices B and C are too specific, and choice D is too general.

21. C In Singapore, the cost of text translation is $9, while the least expensive phrase book is $10.

22. C In Seoul, verbal interpretation is $67, while text translation is $7. This $60 price difference is by far the greatest discrepancy between the two services in all the cities listed.

23. B The article states that the aboriginal people made these tools "for barter." (*Barter* means "trade.")

24. A The article says that the drug was "used to counteract hunger pangs." (*Pangs* means "painful sensations.")

25. C The bone was 60,000 years old, and its discovery "pushed back the date of human habitation in Australia by 20,000 years." Previously it must have been believed that human habitation in Australia began 40,000 years ago. (60,000 – 20,000 = 40,000)

26. C The arrangement of topics and page numbers suggests that this is a table of contents. The topics themselves suggest that it is a table of contents for a company's policy manual.

27. D A person who wanted information on taking a business trip would probably look in the "Travel" section, which begins on page 36.

28. C The section entitled "Profit sharing plan" covers ten pages (26–35), considerably more than any of the other topics listed as answer choices.

29. B Toy-making operations were shifted by Hong Kong manufacturers to Macao, Indonesia, and Malaysia, and away from China, so China did not benefit.

30. D It can be concluded from the article that the GSP ("Generalized System of Preferences") is a system of export benefits provided by the United States to various countries.

31. B A is not true; the article says some—but not all—operations have been shifted from Hong Kong and China. There is no information in the article to indicate that C or D is true. Choice B is the best answer. The article states that toy-making is Hong Kong's fifth largest export industry, so only four other export industries can be larger.

32. B There is no information about getting an engine started. The other aspects of driving in the snow are all discussed in the article.

33. A According to the article, "if your car's rear end slides to the right, gently steer to the right."

34. A This ad is intended for people who want to stay at a vacation resort. This is clear from the mention of leisure activities such as horseback riding.

35. C There is no mention of swimming in the advertisement; tennis, horseback riding, and fishing are mentioned.

36. A "Free trade association" is a term used in international trade; the fact that the term is defined in the reading indicates that this passage is an entry in a dictionary of international trade terms. The "see also" list of references is also a common notation in a dictionary.

37. B Trade unions and free trade associations are similar in that both serve to eliminate trade barriers with other members.

38. C Since people in their twenties are younger than the average age of people in the workforce, an influx of workers in their twenties would lower the average age. Choice A would have no effect, since children are not part of the workforce. Choices B and D would cause the age of the workforce to go up, not down.

39. D Choice A continually goes up; choices B and C continually decline. Only choice D reverses a trend. The percentage of government workers rises between 1985 and 1990, but declines from 1990 to 1995.

40. B The percentage of people working in retail trade changed only .1% in ten years, less than any of the other fields listed as choices.

Practice TOEIC Test

Listening Comprehension
Part I

1. __D__ A. They're digging up the roots.
B. They're repairing the ceiling.
C. They're walking along the route.
D. They're working on top of the building.

2. __A__ A. The telephone is being used.
B. She's pressing a button on the television.
C. The telephone is on her desk.
D. She's pointing at the telephone book.

3. __D__ A. The trees are bare and empty of leaves.
B. The policewoman is on the roof of the house.
C. The horse is racing forward.
D. The policewoman is on horseback.

4. __C__ A. The man who is standing is reading the paper.
B. They're both wearing a coat and tie.
C. They appear to be taking a break.
D. The man who is seated is drinking coffee.

5. __D__ A. She's studying the books.
B. The lecture must be exciting.
C. She's writing down notes.
D. Her chin is resting on her hand.

6. __B__ A. The cats are in the closet.
B. A tag is hanging from one of the jackets.
C. The letters are piled on the table.
D. The plane is in the hangar.

7. __C__ A. He's opening the curtain.
B. He's talking about the article.
C. He's reading the magazine.
D. He's looking out the window.

8. __D__ A. The woman and the child are alone in the forest.
B. The bag is hanging over the woman's shoulder.
C. The carriage is being pushed down the hallway.
D. The woman is looking into the baby carriage.

9. __A__ A. The information booth is round.
B. People are waiting to ask questions.
C. The information booth is unoccupied.
D. Newspapers are sold here.

10. __A__ A. They're getting their luggage.
B. They're at an amusement park.
C. They're buying suitcases at a store.
D. They're looking at the poster.

11. __D__ A. The car is speeding down the freeway.
B. He's working with electronic tools.
C. The doors of the car are open wide.
D. He's making an adjustment to the engine.

12. __C__ A. The restaurant seems to be closed.
B. Tables are set up outside the restaurant.
C. There are signs in the window.
D. A crowd is coming through the door.

13. __D__ A. She's making something out of iron.
B. She's closing up the shop.
C. She's grabbing the fire extinguisher.
D. She's ironing some clothes.

14. __D__ A. People are standing in line to vote.
B. The wind is blowing the sails.
C. The sailors are wearing boots.
D. The boats are reflected in the water.

15. __C__ A. They're waiting for the rain to stop.
B. The train is waiting for the signal to change.
C. The truck is stopped at a railroad crossing.
D. They're loading a truck onto the train.

16. __A__ A. Two people are looking at the screen.
B. They're taking pictures of the scene.
C. The couple is checking the lights.
D. They're watching a program on television.

17. __B__ A. He's standing by the fan.
B. He's holding the door.
C. He's getting out of the van.
D. He's washing the floor.

18. __C__ A. The dancers are arm-in-arm.
B. They're playing instruments.
C. The dancers are wearing costumes.
D. They're dancing up on a stage.

19. __A__ A. She's buying fruit at a market.
B. She's planting a garden.
C. She's picking fruit from the tree.
D. She's marking the paper.

20. B   A. The sculpture is formless.
           B. The statue can be seen from the window.
           C. The sculpture seems to be made of concrete.
           D. The substance is harmless.

Part II

21. B   How long have you lived in this apartment?
           A. A long way from here.
           B. For about six months.
           C. I saw a "For Rent" sign.

22. C   Are air fares going up again?
           A. Yes, the plane already took off.
           B. The fare was around $500.
           C. That's what my travel agent told me.

23. B   How were your seats at the concert?
           A. The music was wonderful.
           B. We had a great view of the stage.
           C. It started at about eight o'clock.

24. C   How about spending the afternoon at the beach?
           A. I think we spent too much for that.
           B. Those peaches look delicious.
           C. That sounds like a great idea.

25. A   Who taught you how to swim?
           A. No one — I learned on my own.
           B. I thought about going swimming.
           C. I taught my friend.

26. B   Is the grocery store far from here?
           A. Just some milk and eggs, please.
           B. It's just a few blocks.
           C. I've already put them away.

27. A   What's that book about?
           A. It's the biography of a famous actress.
           B. About four hundred pages.
           C. Thanks, I'd enjoy reading it.

28. A   How often is he late for work?
           A. Once every few weeks, at least.
           B. About half an hour.
           C. Because of a traffic jam.

29. B   Would you rather take a bus or walk?
           A. Yes, I would.
           B. I wouldn't mind getting a little exercise.
           C. This bus goes to the stadium.

30. A   Don't tell anyone what I told you, all right?
           A. Don't worry, I won't.
           B. That's what I said.

           C. I'm afraid I can't tell you.

31. C   Where did these flowers come from?
           A. At the florist's shop.
           B. From nine to five o'clock.
           C. Someone delivered them.

32. C   Which of these two tools would be better for this job?
           A. They work very hard.
           B. These two are good.
           C. They're both about the same.

33. C   Whom should I contact when I arrive in Malaysia?
           A. It was signed by Mr. Malek.
           B. You'll be there by Wednesday.
           C. Call Mr. Malek.

34. B   Do you have the correct change?
           A. It's ten o'clock.
           B. Yes, I have exactly the right amount.
           C. No, it hasn't changed at all.

35. B   I expect Akiko will be very successful, don't you?
           A. She said it was a great success.
           B. I'm sure she will be.
           C. Because of her experience.

36. C   What do you think of Jim's plan?
           A. He's planning to go.
           B. I like him a lot.
           C. It's too complicated.

37. A   Why didn't you tell me you'd gotten a promotion?
           A. I just found out myself.
           B. Because I did a good job.
           C. Yes, let's do.

38. B   You're not by any chance going downtown, are you?
           A. I'll probably take a taxi.
           B. I sure am — do you want a ride?
           C. There's a chance it will go down.

39. A   How long ago did she graduate from the university?
           A. It was about eight years ago.
           B. Yes, she's a graduate.
           C. For over four years.

40. A   Do you know if Mrs. Simms is planning to go to London?
           A. I think that's still her plan.
           B. She'll be there until next week.
           C. If you want to, go ahead.

41. _B_ Did you put the suitcase in the closet?
       A. Yes, I closed the suitcase.
       B. No, I put it under the bed.
       C. I put my clothes in it.

42. _C_ What gate is your flight leaving from?
       A. It's leaving on time.
       B. I'll be flying to Athens.
       C. Gate 23 on Concourse C.

43. _C_ Hadn't we better go now?
       A. Yes, I feel fine now, thanks.
       B. I've seen better ones before.
       C. You're right, I think we should.

44. _A_ When did your company first start doing business in Hong Kong?
       A. Over forty years ago.
       B. This wasn't the first time.
       C. A shipping business.

45. _A_ Who can help Nancy address those envelopes?
       A. I'll be happy to.
       B. They were addressed to her.
       C. Nancy can wear her green dress.

46. _C_ Isn't this a picture of the Space Needle in Seattle?
       A. I've been to Seattle several times.
       B. I prefer rice to noodles.
       C. I believe it is.

47. _B_ If I have any more questions, can I call you later?
       A. Yes, I'll call you.
       B. Sure, call anytime.
       C. No, I don't have any questions.

48. _C_ Is there anywhere in this town to hear some good jazz?
       A. I've never been there.
       B. I used to listen to jazz years ago.
       C. There's a jazz club on Simon Street that's not bad.

49. _A_ What was it about the hotel you didn't like?
       A. The rooms were too small.
       B. The rates were very reasonable.
       C. Yes, I liked it.

50. _C_ Can you recommend a good family doctor?
       A. The doctor has two children.
       B. He recommended that I quit smoking.
       C. Dr. Kaufmann at the Medical Center is excellent.

Part III

51. _A_ F: Mr. Hofner, your appointment isn't until eleven AM.
     M1: I always like to arrive a little early.
      F: But you're here almost an hour ahead of time!

52. _D_ F: So, Yoshi, did you finally find an apartment?
     M2: Yes, Ann, I did, but it's unfurnished, so I need to buy some inexpensive furniture.
      F: Maybe you should rent some, since you'll only be here six months.

53. _C_ M1: Are you carrying any fresh fruit, vegetables, or meat?
     M2: Yes, I have a basket of tropical fruit I'm taking as a gift to a friend.
     M1: Sorry, sir, but it's illegal to bring fresh fruit into the country.

54. _C_ M1: Have you mailed the brochures for next month's sale yet?
     M2: No, Mr. Metz, they won't be back from the printer until Wednesday or Thursday.
     M1: That's fine, as long as we get them in the mail by next Monday.

55. _B_ F: Call me at my office when you get back to your hotel.
     M1: Won't you be at home by then, Linda? I won't be back at my hotel until late this evening.
      F: No, I'll be working late.

56. _A_ M2: Have you made any big sales so far this week?
      F: Just one!
     M2: That's still better than I've done.

57. _B_ F: Are these your notes from Monday's budget meeting?
     M1: No, Marina, I was out of town Monday, remember? Maybe they're Tom's.
      F: No, I'd recognize his handwriting.

58. _A_ M2: With all these new orders, we'll have to hire more production workers.
      F: Are you sure, Mr. Heath? We still have plenty of back inventory.
     M2: Yes, but that won't last forever, and we just can't ask our current workers to put in any more overtime.

59. _D_   M1: Have you read this new best-seller by Mark Westbrook?
         M2: No, I haven't. I don't really enjoy fiction.
         M1: I think you'd like this. It's a very fast-paced adventure.

60. _D_   F: Mr. Stevens? This is Marcia at Dr. Cheng's office. I'm just calling to remind you that you have a dental appointment tomorrow morning at ten.
         M1: Oh, it's a good thing you called — I'd forgotten all about it.
         F: So we'll see you tomorrow.

61. _B_   M2: Hello, David, this is Sam Briggs at Briggs Electronics Outlets. I'm just calling to see how that new campaign you're working on for me is going.
         M1: It's coming along fine, Sam. The radio spots have already been recorded, and they'll be on the air next week.
         M2: And the newspaper ads?

62. _D_   F: That SA-5 Unit hasn't been shipped yet, has it?
         M2: Yes, Mrs. Spears, the shipping company picked it up first thing this morning.
         F: Oh, no — this invoice was supposed to be in the package!

63. _B_   M2: Rosa, some people from the office are going skiing tomorrow. Would you like to join us?
         F: I'd love to, but I'll be spending the day packing. I'm going to move to another apartment next week.
         M2: Well, maybe some other weekend then. See you at work Monday.

64. _D_   F: You know, that old watch you bought at the auction is worth a lot of money.
         M1: Really? How do you know so much about watches, Amy?
         F: My father taught me. He was a jeweler, and he collected antique watches.

65. _B_   M1: Paul, I'm working on the new schedule. Do you still want to work only four evenings a week?
         M2: Yes, but if possible, I'd like to work for a couple more hours every evening.

         M1: You could come in earlier if you want — say at five or six.

66. _C_   M1: Did you have a private room?
         M2: No, but there wasn't a patient in the other bed.
         M1: Well, that was fortunate for you.

67. _A_   M2: We'll send out someone to repair your copy machine as soon as possible.
         F: Please try to send someone out this afternoon, Mr. Perkins. We have to copy some important documents for a meeting tomorrow.
         M2: If I were you, I'd send them out to a commercial copy center.

68. _A_   M1: I can't find the receipt for my airline tickets from that trip I took last week.
         M2: So? Why do you need it, Phil?
         M1: If I don't have that receipt, my company won't pay me back for buying the tickets.

69. _B_   M1: I've just finished that book called *The One-Minute Manager*.
         F: Oh, yes, I read that a long time ago. It made quite an impression on me.
         M1: Yes, I felt the same way.

70. _A_   M2: Did you get a program from the usher?
         F: Yes, it's right here in my purse. You can take a look at it during the intermission.
         M2: Good. I always like to read about the cast.

71. _D_   M1: Do you want a glass of lemonade, Loraine?
         F: Just some ice water, please.
         M1: I prefer water when it's hot, too.

72. _A_   M1: I wonder if there are any tickets left for the nine o'clock concert Friday night.
         F: Why don't you call the box office right now and find out?
         M1: The box office doesn't open until 3 PM. I'll call then.

73. _D_   M2: I'll *never* have lunch at the Old Oak Room again!
         F: What was wrong this time, Frank? Was the soup cold? Or were the waiters rude?
         M2: Neither. But we had to wait over an hour for our lunch!

74. _B_ F: Good evening, and welcome to the party. You must be George Nielsen's brother Eric.
M1: No, I'm his cousin.
F: Really? You two look enough alike to be brothers.

75. _D_ M1: I love to spend afternoons looking through used bookstores.
F: Me too. And used books are so much cheaper than the new ones.
M1: Well, for me, that's not the point. I'm looking for first editions and other hard-to-find books.

76. _D_ F: I just want a cup of coffee — do I have to stand in that long line?
M2: No, ma'am. Just pour yourself some coffee over there and pay the cashier.
F: Thanks — that will save a lot of time.

77. _B_ M2: We've commissioned Ms. Anspach to do a portrait of our Chief Executive Officer.
M1: Oh? Is he going to pose for her?
M2: No, I took a couple of snapshots of him, and she'll work from the photographs.

78. _C_ M1: Lee, Mr. Devon wants to see you in his office.
M2: Uh, oh — I bet he didn't like the work I did on the McVey project.
M1: That's not it at all. He was so pleased with your work that he wants to take you out for lunch.

79. _A_ M2: Well, the consultants have finally finished their work.
F: And what did they advise us to do about our problem?
M2: That depends on which consultant you ask.

80. _D_ M1: My suggestion to cut expenses is to reduce bonuses for sales personnel by 50% for the next six months.
F: But, John, those bonuses help motivate our sales staff, and a well-motivated sales staff brings in more new accounts for the company.
M1: We'll tell them that this is only a short-term measure. I think they'll understand.

Part IV

[Questions 81 to 83 are based on the following talk:]
[The type of bicycle that you choose depends on the type of bicycling that you plan to do. The simplest bicycle has either three speeds or none at all. This type of bicycle provides basic transportation and is a bargain. For the serious bicycle commuter, a ten-speed bicycle is the best choice. This type of bicycle performs well on city streets and on highways. The sturdiest bicycle is the mountain bicycle, which is designed to be ridden on steep, rocky trails or on no trails at all. The most recently developed type of bicycle is the hybrid, which can be used on both paved city streets or on unpaved mountain trails.]

81. _A_ Choice A is correct; the talk describes four types of bicycles and their uses. Choice B is incorrect because there is no mention of bicycle safety. Choice C is incorrect because there is no mention of bicycle maintenance. Choice D is incorrect because there is no mention of bicycle development.

82. _B_ The speaker says that the mountain bicycle "is designed to be ridden on steep, rocky trails or on no trails at all."

83. _D_ The hybrid bicycle "can be used on both paved city streets or on unpaved mountain roads."

[Questions 84 to 87 refer to the following announcement:]
[And now, radio station KCFX presents this public service message: Bonfort Blood Center has just issued an urgent request for blood donations. Every year in late summer, the blood supply drops to dangerously low levels, and this summer is no exception. The Labor Day holiday weekend is coming up in a few days, and the possibility of numerous accidents is high, so the need is great. The shortage of blood type AB positive is particularly critical. It will only take a few minutes to donate, and every donor gets fruit juice and a cookie as well as a pin that says "I gave the gift of life." And remember, donors are eligible for an unlimited supply of free blood should they require it within the next year. So please, come on down to the Bonfort Blood Center, especially you AB positive donors.]

84. _D_ The speaker says that, "the Labor Day holiday weekend is coming up in a few days."

85. _A_ The speaker says that "every year in late summer, the blood supply drops to dangerously low levels, and this summer is no exception."

86. _C_ The speaker does not say that donors will receive mention on the radio.

87. __A__ In the talk, the speaker says that "the shortage of blood type AB positive is particularly critical."

[Questions 88 to 90 are based on the following news item:]
[Today, North American Airlines made the announcement that it will move its main training facility to Minneapolis next year. Industry analysts were taken by surprise by the announcement. North American had been expected to move the facility to one of its hub cities, Salt Lake City or St. Louis, or to keep it in its present location, Atlanta. Analysts speculate that Minneapolis must have made an offer North American could not refuse, including generous tax breaks. Minneapolis, in return, receives hundreds, even thousands, of desirable, well-paying jobs.]

88. __D__ The speaker says that "analysts were taken by surprise by the announcement."
89. __D__ According to the talk, the present location is Atlanta.
90. __B__ Minneapolis will receive "hundreds, even thousands, of desirable, well-paying jobs."

[Questions 91 and 92 are based on the following recording:]
Thank you for calling PhotoWorld. We offer high-quality, low-cost developing service. For color film, bring in a roll by noon and pick it up after three the following day. Enlargements, reproductions, and black-and-white film developing are done in three or four days. We also offer many types of color film for sale at special discount prices.]

91. __C__ The advertisement says that if you bring in a roll of film in the morning you can pick it up after three the following day; therefore, if you bring it in on Monday morning, you can get it after three on Tuesday.
92. __D__ The speaker says that color film is "for sale at special discount prices."

[Questions 93 to 95 are based on the following talk:]
[Film has its Oscars, music has its Grammies, television has its Emmies, and advertising has its Clios. Clio Awards are given for a wide variety of achievements in advertising, including Television Commercial of the Year. The awards ceremony was televised annually until 1991. In that year, the organization granting the awards collapsed due to financial mismanagement and ownership problems. In subsequent years, the organization was taken over by new management and revived. A new panel of 30 international judges was appointed, and the number of awards was reduced from over 400 to just 72.]

93. __C__ The speaker says that, "advertising has its Clios."
94. __C__ In 1991, "the organization granting the awards collapsed."
95. __A__ The number of awards dropped from over 400 to 72.

[Questions 96 and 97 are based on the following announcement:]
[At the end of the workday, do your hands, arms, or back ever ache? This can be a warning sign of serious problems caused by incorrect posture or hand position while working at a desk, or by the improper arrangement of office equipment or furniture. This Friday at 11, Diana Hartwick will discuss these matters at a seminar for all interested office workers and will explain simple ways to avoid fatigue and pain in the office. Ms. Hartwick is a physical therapist who has specialized in ergonomics — the study of the relationship between workers and their environment. All office staff should make every effort to attend this seminar.]

96. __B__ The speaker says she is "a physical therapist who has specialized in ergonomics."
97. __C__ There is nothing to indicate that she is going to talk about exercise. However, it is mentioned that she will discuss posture, arrangement of office equipment, and hand position.

[Questions 98 to 100 are based on the following news item:]
[More unusually cold temperatures are expected for tonight and tomorrow throughout the deep South. Hard freezes are expected over much of Florida, and despite the growers' best efforts, much of the citrus crop will probably be lost. This cold wave, along with last month's flooding in southern California, means citrus fruits are going to be in short supply. That means more imports and, of course, higher prices in the grocery store. Experts predict that prices for oranges may climb to their highest level in five years. Consumers should start seeing these higher prices in about two to three months. So stock up on that frozen orange juice while you can still afford it.]

98. __C__ The main purpose of the talk is to explain why citrus fruits will be in short supply and more expensive.
99. __C__ The speaker says that "consumers should start seeing these higher prices in about two to three months."
100. __D__ The speaker suggests that listeners "stock up on that frozen orange juice" while they can still afford it.

Reading Comprehension

Part V

101. C	111. D	121. A	131. B
102. D	112. B	122. B	132. A
103. B	113. A	123. D	133. C
104. D	114. B	124. D	134. D
105. A	115. B	125. C	135. A
106. C	116. D	126. B	136. C
107. C	117. C	127. C	137. D
108. B	118. A	128. A	138. C
109. A	119. C	129. A	139. D
110. D	120. D	130. B	140. A

Part VI

141. A   The adjective form *professional* should be used in place of the adverb form *professionally*.

142. B   The indefinite article *a* cannot be used with the plural form *lots*. There are two ways to correct the error: to omit the article *a* or to use the singular form, *a lot*.

143. D   The past participle is required in the passive form of the verb (*were painted*).

144. B   The gerund form *adjourning* is needed in place of the simple form after a preposition.

145. C   The adverb *twice* should be used in place of the adjective *double*.

146. D   The noun form *humor* is needed in place of the adjective form *humorous*.

147. C   When a quantity word such as *all* is followed by the preposition *of*, the definite article *the* must be used: *all of the clerical workers*.

148. C   The correct word choice is *likely*, which means "probable." (*Likable* is an adjective meaning "easy to like.")

149. A   Before an adjective + noun (*a difficult decision*) the word *such* must be used in place of *so*.

150. D   Before a plural noun phrase (*minor errors*), the word *few* must be used in place of *little*.

151. C   When a specific number is used before a plural noun, a word such as *million* is not pluralized.

152. D   Because there are two applicants being compared, the comparative adjective form *stronger* should be used in place of the superlative form *strongest*.

153. A   The adjective form *healthy* should be used in place of the noun form *health*.

154. B   The word *city* should be pluralized (*cities*).

155. B   The plural pronoun *they* must be used to refer to the plural noun *profits*.

156. A   The noncount noun *competition* should not be pluralized.

157. D   The noun form *products* should be used in place of the verb form *produces*.

158. C   The word *number* should be used in place of *amount* in a phrase that refers to a plural noun (*employees*).

159. A   The correct word order is adjective + *enough*: *high enough*.

160. B   The words *major* and *important* are so close in meaning that the use of both of them is considered redundant. One of the words should be omitted.

Part VII

161. A   The notice informs customers of the refund policy.

162. C   The opening sentence states that, if a customer is not fully satisfied, he or she may return it "within 90 days."

163. D   The notice states that "checks will be mailed for all refunds of $100 or greater."

164. B   According to the article, the 300 billion dollars spent in restaurants was "an increase of about 5% from the previous year."

165. B   The article states that ambience is "the synthesis of architecture, furniture [which would include tables and chairs] . . . and even staff attire." (*Attire* means clothing.)

166. C   The advertisement promises "guaranteed room reservations when booked 48 hours [in other words, two days] in advance."

167. D   There is no indication that suite updates are free. Continental breakfasts are "complimentary"; valet parking and facilities at the health spa are also free.

168. B   The focus of the article is agro-tech farming in Singapore. Agro-tech farming is not a traditional method of farming, so A is incorrect. Choice C is too general to be correct. Nothing is said in the article about agro-tech methods, so D is incorrect.

169. A   Singapore exported over S$60 million worth of aquarium fish. This sum is greater than any of the other commodities mentioned.

170. B   The August 11 meeting is described as mandatory; eligible employees must attend.

171. B   The footnote indicates that eligibility for the new benefits is restricted to permanent employees who work 30 hours or more a week.

172. C   The third paragraph of the memo states that "a brochure is attached."

173. A   The article is a brief description of Morocco's foreign investment policy; the other choices are not directly discussed in the article.

174. C The article states that financial service companies, which would include banks, are regulated, and that there are restrictions as well on air transport and mining companies.

175. D The article states that incentives are provided to non-service companies investing DH100,000 or more, and to small- and medium-sized companies with investments of less than DH5 million. Therefore, a large service corporation investing more than DH 5 million would not be eligible for incentives.

176. C Attendees are told to wear casual western wear to events at the Carleton Ranch. These events are scheduled for Friday.

177. A The schedule states that "attendees will be bused to Carleton Ranch."

178. D The "Sales Reps of the Year" awards are scheduled for lunch on Saturday, the final event of the conference.

179. C The schedule says the badge is the ticket to all events.

180. A The attendees will not be reimbursed for taxi fares, for room service charges, or for accommodations on Saturday night. However, they are told to keep their receipts for their airline tickets "in order to be reimbursed."

181. D The main purpose of the article is to report on a survey that showed a decline in newspaper sales in the majority of countries surveyed.

182. B There were 40 countries surveyed, and sales fell in 23. Therefore, sales must have gone up or remained the same in 17 of the countries surveyed.

183. A The increase in Peru was 90%, while in India it was 28.5%. Sales declined in the United States and European Union countries.

184. C There was a small decline in newspaper sales last year, but Japan continued to lead the world in daily sales.

185. D The letter indicates that if the member renews at this time, his or her membership will continue until April 1997.

186. B *Wild!* is described as a bimonthly journal, which means it is published every two months.

187. B The basic membership fee is given as $25.

188. A The purpose of the article is to distinguish between mechanical and design patents.

189. B According to the article, design patents last three years.

190. A The purpose of the form is to record information taken from a previous employer during a reference check.

191. D The form indicates that M. Nakayoshi took the information, and therefore filled out the form.

192. B The applicant's current assistant manager states that Carolina Sanchez "would make an excellent data coordinator," indicating that this is the job she applied for.

193. A The article says that the Pareto Principle is "easy to explain by reference to practical examples."

194. B There is nothing in the article to indicate that the Pareto Principle is also called the "Proportional Effect."

195. A According to the Pareto Principle, some 80% of a firm's sales are often made by only 20% of its customers, so 20 of the customers would purchase $80,000 worth of goods.

196. D This business helps other businesses relocate.

197. B The advertisement offers to "take the worry and inconvenience out of your move."

198. C Qatar is looking for investors for a frozen orange juice and dried milk plant.

199. D Brazil is seeking a joint-venture opportunity.

200. C The notice says, "For non-members, there is a three-tip request limit."

About the Author

Bruce Rogers has taught English as a Second Language and test preparation courses at the Economics Institute in Boulder, Colorado, since 1979. He has also taught in special programs at Bank Indonesia in Jakarta, Indonesia; at the National Economics University in Hanoi, Vietnam; at Yonsei University in Seoul, South Korea; and at the Samsung Human Resources Development Center in Yongin, South Korea. He is the author of *The Complete Guide to TOEFL®* and *The Complete Guide to TOEFL® : Practice Tests*, both published by Heinle & Heinle, an International Thomson Publishing company.